Spurgeon's Theology for Multiplying Disciples and Churches

"Books abound on Spurgeon, so some may wonder if anything new may be said. Rod Earls has provided the church with an important study on the man's beliefs and leadership skills that resulted in disciples made, leaders developed, and churches planted. At a time when evangelicals are asking questions about the multiplication of disciples, leaders, and churches, this book arrives at a timely moment!"

—**J. D. PAYNE**, Samford University

"Rod Earls is opening up a whole different perspective on Spurgeon and his impact in ways that most pastors don't have a clue about. Spurgeon, the church planting pastor! He may have been the prince of preachers, but he was also an apostle for global church planting. Read this and learn. Incredibly relevant for today."

—**BOB ROBERTS**, founder, Glocal.net

"This book is a culmination of years of research and experience that will inform students of Spurgeon's life and ministry as well as guide young Christians as they begin their journey and seek to leave a legacy of faithful service."

—**RODNEY A. HARRISON**, president, Baptist Homes & Healthcare Ministries

"'Have you won souls for Jesus?' Since the church began, it remains the crucial question—one we must answer in the affirmative. From brand new believer to lifelong Christian, the life and ministry of C. H. Spurgeon inspires and challenges us to personally win people to Christ—providing a template to teach, train, and turn loose others to do the same."

—**JESSE HANEY**, pastor of Oasis of Hope Church

"Rod Earls has researched and written about the story of Spurgeon what we were privileged to see take place in Guatemala. God led us to plant the gospel in the hearts of the Kekchi Indian people, discipling them to be missionaries. A dramatic movement of multiplication of disciples and churches occurred. In like manner, these principles and applications from Spurgeon are practical and effective because they come from the Savior and Scripture. Read and be inspired!"

—**TED LINDWALL**, president, Church on the March

Spurgeon's Theology for Multiplying Disciples and Churches

The Story of How Spurgeon and the Metropolitan Tabernacle Followed Christ

ROD EARLS

Foreword by Ed Stetzer

WIPF & STOCK · Eugene, Oregon

SPURGEON'S THEOLOGY FOR MULTIPLYING DISCIPLES AND CHURCHES
The Story of How Spurgeon and the Metropolitan Tabernacle Followed Christ

Copyright © 2022 Rod Earls. All rights reserved. Except for brief quotations in critical publications or reviews, no part of this book may be reproduced in any manner without prior written permission from the publisher. Write: Permissions, Wipf and Stock Publishers, 199 W. 8th Ave., Suite 3, Eugene, OR 97401.

Wipf & Stock
An Imprint of Wipf and Stock Publishers
199 W. 8th Ave., Suite 3
Eugene, OR 97401

www.wipfandstock.com

PAPERBACK ISBN: 978-1-6667-4343-2
HARDCOVER ISBN: 978-1-6667-4344-9
EBOOK ISBN: 978-1-6667-4345-6

09/30/22

As our church recognizes no distinction of clergy and laity.

—Charles Spurgeon, *The History of the Metropolitan Tabernacle*

Contents

Foreword by Ed Stetzer | ix
Preface | xiii
Acknowledgments | xv
Introduction | xvii

1. Background to Spurgeon's Ministry | 1
2. Spurgeon's Family Values and Influences | 24
3. Schooling, Conversion, and Spurgeon's Foundation for a Ministry of Multiplication | 44
4. Early Preaching and Pastoral Experience | 63
5. The Metropolitan Tabernacle and Growth of the Pastors' College | 85
6. The Applied Theology of Spurgeon and the Tabernacle which Multiplied Disciples and Churches | 116
7. A Farm System for Local Churches Using Spurgeonic Principles | 147
8. Confident Pastoral Leadership | 176

Conclusion | 201
Bibliography | 205
Subject Index | 209

Foreword
The Prince of Preachers . . . and Church Planting

"If I have seen further," Isaac Newton wrote in a 1675 letter to a fellow scientist Robert Hooke, "it is by standing on the shoulders of giants." Newton's influence on mathematics and physics is hard to overestimate, yet he acknowledged his dependence on those who preceded him.

We can all reflect upon those who have influenced us, people on whose shoulders we stand as well. Parents, pastors, professors, mentors, and more would check that box. Those of us who serve in ministry each have our list of spiritual heroes who have impacted our lives. They may be individuals who have influenced us directly. But many of us find ourselves also deeply influenced by historical mentors—those individuals who we did not know personally but by whose legacy we are moved and changed for the better.

PRINCE OF PREACHERS

For preachers of the Bible in the evangelical tradition and beyond there are few giants with shoulders broader than Charles Haddon Spurgeon. The "Prince of Preachers" is beloved both by those within his theological world—Baptist and Calvinist—and those outside that orbit. In fact, it would be hard to find a historical figure in the evangelical movement more universally loved and respected—and quoted (and misattributed!)—than Spurgeon.

Spurgeon's preaching ability is legendary. His sermons continue to be read to this day by preachers and students. We have more of his writings available today than any other Christian writer outside the Bible. Helmut Thielicke once said of books, "Sell all that you have ... and buy Spurgeon."

In his youth, Spurgeon had an interesting theological odyssey. Raised an Independent (his parents were Congregationalists), he came to Christ at age 15 when he stopped in a Primitive Methodist church during a blizzard. A layperson was filling in for the pastor who was prevented by the blizzard from showing up. The lay preacher called the tiny congregation—and specifically unfamiliar young Spurgeon in attendance—to look to Jesus. Within months he became convinced by a burden to preach the gospel himself. He would become a Baptist and, eventually, the most famous Baptist preacher of his era.

I can relate to Spurgeon's journey as a youth. I came to Christ through the ministry of a charismatic Episcopal church in Florida. I would eventually become a Baptist like Spurgeon. And like Spurgeon, I have an appreciation for all those who love Christ, Baptist or not.

While Spurgeon is known best for his preaching ability, he was so much more than a great preacher. He founded schools, pastored a megachurch in London long before the modern megachurch movement, authored many books, stood tall in theological controversy, and oversaw the planting of many churches.

MEGACHURCH PASTOR

When a young nineteen year old Spurgeon came to the New Park Street Church in 1854, the congregation had 232 members. When his pastorate ended almost four decades later, it was probably the largest congregation in the world. A true megachurch, what is now called the Metropolitan Tabernacle had grown to over 5,000 members during Spurgeon's tenure as pastor. Some have estimated that he preached to more than 10 million people in his lifetime.

He spoke to his congregation in a common language that was uncommon in the established church but fit his setting well. He gained strength from the "boiler room," the people who gathered in the basement to pray for their pastor as he preached. Spurgeon knew that the growth and health of a church must be rooted deeply in prayer.

COLLEGE FOUNDER

A couple of years after becoming the pastor of his church, Spurgeon also founded Pastors' College, which is now called Spurgeon's College in honor of its founder. His goal for the College was both to train ministers and to found new churches through its training of future ministry leaders. By the time Spurgeon died, the college had already trained nearly nine hundred ministers and released them into the world for ministry service, multiplying Spurgeon's legacy for generations to come.

CHURCH PLANTER

When thinking of Spurgeon, few associate his legacy with church planting. And, personally, I've been shaped by Spurgeon's theology, preaching, and evangelistic passion. But, twenty years ago, long after I loved Spurgeon, it was Rod Earls who introduced me to the church planting Spurgeon.

Yes, the Prince of Preachers was passionate about replicating new churches, even writing in 1881 that, "It is my greatest pleasure to aid in the commencing of new churches." He went on to add that the goal of his college was "not alone for the education of ministers, but for the general spread of the gospel." Church planting was foundational to that vision of the gospel message multiplying throughout the world. By 1881, Pastors' College alumni had planted more than two hundred churches around the world (80 within the vicinity of London!) and baptized more than forty thousand people.

WHY SO INFLUENTIAL?

Why does Charles Spurgeon continue to be so influential? There are many reasons, but here are three that have influenced many, including me.

Spurgeon's life and ministry focused on Christ and him crucified. In his book *The Soul-Winner*, Spurgeon said he was often asked the secret of his success. His reply: "I always answer that I have no other secret but this, that I have preached the gospel—not about the gospel, but the gospel—the full, free, glorious gospel of the living Christ who is the incarnation of the good news."

Spurgeon's life and ministry remind us even the giants had their struggles. Though known for his sense of humor and focus on a joyful life, Spurgeon battled depression—to such an extent that his wife at times wondered if he would continue preaching. He faced a number of personal tragedies, severe criticism, and physical infirmity. He was brilliant in mind yet weak in body. Yet, he did not simply minister in spite of these trials. He allowed the trials to become a point through which God would use him to minister to others.

Spurgeon's life and ministry give us a profound example to follow. It is this factor that makes Rod Earls' book such a helpful contribution. We can read Spurgeon's sermons, devour his books, and admire his preaching ministry, but there is much to learn from Spurgeon in the realm of leadership.

Many today criticize the modern megachurch as being more a model of consumerism than a reflection of the New Testament church. As Earls points out, Spurgeon offers a model for a disciple making approach—a "farm system" to use Rod's term—to multiple disciples. His preaching, his college, and his passion all point to Spurgeon's goal of having all believers engaged in Great Commission work. Whether you are a preacher, a pastor, a prayer-warrior, a church planter, or a believer who simply wants to know and serve God more faithfully, you can learn much from the life and lessons of Spurgeon.

Ed Stetzer
Dean and professor, Wheaton College

Preface

I HAVE WATCHED GOD use the insights from this research work for over thirty years. The ecclesiological, soteriological, and pastor leadership principles have helped others come closer to the Savior and more confident of His leading and using them further in His service. The Spurgeonic principles shared at the end, built upon his early lessons presented in the front end of the book, will serve any and every pastor and church to experience more of God's power and presence for serving His Son's calling.

The research and prose in this work aims to help the reader fall more in love with the Savior, and be more enabled to fulfill His Great Commandment, Great Commission, and 2 Tim 2:2 better. Let this read challenge and guide you further in His calling on your life.

Acknowledgments

THIS BOOK IS A collaborative effort by many people who have modeled the principles surfaced in this writing and presented for application to life and ministry from Spurgeon and the Metropolitan Tabernacle church family. It has been a wonderful journey since childhood to watch God-honoring lay people serve and live for the Savior. Growing up in a small country church allowed me to see God up close in those around me. There's a culture in smaller churches whereby life is lived more 'out in the open'.

Planting a church in Texas and then coming to California to serve in an established church allowed these early life lessons to be experienced at a deeper level and more appreciated. With all my heart I believe the heroes in heaven will be lay people. They need and deserve good leaders as they are Christ's and must be stewarded as such. When they are duly appreciated and seen for their worth as servants of the Savior, the church becomes a wonderful small taste of heaven. The insights from the life and ministry of Spurgeon reflected in this reading helps realize this experience. The lay people give a deep and dear picture of the Savior's heart and ability to use lives in His service and kingdom advancement. These dear people have taught me so much about the Savior.

The seed thought and challenge for writing this work on Spurgeon was shared by a dear friend J. V. Thomas. J. V. served the Baptist General Convention of Texas and worked to see more churches planted in the state. While studying at Dallas Seminary we were gifted to participate in a new church J.V. Thomas had assisted to launch, one ably led by Steve Stroope, and which proved an example of multiplying disciples and churches.

I am grateful to the many college and seminary professors who modeled reverence for the Lord and the commitment to serve Him and His people with excellence. Each of them contributed wisdom and character formation in seminating God's Word line upon line into my heart and mind. Many dear colleagues in the pastorate as well in varying denominational agencies along with teaching fellows have inspired me greatly.

Dr. Jerry Falwell Sr. constantly reminded us as young husbands who were part of the student body of Liberty University in its early years: "the wife is the neck that turns the head boys; so make sure you appreciate her." His words were loaded with gold. God gifted me Carol as my life teammate and this book's labors come out of her always showing up for the game of life as we together tried to follow and serve the Savior. Any credits on the book's value go to the Lord and her. Her example and spirit has equipped and strengthened our three beautiful children, children-in-law, and grandchildren to be learning Micah 6:8: love mercy, do justly, and walk humbly with God, just as our parents taught us.

Introduction

THIS BOOK WAS DERIVED out of a dissertation work written in 1989 on Spurgeon's life and work in making and multiplying disciples and churches. The original study was devoted to understanding how Spurgeon and the Metropolitan Tabernacle (noted as MT later) were able to start 200 churches in and around London. After working with pastors and churches over the last twenty-five years, these experiences and additional research have given added practical applications from Spurgeon for today's church. This book is written with the prayer that pastors and churches can gain wisdom and encouragement for carrying out the Savior's Great Commission through better experiencing His Great Commandment. Hopefully it will inspire how farm systems can be formed, as God taught Spurgeon and MT, by which more disciples and churches can come into existence. The book aims to present the mirror Spurgeon holds up of the Lord Jesus and how this can help us see Him more clearly and serve Him more effectively.

Eric Hayden was a devoted student of Spurgeon and pastored at the Metropolitan Tabernacle in the 1960's. In his book on the Tabernacle's history, he lists over thirty books published by Spurgeon; these were compiled from lectures, addresses, and from research on particular themes. The great majority of what we know of Spurgeon's beliefs, insights, and practices for Christ's work come from his sermons. These were published weekly following the first year (1854) of his London pastorate. In order to effectively use Spurgeon's wisdom, this book will quote extensively from Spurgeon's sermons. I pray God will speak to you of how He wants to use you in light of what He did for Spurgeon and that it may inspire more faith and love for the Lord Jesus and His calling to share Him with your generation.

Spurgeon's theology was simple and sure: *Jesus Christ and Him crucified.* He declared this in his early ministry at New Park Street Baptist (the church was called Metropolitan Tabernacle after entering their new building in 1861) in London; it became the motto of the Pastors' College he established, and it was the message he trained the students to preach. He loved Puritan writings, being a twelfth generation Puritan preacher in his family lineage, and he loved John Calvin's teachings—especially Calvin's teaching in his later years. But all this was subservient to and was solely used for responding to the call of Scripture in Galatians 6:14: knowing Jesus Christ and His cross made real in life.

You and I are not Spurgeon, but we can learn much from him for being what God wants each of us to be and do. We are all different gifted and unique in our talents and passions. We will not perhaps experience the size of ministry Spurgeon did, but all ministry and mission work is significant. It is important to be reminded often, especially in American Christianity, that God begins with small things in order to do big things. We only hear of Ananias twice in Acts, but if he hadn't done his part we would not have one-half of the New Testament today. Moody led one million to Christ during his ministry, but who remembers the person who led him to Christ—Edward Kimball? Our commonality with Spurgeon is our Savior and His calling on each of us to live the Great Commandment and carry out His Great Commission. This is where Spurgeon can be a friend to guide us from his experiences and wisdom; he can help us avoid frustration and unfruitfulness in doing the great work we are invited and called to by our Savior.

This book, *first,* looks at Spurgeon's world context to better understand the needs and challenges of the era in which he ministered: this gives the reader encouragement that if God did it then against such obstacles, He can and will do it again now. It *then* looks at his heritage in order to allow the reader to see how convictions from Scripture, formed in his childhood, guided his entire life: this gives us the value of Scripture and imputing the Word into our lives (especially into lives of children). The *book then proceeds* to carefully look at his teenage schooling experiences and his conversion: this will show how Spurgeon's salvation experience influenced his life in living and ministering the gospel. *Next* the book considers Spurgeon's early ministry experiences and how this shaped his vision: this gives understanding of the foundation for the farm system God brought together for multiplying disciples and churches through the Metropolitan Tabernacle and the Pastors' College. *Following this* the book addresses the system of training carried out by the Pastors' College and how it was distinct in its approach to theological training: this shows how churches and schools can invest into young people solid preparation for ministry and church leadership. *The book then* gives a closer look at the theology Spurgeon and the Metropolitan Tabernacle believed, understood, and shared with others: this gives insight and confidence in God's Word and how He can add lives to the church and strengthen members to be leaders and workers in our Lord's harvest fields. *This is followed* with examining seven principles practiced by Spurgeon and MT which answered the Savior's call to make and multiply disciples and churches: this shows how every church can follow the 2 Timothy 2:2 principle to raise up leaders who can lead others to Christ. The *final chapter* addresses pastors and how they can lead churches using the biblical leadership principles and wisdom which guided Spurgeon to experience God's blessings. Spurgeon's story and the leadership he practiced and the principles he followed can keep pastors and church members encouraged in Christ's person and work.

1

Background to Spurgeon's Ministry

THE OBJECTIVE FOR LOCAL churches is to love and follow Christ in making disciples and disciple-making centers (churches). The book of Acts, what Jesus Christ led His church to do in its first thirty years of existence (and what He calls us to today), is a story of reproducing disciples and disciple-birthing congregations. The early disciples simply and sincerely embraced Jesus' words in Acts 1:8: "But you will receive power when the Holy Spirit comes on you; and you will be my witnesses in Jerusalem, and in all Judea and Samaria, and to the ends of the earth." They straightforwardly went about the work He instructed them to carry out leaning on Him for the wisdom and strength to do it. The instruction Jesus had given them for His great desire for all peoples was "matheteusate," i.e. "make disciples" (Matt 28:19). Understood correctly, the instruction is to make disciple-making disciples by teaching them all the things He commanded which includes being sent out by Him to do make more disciples. It was directive, a command for each of His followers to embrace as a lifestyle: to love Jesus and love others to Him. Donald McGavran said "Anyone who would comprehend the growth of Christian Churches must see it primarily as faithfulness to God. God desires it. The Christian, like his Master, is sent to seek and save the lost."[1]

Conversion church growth in local churches is the expected norm; it is not to be the exception. Studies inform us in American Christianity,

1. McGavran, *Understanding Church Growth*, 5.

85–90 percent of our local churches have been plateaued or declining. There is great need for aligning our church experiences and practices with the Word of God and the Spirit of God; we need and want to be making strong followers of the Lord Jesus Christ. The life and ministry of Charles Haddon Spurgeon gives a rich study of principles and practices how this life of love and obedience to Christ can be experienced.

It is helpful to readers of Spurgeon to understand the times in which he ministered. They were as challenging as the current world we live in. In his message at New Park Street Baptist in London on 19 August 1855, Spurgeon stated:

> Any man, who has his eyes open to the world at large, will acknowledge that there are many clouds brooding over England, and over the world. I received lately a letter from a gentleman at Hull, in which he tells me that he sympathizes with my views concerning the condition of the church at large. *I do not know whether Christendom was ever worse off than it is now* [emphasis added]. At any rate, I pray God it never may be. Read the account of the condition of the Suffolk churches where the gospel is somewhat flourishing, and you will be surprised to find that they have had scarcely any increase at all in the year. So you may go from church to church, and find scarcely any that are growing... Wherever I have gone throughout England, I have always been grieved to see how the glory of Zion is under a cloud... It is not for me to set myself up as a universal censor of the church, but I must be honest and say, that spiritual life, and fire, and zeal, and piety, seemed to be absent in ten thousand instances.[2]

The Baptist denomination in particular was in a deplorable condition in England when Charles Spurgeon began his ministry at New Park Street Chapel in 1854. The Baptist Union's report for 1853 revealed the smallest rate of increase in membership since its inception in 1813 (although being reorganized several times during this period). The Baptist Union was overshadowed in its popularity and acceptance in England by the much more widely established and well-known Baptist Mission Society (BMS). The BMS had been founded by the efforts and appeal for intentional missions work by William Carey and others holding similar convictions. Originally called the "Particular Baptist Society for the Propagation of the Gospel among the Heathen," the first secretary for this society was Andrew Fuller who ably served this role for twenty-two

---

2. Spurgeon, *New Park Street Pulpit*, vol. 1, 281.

years. Joint efforts of Christians for mission work were accomplished through the society. Such societies were independent organizations of like-minded Christians who jointly committed to carry out Christ's work. They were composed of people who were dedicated members of various churches. Local associations of churches and the Baptist Union in England was an effort to more formerly partner churches together for the cause of furthering Christ's work which these societies championed.

The London Association of Baptist Churches meeting on October 17, 1855, had thirty-three member churches and only nine persons attended this annual meeting: six pastors and three laymen. Spurgeon explained the times in his 1856 sermon "What Are the Clouds?": "we have abundance of agencies, we have good mechanism, but the church, now-a-days is very much like a steam engine, without any fire, without any hot water in the boiler, without any steam."[3]

ORIGINS OF EVANGELICALISM AND BAPTIST WORK IN ENGLAND

The theological atmosphere and state of the church preceding Spurgeon's London ministry should be understood in order to gain from his evangelism experiences. Spurgeon entered upon a time of ministry that brought with it religious uncertainties regarding denominational work as well as theological questions for Christ's work.

Understanding the historical context of a person and their ministry gives significant help to correctly interpretating and applying the wisdom they can give to the modern minister and ministry. Charles Spurgeon was born into a race of Non-Conformists. Non-Conformists were believers in England dissenting from the established Church of England. Congregationalists, Baptists, and Methodists were all to be found under the umbrella of Nonconformity. Nonconformity (known as the Free Church movement) began to express itself before the Reformation. The Anabaptist-Mennonite development from the European continent and England's Puritan Separatist gave strength and impetus to Nonconformity. Nonconformists owed their inspiration for existence to several: "Wycliff as well as Luther, Huss as well as Calvin, Gubmaier as well as Menno Simons contributed consciously or unconsciously, directly or indirectly, to the

---

3. Spurgeon, *New Park Street Pulpit*, vol. 1, 281.

stand taken by Robert Browne and his friends . . . that caused the Puritan and Separatist movement to develop as they did."[4]

Robert Browne, born about 1550, worked for the separation of church and state through his writings and early ministry efforts. He was a rare individual being called by church historian Leon McBeth "an ignoble prophet of a noble vision." McBeth reports Browne was a painful controversialist, insensitively censorious and judgmental, and known to beat his wife. As McBeth says, "Seldom does one find purer doctrine associated with a more unlovely character."[5] Browne was trained at Cambridge and his influence passed to another Cambridge man, John Greenwood. Greenwood joined himself with a Separatist group in London. They had to meet secretly for Bible study and worship. Eventually he, along with Henry Barrow and John Perry, were martyred for their confession of exalting Christ over the bishops of the Church of England. Their influence raised questions about baptism and inspired another Cambridge man, John Smyth, to take Thomas Helwys and a body of believers to Amsterdam so they could baptize believers as they understood the Bible taught. Helwys eventually returned with a portion of this group to establish the first Baptist church in England at Spitalfields, London, in 1612.

English Baptists were the beneficiaries of the influence of strong radical dissenters, especially the Puritans, from the Church of England. Because of the contributions of Ulrich Zwingli's and John Calvin's Reformation theology and the release of the English Bible, these Non-Conformists in England came to be called 'Baptists' because of their adapting a baptism practice of total immersion.

Two major groups of Baptists emerged in England in the early 1600s. They shared much in common, but they differed in their views on atonement and church organization. The earlier group was called General Baptists because they embraced anyone who voluntarily believed in Christ could be saved. They were less influenced by John Calvin, who taught only the predestined could be saved, and were more influenced by the Dutch theologian, Jacob Arminius who expressed a unique free will theology. Consequently, General Baptists taught the possibility of "falling from grace." Their church governance was more guided by associations than local congregational autonomy. They saw their churches as local units of the larger church.[6]

4. Payne, *Free Church Tradition*, 1–15.
5. McBeth, *Baptist Heritage*, 27.
6. McBeth, *Baptist Heritage*, 21, 76.

Particular Baptists began forming in the 1630s. They embraced Calvin's teachings and held to a "particular' atonement, i.e., they believed Christ died only for the ones who were elected. Those elected to the salvation Christ died to provide them, would not lose this salvation. They benefited from the teachings of the sixteenth century Puritan believers who desired to purify and reform the Church of England from within rather than breaking away from it. Puritans had wanted to simplify worship and modify church polity from episcopal to presbyterial forms and embrace more of Calvin's doctrines.

Believers, realizing their hope for a purer church would not happen through reform efforts, began to separate from the Church of England. Separatists were prompted to pull out of the established church through the actions of Queen Mary Tudor, 1553–1558, (she was known as Bloody Mary,) and the subsequent leadership of her sister Queen Elizabeth (1559–1609). Elizabeth had reversed the work of their brother Edward VI who had moved the Church of England toward Protestantism. Believers who had genuinely tasted Christ's power and experienced freedom of worship under the Edwardian era did not want to return to the state governed church. Not until 1689 and adoption of the Act of Toleration did Baptists and other Protestants have the freedom to worship openly as they chose in England. In that year they released their London Baptist Confession.

Throughout their beginnings, Baptists were served by lay pastors who worked other secular jobs while serving as the leading minister of their churches. In seeking to give encouragement and assistance in the work of Christ, the Particular Baptists (who held to the autonomy of each local church), valued cooperation with other churches. Their confession of 1689 regarding this states:

> It is according to the mind of Christ, that many Churches holding communion together, do by their messengers meet to consider, and give advice in, or about that matter in difference, to be reported to all the Churches concerned; howbeit these messengers assembled, are not entrusted with any Church-power properly so called; or with any jurisdiction over the Churches themselves, to exercise any censures either over any Churches, or Persons: or to impose their determination on the Churches, or Officers.[7]

---

7. McBeth, *Baptist Heritage*, 98.

This spirit and attitude continued to guide and influence Baptist life. The first meeting of the Abingdon Association of England was in 1652. Some of their logic for an association of churches affirmed that all churches were under the headship of Christ and by working together they could demonstrate their unity under Him. They also believed an association of churches could assist one another in mutual discipline matters, aid in controversies, pool resources for more effective ministry, help keep each other pure, encourage fellow churches to stay on fire for Christ, assist when there was need, and provide counsel in unclear matters.[8]

While early English Baptists were marked with evangelical passion and doctrine, the same was not true of Baptists following toleration. The eighteenth-century Baptists fell into a fog of religious indifference and decay. The leaders who had weathered persecution and kept the course of evangelism and planting more churches were now gone. Another factor contributing to the demise of Baptist work was the fact they were not allowed to attend the major English universities as their Puritan and Separatists predecessors had done. The quality of Baptist leadership began to show decline.

General Baptists normally followed an Arminian doctrine. They were influenced by Arianistic teachings that were being embraced by some Anglicans and Presbyterians during the latter seventeenth and early eighteenth centuries.[9] They were closer to Continental Mennonites and the English Quakers in stressing subjectivity of response to the Spirit's guidance and working; this was right in principle but was not always grounded in solid exegesis of Scripture.

Doubts about the deity of Christ began to plague all Protestant groups. General Baptists proved vulnerable to this vein of thinking. Evangelistic zeal began to wane as more energies and attention were given to theological speculations. Many were enraptured with the intellectual problem of the person of Christ. There evolved an increasing arrogant and critical spirit.[10] This serves an important lesson for every generation of churches: if we are not preoccupied with following Christ and making disciples of Him, we are not in our Savior's favor. He stated He will be with us (John 15) as we are about His call of going and making disciples with our lives; if we become focused on other aims and issues

---

8. McBeth, *Baptist Heritage*, 97.
9. Torbet, *History of Baptists*, 62–63.
10. Torbet, *History of Baptists*, 213–14.

in our ministries and efforts, we will not know His presence or power. Without such, we will experience wilderness wonderings as churches and individual believers.

In the Particular Baptist body some took their Calvinistic theology to the extreme. Many lost their evangelistic drive, and some became antinomian emphasizing grace over the law. Those holding this view were at times guilty of scandalous conduct including deceit and even immorality.[11]

Between 1715 and 1792 Baptists were evangelistically stagnant. There were some positive signs after 1770 of new churches being planted in London through the influence of Dan Taylor and Abraham Booth.[12] Interestingly one of Charles Spurgeon's predecessors in the pulpit of the New Park Street church (John Gill) was a man noted for his theological knowledge but lacking demonstrated evangelistic passion.

John Gill served what was then known as the Horselydown church in Southwark, London from 1719 until his death in 1771. Gill was influenced by the writings of Tobias Crisp (1600–1642) who could be described as a hyper-Calvinist. Crisp was an Anglican pastor who taught not only extreme Calvinism, but also exaggerated antinomian concepts. He wrote "Whatsoever sins they do commit, being Believers, their sins shall do them no hurt."[13] Reading Gill one hundred years later was like reading Crisp all over again. McBeth describes Gill by saying "He was so jealous to maintain the sovereignty of God that he refused 'to offer Christ' to unregenerate sinners and taught others to make the same refusal."[14] John Fawcett, 1739–1817, Baptist theologian and pastor (author of the hymn "Bless Be the Ties that Binds"), said Gill was read by Particular Baptists almost to the exclusion of all other works of divinity.[15] Gill was unable to rival the Calvinistic application of the gospel of his own predecessor at Horselydown church, Benjamin Keach. Keach served the same church from 1668 to 1704 and was able to balance his Calvinism with a warm and fervent evangelism.

History shows Particular Baptists grew in their discontent over the theology of Gill and others by the middle of the eighteenth century. Abraham Booth, a Particular Baptist pastor, wrote a work in 1768 called *The*

---

11. Whitley, *Baptists of London*, 55.
12. Whitley, *History of Baptists*, 56–57; 195–203.
13. McBeth, *Baptist Heritage*, 174.
14. McBeth, *Baptist Heritage*, 176.
15. McBeth, *Baptist Heritage*, 177.

Reign of Grace. In this work he argued strong Calvinism, but also fervent evangelism. Booth had been converted through the efforts of a conservative group of evangelical General Baptists, but eventually accepted Calvinistic views. Booth reinforced the views espoused in *Reign of Grace* with a subsequent work *Glad Tidings to Perishing Sinners* published in 1796. The subtitle to the book was "The Genuine Gospel, a Complete Warrant for the Ungodly to Believe in Christ." His understanding of election allowed him to call sinners to repentance—a position Spurgeon himself later embraced as a fellow Calvinist. Booth was not educated but was a very careful student of Scripture and sincerely devoted to his people. "*He appeared always willing to give up almost everything to the decision of the church; the consequence was . . . the church gave up almost everything to his decision* [emphasis added]".[16] When there is trust between pastor and people, decision-making for the direction of the church is more a team experience and growth in unity. When the unity of Christ and the Father is known in a church, the Spirit of God can empower and use the members for effective evangelism and disciple-making work (John 17:21–23). This book will develop further understanding of how this is experienced from Spurgeon's experience with the church in the final chapter.

With Unitarian views affecting General Baptists, a conservative group under the leadership of Dan Taylor (1738–1816) withdrew to form the New Connection group. It was Taylor's leadership that helped launch their mission efforts at the end of the eighteenth century. The New Connection body eventually merged with the Baptist Union and became more closely aligned with Particular Baptists in 1813. This was strengthened when the Union reorganized in 1832. Robert Hall (1764–1831), a leading Baptist pastor at Cambridge, along with Taylor, contributed a growing influence and understanding of evangelism as a mandate for Baptists to practice.[17] Hall's teachings and leadership set in motion a farm system at St. Andrews Baptist Church which would shape Charles Spurgeon's outlook for ministry when he became involved with this church in 1849.

As Baptists moved into the nineteenth century there were continuing disagreements concerning the communion issue along with doctrinal questions related to John Calvin's teachings. Along with practicing open communion, many Baptist churches embraced an open membership, i.e., accepting those who were unbaptized into membership.

---

16. McBeth, *Baptist Heritage*, 179.

17. Underwood, *History of Baptists*, 169–72.

Evangelicalism and Baptists in London

As indicated above, Baptists' collective efforts of ministry were waning when Spurgeon came to his pastorate in London in 1854. Only thirteen of the thirty-seven total Baptist Associations in England contributed funds to the Baptist Union in 1863.[18] Spurgeon spearheaded a new thrust of resources toward Baptist Union causes through his leadership in the London Baptist Association. He was motivated to help reorganize and form a new London Baptist Association which could help start more churches in the London metropolis. He had visited Bradford in the Yorkshire Association and witnessed their cooperative efforts in starting new churches. The example galvanized a conviction in Spurgeon,

> The Yorkshire churches cooperated in raising a Loan Fund for building. Spurgeon, already mindful of the rapid expansion of London, saw in this a reason to rally London Baptists to meet an urgent need to raise money for church extension and, united by a common purpose to build churches for the preaching of the Gospel and the extension of the Kingdom, forge a fellowship of London Baptists which would endure. In this he succeeded more than he knew, because the record of the Association during the past century constitutes a thrilling story of achievement in church extension, through common endeavor, sacrifice and fellowship.[19]

There would remain theological challenges impacting the life and work of Baptists during the time Spurgeon served in London. In his message on November 6, 1870, the day before the London Baptist Association Day of Prayer, Spurgeon expressed his concerns:

> Just now, I do not know how you feel, but I am ill at ease. The Church of England is eaten through and through with Sacramentarianism, but Nonconformity appears to me to be almost as badly riddled with philosophical infidelity. Those of whom we thought better things are turning aside one by one from the fundamentals of the faith. At first they gave up the doctrine of the eternity of future punishment, now it must be the doctrine of the fall: first one thing then another. If some men have their way, all the doctrines of the word must go. They treat the doctrines of Scripture as though they were all disproved, and only held by a few ignorant bigots. Through and through, I believe, the heart of England is honeycombed with a detestable infidelity, which

---

18. Payne, *Baptist Union*, 43.
19. Johnson, *Encounter in London*, 23–24.

> dares still to go into the pulpit, and call itself Christian. I pray that God may preserve our denomination from it. *But my prayer shall go up that he will give us the Holy Spirit, for men never go wrong with the Holy Spirit; he will keep them right, and lead them into all truth. Soundness of doctrine is only worth having when it is the result of the living indwelling of God in the church; and because too much the Holy Spirit has departed, we see the signs that the orthodox faith is given up, and the inventions of man preached instead thereof* [emphasis added].[20]

Spurgeon ever leaned on and valued the Holy Spirit's ministry in all he attempted as will be seen later.

Kenneth Scott Latourette notes throughout the latter half of the nineteenth century an evangelical movement was affecting all churches except Roman Catholicism. Religious inquiry along with serious thinking was the atmosphere of the times. Rationalism had developed further in Europe during the eighteenth and nineteenth centuries. It was beginning to make its presence known in England. Poole-Conner writes, "Of the prevalence of Evangelicalism in the Victorian era there is no question; but it was far from finding universal acceptance."[21] Various church leaders including many Baptists were grappling with the relevance and authority of Scripture.[22]

In Germany Friedrich Schleiermacher (1768–1834) produced an anthropocentric interpretation of the gospel as opposed to a Christocentric teaching. As succeeding scholars developed this strain of theological understanding, the church began to lose confidence in a dogmatic theology based on Scripture. Georg Hegel (1770–831), influential German philosopher, identified the Holy Spirit as simply the process of life itself.[23]

Michael Stroope gives an excellent assessment of the theological milieu that produced a mission theology of humanistic reform as opposed to radical conversion to Christ and His cross: "The church equated the essence of Christian faith to the modern psyche of man, and thereby, obligated God to creaturely social and mission programs. Because there was no real separation of God and man, and time and eternity in these efforts, the objectifiable became real and eternal, and the eternal was objectified.

---

20. Spurgeon, *Metropolitan Tabernacle Pulpit*, vol.16, 623.
21. Poole-Conner, *Evangelicalism in England*, 230.
22. Bailey, "The Challenge of Change," *Expository Times* 86, 18–22.
23. Livingston, *Modern Christian Thought*, 155.

Man's hope was located in the progressive realization of human goals."[24] When Scripture is not viewed as authoritative for all life practices, people have to rationalize its teachings so accountability to the Scriptures and to God is precluded. Without seeing miracles of grace, people lose hope and confidence that such exists even at the direction of Scripture. This is why Jesus always taught us to hear and obey the Word in order to trust God so miracles of grace could be experienced. When a generation of leaders devalue such living by the Book, succeeding generations live life without God. This is the lesson of Judg 2:10, "After that whole generation had been gathered to their ancestors, another generation grew up who knew neither the Lord nor what he had done for Israel." Each generation must have deep and real experiences with God so they can genuinely and confidently proclaim Him (1 Pet 2:9).

The publication of Charles Darwin's *The Origin of Species* in 1859 eventuated higher criticism being absorbed into the thinking of Baptist ministers in England. Those who accepted the thinking of a non-divine creation lost the understanding of a Creator. Without acceptance of Creation as a work of God, discounting revelation was the natural outcome. Not affirming the authority of the Scriptures as being the revelation of God, it was only natural to think there was no fall of Creation because there was no God involved in the creation of man. In this vein of thinking and rationale there was no need of redemption—man was his own (and only) hope.

Leading pastors like John Clifford and Archibald Duff helped Baptists and Congregationalists accept higher criticism views of scriptural interpretation. Glover states, "The really important presuppositions of higher criticism were shared by critics and traditionalists alike, for they were a part of the spirit of the age."[25] Many practiced a non-critical acceptance of new theological views. Baptists tended to become indifferent to theology as the spirit of revival prevailed through the latter half of the nineteenth century. Glover goes on to say, "The pietistic quality of the revival put primary emphasis on individual Christian experience and valued correct doctrine only as a means to the creation of such experience. As a result evangelicals would tolerate almost any divergence in doctrine provided the individual concerned was known to have a fervent evangelical experience, and above all if his ministry awakened the same

---

24. Stroope, "Eschatological Mission," 3.
25. Glover, *Evangelical Nonconformists*, 32.

experience in others."[26] The need in Christian experience is to balance biblical knowledge and obedience. Throughout church history, God has demonstrated He did not give us His Word to increase our brain data, but to change our lives, i.e., to make us holy—like Himself. 1 Cor 8:1 tells us this: "knowledge puffs up while love builds up." If our Bible study doesn't lead to our being more in love with Jesus and more like Jesus, it's not true nor profitable handling of the Word of God.

Evangelical scholars and writers during Spurgeon's time more and more questioned inspiration of Scripture. John Clifford, who led the opposition within the Baptist Union against Spurgeon's claims made during the Downgrade Controversy, declared "For no doubt our theological apathy is due first and mainly to the overshadowing importance accorded in our system to the regenerate life . . . Systems of doctrine are trifles light as air to souls that see God face to face in immediate fellowship with the Eternal Spirit.[27] They gravitated toward understanding God as a genie providing power for enjoyment rather than Great Commission employment.

Up to this time in Christendom there had not been a carefully processed and developed hermeneutic work of Scripture. The evangelical church had simply accepted the Bible as being the Word of God. A careful scientific examination of truth, as recorded in Scripture related to its authority, had never been implemented. As questions prevailed more and more regarding the veracity and relevance of Scripture to life, it forced the church into a study of Scripture's inspiration, authority, and application for life. Hermeneutical studies and developments would progress more as a result of the church's experiences of the nineteenth century.

Charles Haddon Spurgeon worked through these matters of theological relativism and held strongly to his confidence in the Christ of Scripture. Delivering his first message in the opening service of their new Metropolitan Tabernacle building in Newington, London, Spurgeon gave his creed for what he felt deeply confident of and what he believed God wanted him to be guided by for his life and ministry:

> In the days of Paul it was not difficult at once, in one word, to give the sum and substance of the current theology. It was Christ Jesus . . . but if I am asked to say what is my creed, I think I must reply—"It is Jesus Christ." My venerable predecessor, Dr. Gill, has left a body of divinity, admirable and excellent in its way; but the body of divinity to which I would pin and bind myself for

26. Glover, *Evangelical Nonconformists*, 93–94.
27. Fisher, *History of Christian Church*, 635.

ever, God helping me, is not his system of divinity or any other human treatise, but Christ Jesus, who is the sum and substance of the gospel; who is in himself truth, the all glorious personal embodiment of the way, the truth, and the life.[28]

Spurgeon's commitment to Christ and extending His Kingdom manifested itself clearly during his lifetime. He was used of God to inspire, equip, and lead other men, along with the help of dedicated laymen and laywomen, to start over two hundred churches in and around London. In addition, Spurgeon and the Metropolitan Tabernacle saw other men go out from them to plant churches throughout England and the British Empire and in other nations. They also sent out many pastors from their farm system who saw revitalization come to the existing churches they went to serve. The study of this man's life and ministry can meaningfully contribute to the strengthening of churches in our day and give guidance to multiplying disciples and more churches.

Sir William Robertson Nicoll, a highly regarded publisher during Spurgeon's time, said next to the Bible a Christian should study Spurgeon. Nicoll had read through the available sermons by Spurgeon in one six-month period when he was without other works to read. This convinced him of the profit Christians could have from studying what God had taught this man.[29] The respected and noted evangelist and theologian Helmet Thielicke, who preached to large crowds throughout Germany, said about Spurgeon, "Sell all you that you have and buy Spurgeon. Let him be a Socrates who helps you find your own way."[30]

HISTORY OF METROPOLITAN TABERNACLE CHURCH

A short review of the history of the church Charles Spurgeon served for thirty-eight years as pastor will be helpful to the contemporary reader. Much of the following information comes from Spurgeon's *The Metropolitan Tabernacle: It's History and Work*. It gives additional understanding to effectively apply lessons from this man and his ministry. Spurgeon wrote this history of the church in 1876 and in it commented, "the facts here placed on record are well worthy of being known. In us they have aroused fervent emotions of gratitude, and in putting them together our

---

28. Spurgeon, *New Park Street Pulpit*, vol. 7, 169.
29. Nicoll, *Princes of the Church*, 50–57.
30. Thielicke, *Encounter with Spurgeon*, v.

faith in God has been greatly established . . ."³¹ Spurgeon was never unclear on what he believed or where he stood. In the opening remarks of his history of the church he states,

> "We do not expect in reading a life of Wesley to find his Arminianism and his Methodism left out, nor ought any one to expect us to weed out Believers' Baptism and Calvinistic doctrine from the annals of a Particular Baptist church. We are Calvinistic Baptists, and have no desire to sail under false colors, neither are we ashamed of our principles: if we were, we would renounce them to-morrow."³²

When Spurgeon came to the New Park Street Baptist Church, as it was called in 1854, he came to one of England's foremost Baptist churches in the country's history. Its history actually began in the year 1652. A group of people decided to separate from one of the most ancient Baptist congregations in London and to meet in homes or other buildings available to them. Their first recorded pastor was William Rider. The church was located in the community of Southwark, south of the Thames River in London.

Benjamin Keach

In 1668 the congregation called Benjamin Keach as their pastor following the decease of Rider. Keach as mentioned earlier was Calvinistic as well evangelistically passionate. Keach at times suffered imprisonment and abuse because of his writings and his publicly preaching the gospel. Baptists were not yet free to worship openly and Keach faced opposition from the leaders of the Church of England. Through all this, he suffered joyously for His Lord and continued preaching His gospel. Spurgeon described him:

> Benjamin Keach was one of the most useful preachers of his time, and built up the church of God with sound doctrine for thirty-six years. Having been in his very earliest days an Arminian, and having soon advanced to Calvinistic views, he preserved the balance in his preaching, and was never a member of that exclusive school which deems it to be unsound to persuade men to repent and believe. He was by no means so highly Calvinistic

---

31. Spurgeon, *Metropolitan Tabernacle*, 5.

32. Spurgeon, *Metropolitan Tabernacle* 5–6.

Background to Spurgeon's Ministry 15

> as his great successor, Dr. Gill; but evidently held much the same views as are now advocated from the pulpit of the Tabernacle.[33]

Charles II ruled in England from 1660 to 1685 and made efforts to lessen persecution against Nonconformists. Successful for a brief time in 1672 through the Indulgence bill, the church under Keach built a building at Horselydown capable of holding one thousand. (This was also the time when John Bunyan was allowed out of jail after a twelve-year incarceration.) At this time, buildings for worship did not normally have seats because congregations stood due to fear of reprisal taking place during a worship service. Pews were a later addition.

Keach wrote a total of forty-three books and proved influential in leading his denomination to pay ministers a decent remuneration for their labors. He was also very instrumental in helping Baptists adopt the practice of congregational singing. He was patient and wise in leading his church into a worship expression that had not been done for decades due to fear of being discovered by the magistrates and incarcerated for unlawful assemblies. They began singing at the conclusion of the Lord's Supper only; this went on for six years. Only then did he lead them to add singing at special services—this continuing for fourteen years. After a total of twenty years, he began leading the church to sing at the conclusion of every Lord's Day. Keach understood culture takes time to change and kept the church moving toward the vision God had placed in his heart as their pastor. Even then some withdrew from the church because of their uncomfortableness with this practice. Interestingly, they formed new church that became a strong work—and one which soon learned to enjoy singing to the Lord as well. In 1691 Keach published a book of hymns containing almost 300 songs.[34]

> The pastor was a power in the church, and by the weight of his mind and character directed it aright, so that troublers found it expedient to carry out their mission in some less consolidated community. He could also wax warm, and deliver his mind with vehemence, and then it was somewhat dangerous to be his opponent. Mr. Keach was not, however, apt to spend his time in contention, he was a practical man, and trained his church to labour in the service of the Lord. Several were by his means called into the Christian ministry, his own son, Elias Keach, among

---

33. Spurgeon, *Metropolitan Tabernacle*, 25.
34. Hayden, *Centennial History of Tabernacle*, 3.

them. He was mighty at home and useful abroad. By his means other churches were founded and meeting-houses erected.[35]

Benjamin Stinton

The next pastor called to the church at Horselydown was Benjamin Stinton in 1704, the son-in-law of Benjamin Keach. He had helped his father-in-law in the church for some years and so was not new or untested with the church. Spurgeon wrote of this transition of leadership in the church, "*It is no small blessing when a church can find her pastors in her own midst; the rule is to look abroad, but perhaps if our home gifts were more encouraged the Holy Spirit would cause our teachers to come forth more frequently from among our own brethren* [emphasis added]."[36] This is surely a wise consideration for our churches today and would be effective application of 2 Tim 2:2.

The church's history included many pastors who were quite young when coming to serve (as was the case of Spurgeon being only nineteen when he began at New Park Street). Stinton was diligent in personal studies to increase his effectiveness. He mastered different languages and other disciplines to assist in his biblical studies and their application in ministry. Stinton was also instrumental in leading London Baptist pastors to organize into a fraternal fellowship in 1714 to help one another in Christ's work. (He helped establish the Particular Baptist Fund in 1717 to assist needy pastors.)[37]

John Gill

John Gill became pastor of the church in 1720 following a probationary period of two years—partly due to his only being twenty years of age when first introduced to the congregation. Stinton's sudden death in 1718 led the church to search out another suitable minister. When the church finally decided to call Gill, almost half of the congregation withdrew; eventually the sides reconciled. Gill, although not trained at the

---

35. Spurgeon, *Metropolitan Tabernacle*, 32–33.
36. Spurgeon, *Metropolitan Tabernacle.*, 35.
37. Hayden, *Centennial History of Tabernacle*, 3.

universities, had read most of the Latin classics and was able to work in the Greek by age eleven. Spurgeon says of Gill,

> His entire ministry was crowned with more than ordinary success, and he was by far the greatest scholar the church had yet chosen, but he cannot be regarded as so great a soul-winner as Keach had been, neither was the church at any time so numerous under his ministry as under that of Keach. *His method of address to sinners, in which for many years a large class of preachers followed him, was not likely to be largely useful* [emphasis added]. He cramped himself, and was therefore straightened where there was no scriptural reason for being so.[38]

Gill was constantly in his study. He obtained such a great deal of knowledge that various men arranged to subsidize Gill to give lectures on Wednesday evenings in the Great Eastcheap building. Gill did this for twenty-six years beginning this series in 1729. The Marischal College, Aberdeen (which became the University of Aberdeen after merging with King's College in 1860), gave him the Doctor of Divinity in 1748 because of his knowledge of the Scriptures, Oriental languages, and Jewish antiquities.[39]

Though not known for making pastoral calls, Gill was loved and respected for his faithful care of the flock through his pulpit ministrations and his leading the church with dignity and affection. He lived with a total assurance of God's faithfulness and grace in his life. Toward the end of his life he wrote a family member saying "I depend wholly and alone upon the free, sovereign, eternal, unchangeable, love of God, the firm and everlasting covenant of grace, and my interest in the persons of the Trinity, for my whole salvation; and not upon any righteousness of my own; nor upon anything done in me, or done by me, under the influences of the Holy Spirit."[40] He died at the age of seventy-three (1771) without ever having to use glasses for the massive amounts of reading and studies he carried out.

---

38. Spurgeon, *Metropolitan Tabernacle*, 39.
39. Spurgeon, *Metropolitan Tabernacle*, 41.
40. Spurgeon, *Metropolitan Tabernacle*, 46.

John Rippon

John Rippon came to the church in 1773 and served until 1836. The church had relocated to Carter Lane under Gill's leadership. Like Gill, Rippon was twenty years of age when he came to the church. Rippon, one of the few in the church's history having formal schooling for the ministry, had been trained at Bristol College. (This was the first Baptist college established in history being founded in 1679.) Rippon came to the church with his teachers' recommendation because the church had written the school requesting a pastoral prospect for the congregation.

The church had dwindled in attendance under the closing years of Gill's pastorate, but under Rippon renewed zeal for evangelism was experienced and growth began to be experienced. "The chapel in Carter Lane was enlarged, and various agencies and societies set in motion; there was in fact, a real revival of religion in the church, though it was of that quiet style which became a Baptist church of the straighter sort. Rippon was rather clever than profound; his talents were far inferior to those of Gill, but he had more tact, and so turned his gifts to the greatest possible account."[41] His preaching was interesting and witty along with being lively and affectionate. Spurgeon records, "Many souls were won to Jesus by his teaching, and *out of these a remarkable number became themselves ministers of the gospel*. The church-book abounds with records of brethren preaching before the church, *as the custom was in those days* [emphasis added]."[42] As will be seen throughout this work, giving men preaching experiences is a key element in their journey and calling into the ministry of pastoring and planting churches.

Rippon started a publication called *The Baptist Register*, which in the twentieth century became *The Baptist Times*. This gave information to churches regarding affairs of the Baptist denomination. It was addressed to all baptized ministers and people in England, America, and beyond. Some feel this was the genesis of the Baptist World Alliance. He was also instrumental in calling together a meeting of some sixty ministers at Carter Lane in 1812 where they discussed the benefits of a general union of Baptist pastors being formed. The next year "The General Union of Baptist Ministers and Churches" was established.[43]

---

41. Spurgeon, *Metropolitan Tabernacle*, 49–50.
42. Spurgeon, *Metropolitan Tabernacle*, 50.
43. Hayden, *Centennial History of Tabernacle*, 6.

Pastor Rippon was concerned over the care of the aged and began a ministry of almshouses in 1803 in order to care for those who did not have needed assistance from family or otherwise. Because his church officers did not think this was prudent, Rippon carried out the work through his own resources. Spurgeon said of his pastoral leadership,

> The Pastor occupied no mean position in the church, but ruled with dignity and discretion—perhaps ruled a little too much. "How is it, Doctor, that your church is always so peaceful?" said a much-tried brother minister. "Well, friend," said Rippon, "you see, we don't call a church-meeting to consult about buying a new broom every time we want one, and we don't entreat every noisy member to make a speech about the price of the soap the floors are scrubbed with." [Spurgeon added] In many of our smaller churches a want of common sense is very manifest in the management, and trouble is invited by the foolish methods of procedure.[44]

(Wise pastoral leadership and church structures are dealt with later in the book.)

Six years before his death (1836), the church building at Carter Lane was torn down to make room for the completion of the London Bridge project. Compensation was made, but a new building could not be constructed for some time. For three years, through the hospitality of other churches, the congregation met in other buildings. The New Park Street building, which Spurgeon came to when called to the church in 1854, was erected in 1833. Spurgeon's observation about its location reveals his perspective about where church buildings should be positioned in communities (it also explains the dismal prospect of the church's reaching people and growing when Spurgeon came):

> After so long a time for choice, the good deacons ought to have pitched upon a better site for the new edifice; but it is not hardly judging them when we say that they could not have discovered a worse position. If they had taken thirty years to look about them with the design of burying the church alive they could not have succeeded better. New Park Street is a lowlying sort of lane close to the bank of the river Thames, near the enormous breweries of Messrs. Barclay and Perkins, the vinegar factories of Mr. Potts, and several large boiler works. The nearest way to it from the City was over Southwark bridge, *with a toll to pay*. No

---

44. Spurgeon, *Metropolitan Tabernacle*, 52.

cabs could be had within about a half-a-mile to the place, and the region was dim, dirty, and destitute, and frequently flooded by the river at high tides. Here, however, the new chapel must be built because the ground was a cheap freehold and the authorities were destitute of enterprise, and would not spend a penny more than the amount in hand.[45]

Unfortunately, Rippon outlived his usefulness and became somewhat obstinate and disagreeable. Prior to his death his leadership became acutely more controlling and demanding, and the congregation decreased. He had served the church with vigor and fruitfulness for sixty-three years as their pastor. The church in one hundred and seventeen years had been presided over by only two pastors. This would be a wonderful blessing for churches to have pastors serve lengthy ministries and be able to effectively pass the mantle of pastor to younger men they and their churches have helped influence and prepare for such a role.

The years between 1837 to 1853, saw the church congregation, now worshipping at New Park Street, have three short pastorates. Joseph Angus came to the church in 1837, but two years later was asked to become secretary (executive director) of the Baptist Missionary Society. Angus had schooled at Stepney and at Edinburgh University and the church enjoyed increase under his leadership. The church had prayed seriously for the successor to Rippon and news of the BMS inviting Angus away from them so soon after his coming to them was not easy to accept. After Dr. Angus served the BMS for several years, he went onto become the principal (president) of Stepney College for a period of forty-four years. (He and Spurgeon would later connect with one another in a unique way, discussed later in the book.)

James Smith

James Smith came to New Park Street church in 1841 and ably served the congregation for the next nine years. In his second year of service, sixty-six people were added to the membership of the church. (What will be explained in more detail later, membership came with high expectations of commitment and involvement—a stark contrast to practices in many churches in modern times.) He was not as educated as Angus but was

---

45. Spurgeon, *Metropolitan Tabernacle*, 53.

wisely practical in ministry and an able communicator with evangelistic passion. Smith wrote in his diary on November 19, 1844,

> The church now increases faster than it has done since I have been its pastor, but not so fast as I wish to see it. *I try a variety of means, and feel determined to leave no stone unturned for its welfare and advantage* [emphasis mine]. I am surrounded by a great many young people, very hopeful characters. This encourages me, and I continue to plead with God for many of them by name, and I preach to them monthly. O to have many of them given unto me as my joy and crown of rejoicing in the day of the Lord![46]

For churches to grow in seeing lost souls added to the body, there must be effort in trying many methods to find what will work effectively for them in their field context for carrying out the Great Commission.

Smith maintained his evangelistic focus throughout his pastorate at New Park. He wrote in his diary in July 1848 "I begin to feel sad and somewhat unsettled, for I feel as if I could not live, much less be happy, if souls are not constantly brought to God."[47] He explained that signs of life imparted to those who are dead in sin is what is desired through the work of the church. Between four to five hundred members were added to the church during his tenure.

William Walters

In July 1851 the church called William Walters to become their pastor. Unfortunately, this was not a good match for pastor and people, and the deacons communicated this understanding to Walters. He relocated to a church in Halifax in June 1853. A church, which had an auditorium seating 1200, was now seeing less than 200 in worship attendance prior to calling Charles Haddon Spurgeon at the beginning of 1854.

Charles Spurgeon

Spurgeon includes a significant and unique chapter in his history of the church. He devotes this chapter to a deacon named William Lepard (1700–1799) who was active during the pastorates of Stinton, Gill, and Rippon. The very first lines of this chapter are paramount in helping

---

46. Spurgeon, *Metropolitan Tabernacle*, 69.
47. Spurgeon, *Metropolitan Tabernacle*, 69.

us understand Spurgeon's view of laymen (and laywomen) and his understanding of the doctrine of the *Priesthood of the Believer*. Spurgeon explains the work of the local church is never accomplished only by the efforts of a pastor. His very first sentence to the chapter gives strategic theological insight in accomplishing a multiplying ministry reproducing disciples and churches: "*As our church recognizes no distinction of clergy and laity*, . . . [emphasis added]."[48] Spurgeon never accepted ordination largely due to his convictions regarding Scripture's treatment of believers and their life calling by the Lord. The manner in which he ministered to and led the church at New Park Street/Metropolitan Tabernacle was greatly influenced through his understanding of this teaching in Scripture which informed and guided his attitude toward, and leadership of, the laity. It enabled him to raise up many, many kingdom leaders in his church. This will be very important to note.

I close this chapter sharing from Howard Hendricks. It was a great help in my theological and ministerial development to sit under Dr. Hendricks at Dallas Seminary. He placed before us as students the value of seeing God's Word applied in the lives of those we were entrusted to serve as pastors and church leaders. The challenge in ministry is helping them apply the Word to their lives—and through them to others. Dr. Hendricks stated,

> In fact, my greatest joy as a professor is to see my students excelling in the arenas to which God calls them. When they succeed, I succeed. When they break new ground, I feel like a part of the team. When they win praise and acclaim, I feel a swell of pride, knowing that I've had a strategic part in helping them along the way.
>
> But sometimes I wonder whether as a society we have any appreciation left for the development of people. I often hear business executives mouth the old bromide that "our people are our most important asset." But if that's true, then it's fair to ask, what are you doing to cultivate that asset? *What specific, practical plans and budgets do you have in place to identify and build the strengths of your people, and place them where they can be most effective? And if those questions apply to business, how much more to the local church* [emphases added]? If you are a pastor, I challenge you to consider: Is your church a net consumer of human resources, or a net producer of them? Are you building a great church, or great people? Are you building people only to

---

48. Spurgeon, *Metropolitan Tabernacle*, 55.

the extent that they serve the purposes and programs of your institution, or in light of the gifts and opportunities that God has given to your people? Ephesians 4 speaks to this very issue.[49]

---

49. Hendricks and Hendricks, *Iron Sharpens Iron*, 150.

2

Spurgeon's Family Values and Influences

STUDYING THE EARLY LIFE and heritage that shaped Charles Haddon Spurgeon is very helpful to understanding his later convictions which guided his ministry for leading a church and making and multiplying disciples and churches. What he experienced in this time of his life marked and guided the work he would undertake in adulthood.

Charles Spurgeon was born into a family saturated with Nonconformist convictions. Revolutionary changes occurred in England through Henry VIII (1509–1547) and his efforts to break away religiously and politically from Rome. Other events in the world occurred bringing further ideas of Protestantism into England. Spain's Phillip II (1556–98) instigated persecutions against Reformationists in the Netherlands and forced their Calvinists to migrate to England as did France's Louis XIV's (1643–1715) action revoking freedom of religion assured by the Edict of Nantes. Spurgeons began appearing in the Norfolk and Essex areas (north of London) during these revolutionary changes. Charles Haddon Spurgeon was preceded by an ancestry of eleven generations of Puritan preachers from 1568 to 1834: they were Nonconformists aligned with the Congregational order.[1]

---

1. Day, *Shadow of Broad Brim*, 21.

The great-grandfather of Charles Spurgeon's grandfather, Job Spurgeon, was incarcerated for attending a Nonconformist meeting in 1677. This happened at the same time John Bunyan was in the Bedford jail. Six years later Job Spurgeon was charged again for the same offence. This time he was incarcerated in the Chelmsford jail along with three others on July 22, 1683. "They were, after a few weeks, bailed out till sessions, but on their appearance there on the 3rd of October they were required to give sureties for their good behavior, which, refusing to do, they were recommitted to prison."[2]

Charles Spurgeon described his relationship with this Job Spurgeon:

> In my seasons of suffering, I have often pictured to myself this modern Job in Chelmsford jail, and thanked God that I bore the same name as this persecuted Spurgeon of two hundred years ago. So far as I can make out the genealogy, it appears to me that this Essex Quaker was my great-grandfather's grandfather, and I sometimes feel the shadow of his broad brim come over my spirit . . . There is a sweet fitness in the passing on of holy loyalty from grandsire to father, and from father to son. I like to feel that I serve God "from my fathers." I can cast my eye back through four generations, and see that God has been pleased to hear the prayers of our grandfather's father, who used to supplicate with God that his children might live before Him to the last generation; and God has never deserted the house, and has been pleased to bring first one and then another to fear and love His name.[3]

Nonconformity brought hardships to its adherents. Educational opportunities were withheld and a lower level in society was levied upon them. But this experience trained people for richer lives spiritually and the ability to make greater contributions to their world. Charles Spurgeon's character and attitudes were influenced and molded by values inherited from the Puritan Nonconformist elements in his family line.

SPURGEON'S CHILDHOOD

Charles Haddon Spurgeon was born June 19, 1834, at Kelvedon, Essex. It was a community of about two thousand in population. Charles was the first of seventeen children born to John and Eliza Spurgeon. Nine children died in infancy; two boys and six girls survived. Shortly after

2. Pike, *Life and Works of Spurgeon*, vol. 1, 5.
3. Spurgeon, *Autobiography*, vol. 1, 8.

Charles's birth his parents moved to Colchester in the spring of 1835. Conditions were more feasible and some of their family resided there. But the young couple was still financially strained. Six to eight months after arriving at Colchester, Charles went to stay with his grandparents, Mr. and Mrs. James Spurgeon, at nearby Stambourne. This move would be strategic in the shaping young Spurgeon's values and personality.

While Charles lived at Stambourne, his dad worked as a clerk in a coal yard at Colchester during the week. He conducted a kind of itinerant pastoral ministry at a small Independent church at Tollesbury each Sunday. He would travel nine miles by horse and buggy to carry out his responsibilities in this Congregational church. John Spurgeon pastored sixteen years at Tollesbury, then five years each in two more locations, and then went to London for nine years to finish his life's work.

In his experiences at Stambourne, a great deal of what Charles Spurgeon came to believe, and later practice and accomplish in life, took shape during these six years of his life. Through the example and influence of his grandparents James and Sarah Spurgeon, his aunt Ann, and the environment of Stambourne, Charles Spurgeon received a definite orientation to Puritanism and to the ministry. In the last book he wrote before his death, *Memories of Stambourne*, Spurgeon stated "recalling these things, one could not but be struck with the strange, yet natural and strong connection which exists between this little village and the Great City [London]."[4] Stambourne was a small village not far from Halstead in Essex. This quiet place, nearly shut out from the world, provided the setting for Charles Spurgeon's childhood years.

Pike describes the relationship between Charles Spurgeon and his grandfather:

> Many special providences would happen in the life of such a man, and one of the most signal of these was when grandfather and grandson were brought together under the same roof. The two appear to have been made the one for the other. Though the one was close upon sixty years the elder of the other, they seem to have had much in common; at all events, little Charles appears to have taken readily to such things as pleased the venerable pastor. The child was a daily comfort to the veteran Christian, and was, at the same time, learning in the school which, on the whole, was probably the best fitted to educate his heart and mind.[5]

4. Spurgeon, *Memories of Stambourne*, 62.
5. Pike, *Life and Works of Spurgeon*, vol. 1, 13.

This elder investment into Spurgeon's life should encourage all churches to explore and creatively encourage intergenerational ministries between senior saints and young people.

G. Holden Pike was especially suited to make these judgments about Spurgeon. He had listened to Charles Spurgeon preach at New Park Street, Surrey Hall, and at the Metropolitan Tabernacle. As a writer of Nonconformity he began to submit articles to Spurgeon for publication in the *Sword and Trowel* (Spurgeon's monthly ministry journal) in 1868. In 1872 Spurgeon invited Pike to become 'sub-editor' of the *Sword and Trowel*. He accepted and grew in this working relationship with Spurgeon for twenty years.

The parallels and similarities between the lives of James and Charles Spurgeon are obvious. Charles would go to New Park Street Baptist in later life to serve a church that had experienced long tenures by previous pastors. He would also choose to affectionately love and serve his congregation and remain their pastor for thirty-eight years until he died. This was guided and influenced by the example of his grandfather. What Charles learned in his grandparent's home colored and informed his practice as a pastor and multiplier of disciples and leaders for Christ's work.

The James Spurgeon family

Charles's grandfather was born September 29, 1776. He worked as a tradesman until the age of twenty-six. He then entered Hoxton Academy, a Nonconformist school in London, to train for the ministry. He acquired a strong background in the Bible and Puritan writings. In 1804 he supply preached at the Independent Chapel at Clare, Suffolk, becoming its pastor in 1806. Four years later he went to Stambourne.

Charles's grandfather was called to pastor the church at Stambourne in 1810. The church had only four pastors in its preceding two-hundred-year history before Charles's grandfather became pastor. He served the church fifty-four years until his death at the age of eighty-eight. His grandfather preached with power and was effective throughout his ministry there. Though other churches wanted him as pastor, "the love, harmony, and prosperity which prevailed between pastor and people induced him to decline them all, and he remained true to the people of his choice . . . I have not had one hour's unhappiness with my church since I have been over it."[6]

6. Needham, *Life and Labors of Spurgeon*, 24.

Meeting James Spurgeon was like encountering someone right out of *Pilgrim's Progress*. A man of sparkling wit, he preached with unique force. He taught young Charles to act according to beliefs no matter what the consequences might prove. The inspiration for Charles Spurgeon's successful *John Ploughman's* books came from his grandfather and a farmer he came he came to know and love while at Stambourne, Will Richardson. Some of Charles's theology can be understood from the following story recounting an experience from his grandfather's youth:

> Like his distinguished grandson, the Rev. James Spurgeon firmly believed in and taught the reality and personality of the devil. An incident in his career is recorded which vividly recalls some of Luther's experiences. The story is best told in the words of Charles Haddon Spurgeon: "My grandfather," he says, "remarked that there was formerly a wood in what I think he called Honeywood Park, which was a very memorable place to him. In that wood he had groaned and wept before the Lord while under the burden of sin and under a tree of oak, then only a sapling, he had received the grace of faith and entered upon the enjoyment of peace with God. It was a lonely spot, but henceforth it was to him no other than the house of God and the very gate of heaven. Often he resorted thither and praised the name of the Lord . . . .he dreamed very vividly that the devil appeared to him, and threatened to tear him in pieces if he dared to go along that footpath and pray under the oak as he had been wont to do. . . . 'Whether it be a dream or really a temptation from Satan, I cannot tell, but, anyhow, I will not yield to it, but will show the devil that I will not do his bidding in anything, but will defy him to his face.'[after facing his fear and going back to the oak tree and praying again as was his practice] . . . Then followed a fervent prayer and song of praise, and the young man was about to go on his way when his eye was caught by something shining on the ground. It was a ring, a very large ring, he told me, nearly as large as a curtain ring, and it was solid gold; how it came there it would be hard to guess. Enquiries were made, but no claimant ever appeared, and my grandfather had it made into my grandmother's wedding-ring in memory of the spot so dear to him. Year by year he continued to visit the oak tree on the day of his conversion to pour out his soul before the Lord."[7]

Charles often watched his grandfather walk in the grass near the parsonage located by the worship building. It was here his grandfather

---

7. Ray, *Life of Spurgeon*, 11–14.

spent many times in prayer and meditation, especially the half hour before preaching. This marked Charles deeply and instilled within him an awe for the same practice. He valued prayer but confessed later in adulthood that he found it difficult to spend thirty minutes on his knees in prayer, but that he prayed often throughout the day. "The habit of prayer is good, but the spirit of prayer is better."[8] Spurgeon explained himself further by saying,

> You know a man who spends three hours on his knees? I could not do it if my eternity depended on it! Besides, if I go to the bank with a [checque], what do I want with loafing about the premises when I have got my money? I go to God with a promise, which is in reality a [checque] by God Himself on the bank of heaven. He cashes it for me, and then I go and use what He has given me, to His glory. This I take to be the true way of praying. The fact is long prayers are often the result of unbelief . . . *I think I can say that seldom many minutes elapse without my heart speaking to God in either prayer or praise* [emphasis added].[9]

James Spurgeon passed onto Charles the value and conviction of a Spirit-anointed life for the Savior's service. Charles explained about his grandfather, "the dew of the Spirit from on high never left his ministry. Wherever my grandfather went, souls were saved."[10] He was widely known and respected throughout Essex as a very earnest and practical preacher of the gospel. He was popular with young people and with the children; they loved him. He was known as a pastor who faithfully cared for all his flock.

His grandfather's humor was another example which marked Charles's character and influenced the younger Spurgeon to enjoy himself with people as well. William Williams knew Charles Spurgeon intimately as a former Pastors' College student and then later serving as a fellow pastor in London. Regarding humor, Williams said he laughed more in Spurgeon's company than any other time in life: "He had the most fascinating gift of laughter I ever knew of any man, and he had also the greatest ability for making all who heard him laugh with him."[11] One example of his grandfather's humor, someone once asked the elder Spurgeon how much he weighed and his quick response was "Well, that

---

8. Bacon, *Spurgeon: Heir of Puritans*, 151.
9. Williams, *Spurgeon*, 16.
10. Spurgeon, *Autobiography*, vol. 1, 31.
11. Williams, *Spurgeon*, 24.

all depends on how you take me: if weighed in the balances I am afraid I shall be found wanting, but in the pulpit they tell me I am heavy enough." Spurgeon learned many wonderful qualities from his granddad.

Charles was the first grandchild in the James Spurgeon family. His aunt Ann, along with her parents, became sincerely and affectionately attached to the young child. She was eighteen when Charles came to stay at Stambourne. She had the primary responsibility of caring for the youngest member in the home. She sought to promote his spiritual welfare through her devout life and daily example.

Spurgeon's grandmother offered him a penny for each hymn of Isaac Watts he could permanently memorize. He was also offered a similar reward for memorizing long passages from Bunyan's *Grace Abounding*. His grandfather encouraged young Charles to read Scriptures at the family worship time. By age six he was able to read with an arresting impact on those who heard him. He developed an appetite for books and had a strong desire to understand why things happened in what he read about. His desire for reading and learning manifested itself in problem-solving: once he encountered a problem, he stayed with the challenge until he had come to a sure solution of its remedy.

Aunt Ann taught Charles how to read at home. He also attended a school for young children taught by a Mrs. Burleigh. It was described as a Sunday school class where Mrs. Burleigh would sing or repeat Scriptures over and over to the children and they were expected to repeat them at the next meeting. Under the care and guidance of his grandfather, Charles developed reflective abilities, evaluating matters of right and wrong, good and bad. Through these experiences he became fonder of books than of play. He would sit for hours going through Fox's *Martyrology*, Bunyan's *Pilgrim's Progress* and *Robinson Crusoe*. He evidenced a determination for godly values and boldness in expressing his convictions even as a child. With this kind of childhood background, one can understand the dogmatic conviction for truth and the certitude and confidence with which he later proclaimed the gospel in his ministry.

During these developmental years, God was shaping him for a purpose before Charles had come to know Him in salvation. The development he experienced would help him fulfill a life mission and purpose. A prelude to that mission was demonstrated in little Charles's life while living with his grandparents. Charles observed his grandfather burdened and lamenting over the waywardness of one of his parishioners. In response, young Spurgeon went on a ministry errand:

Little Charles, not yet six years old, had witnessed the grief of the good old minister over the inconsistent conduct of one of his flock, a man who frequented the village inn, drinking and smoking among ungodly companions. One day the boy astonished his grandfather by declaring "I'll kill old Roads, that I will!" The pastor reproved the child, telling him that if he did anything wrong, he would be taken by the police. But the child, very serious and very much in earnest, repeated that he would kill old Roads, though he would not do anything wrong. The grandfather was puzzled, but he let the subject drop and it passed from his mind. Shortly afterwards, however, the child came into his grandfather's room, saying, "I've killed old Roads, he'll never grieve my dear grandpa any more."[12]

The grandfather questioned the child with some concern but was assured by young Charles he had done nothing wrong. He duly told his grandfather he had been about the Lord's work. Mr. Roads, himself, cleared up the entire matter by soon coming to the parsonage. He ashamedly explained,

> I was a-sitting in the public [tavern], just having my pipe and mug of beer . . . when that child comes in—to think an old man like me should be took to task and reproved by a bit of a child like that! Well, he points at me with his finger, just so, and says, "What doest thou here, Elijah, sitting with the ungodly? And you a member of a church and breaking your pastor's heart. I'm ashamed of you! I wouldn't break my pastor's heart, I'm sure." And then he walks away. Well, I did feel angry; but I knew it was all true and I was guilty; so I put down my pipe and did not touch my beer, but hurried away to a lonely spot and cast myself down before the Lord confessing my sin and begging for forgiveness.[13]

The repentance of Roads and the ministry effort of young Spurgeon proved genuine. The pastor who succeeded Charles's grandfather at Stambourne years later reported that Thomas Roads was an earnest and zealous Christian and sought to encourage others in the ways of God, especially young people. This incident gives a clear look at the character bent and personality of Spurgeon and gives understanding of his pastoral leadership of the Metropolitan Tabernacle and serving as president of the Pastors' College.

---

12. Ray, *Spurgeon*, 16–17.
13. Ray, *Spurgeon*, 17.

Young Spurgeon was often at his grandfather's side while the elder counseled and prayed with his parishioners. Sometimes he would sit with his grandfather in the pulpit. To many in the Stambourne congregation, the young Spurgeon was merely a forward child who had caught something of their pastor's eccentricity. Charles's grandfather often hosted visiting ministers at the parsonage. Godly elders were frequent visitors at Stambourne. Charles was privileged to sit with these men and listen to their deliberations. From these discussions he took in evangelical concepts and convictions. This compounded biblical values and convictions upon young Charles's heart.

These early years of Charles Spurgeon's life impressed him deeply with the reality of God and the work and objectives of Christianity and churches. The pulpit ministry became a rich fascination to young Spurgeon. He had an early interest in educating himself about those who preached the Word of God. These early influences instilled in him a strong commitment to reading and endeared a deep interest in spiritual matters. It prepared his heart for a life mission and evangelistic endeavor that made him a multiplier of disciples and churches. These convictions and understandings allowed him to see the renewing of churches he served and those he sent his Pastors' College men to serve.

The experience of living the first six years of his life with his grandparents and aunt in Stambourne left an indelible mark on young Spurgeon's temperament and spirit. Spurgeon gave some insight into how he viewed these early life lessons at Stambourne:

> For more than two centuries, "the tabernacle of righteousness" has been on this spot. If the stone should cry out of the wall, and the beam out of the timber should answer it, what tales they might tell!—happily, in this case, not tales of accusation, exposing wickedness, or denouncing woe. What conflicts and victories have these walls known! What sufferings of the godly, what hopes and anxieties, what fears and joys, and what communion with God! Every room has been hallowed by the breath of prayer: its rooftree has been vocal with the song of praise without ceasing. Almost every Lord's day, for many years, the large central room was occupied, in the interval of public service, by Christian people, who edified and comforted one another by godly conference, combined with the voice of intercession and the melody of psalms and hymns.[14]

14. Spurgeon, *Stambourne*, 29.

Spurgeon was taught by his grandparents right from wrong and trained to act according to convictions. They modeled this by their daily lives. This led Spurgeon to say of all life practices there is need to realize the value and power of example. He said of his early years, "Example is the school of mankind, and many will learn at no other. Examples preach to the eye and leave a deeper impress than counsel addressed to the ear. Children like pictures better than letter press, so do men prefer example to precept."[15]

Whatever goes on in local churches, this rule will always apply *what the leaders model, the members do*. Example does matter. This must be understood and prayerfully worked out by pastors. They must love and mentor the leaders of the church because what the leaders of the church practice in attitude and action will become the culture and practice of the congregation. In the church, this principle is unbreakable—and every pastor and church leader must appreciate and understand how to apply it in their respective ministries. Jesus regarded this and worked it in His ministry. He spent more time with Peter, James and John because they would help and influence the other disciples by their example. The pastor must make sure he helps his leaders be successful in following Christ and to model what the Savior wants everyone else in the church to be learning and practicing. This is what the Savior did with His disciples, and we cannot bypass or ignore His example in working with the believers entrusted to our care and leadership. Our churches will profit immensely if we honor and implement the instruction of 2 Tim 2:2.

Charles's Parents: John and Eliza Spurgeon

When Charles Spurgeon left his grandparents to rejoin his parents in Colchester at age six, he and his grandfather shared some time crying together at his departure. Through their creative and loving training, Charles's grandparents (and Aunt Ann) had nurtured him into a servant of God. Young Charles would return to Stambourne to spend holidays and summers with his grandparents. He was now ready to begin his formal schooling process. Upon his rejoining his parents, Charles received initial training at home that strengthened his academic resolve and dedication.

Charles Spurgeon explained to his Pastors' College men the impression his parents John and Eliza made on him: "I can tell you two reasons

---

15. Conwell, *Life of Spurgeon*, 54.

why I am what I am. He paused and slowly added 'My mother and the truth of my message.'"[16] Spurgeon acknowledged he was blessed with godly parents and watched over with careful eyes, "scarcely ever permitted to mingle with questionable associates, warned not to listen to anything profane or licentious, and taught the way of God from my youth up."[17]

Charles's father, John, followed in the example of his own father. He worked for many years in Colchester before entering the ministry, serving bi-vocationally at the church in Tollesbury from 1835 to1851. Serving a church and working full time while the children were growing up concerned John that he was neglecting his family. He relates,

> I had been away from home a great deal, trying to build up weak congregations, and felt that I was neglecting the religious training of my own children while I was toiling for the good of others. I returned home with these feelings. I opened the door, and was surprised to find none of the children about the hall. Going quietly upstairs, I heard my wife's voice. She was engaged in prayer with the children; I heard her pray for them one by one by name. She came to Charles, and specially prayed for him, for he was of high spirit and daring temper. I listened till she had ended her prayer, and I felt and said, "Lord, I will go on with Thy work. The children will be cared for."[18]

John Spurgeon was an effective pastor who faithfully cared for his congregations. He was able to draw sizeable crowds and was especially popular with young people—like his father. He was viewed with affection and esteem by his people. His preaching was earnest and direct. His wife, Eliza, was right at her husband's side in the ministry.

Eliza Spurgeon was known and respected for her piety. She was a woman who had a kind smile for everyone, and she was clearly unassuming. Her humility was rare, and she etched this character quality upon her children's souls. She prayed carefully over each of her children for their salvation and service to Christ. One of the daughters of John and Eliza became a pastor's wife like her mom; both sons became pastors. Needham relates an insight on the family's internal strength and humor, "Speaking one day to her son Charles of her solicitude for the best interests of all her children, Mrs. Spurgeon said, 'Ah, Charley, I have often prayed that you might be saved, but never that you should become a Baptist.' To this

---

16. Carlisle, *Spurgeon*, 24.
17. Spurgeon, *Autobiography*, vol. 1, 67.
18. Needham, *Life and Labors of Spurgeon*, 28.

Charles replied, 'God has answered your prayer, mother, with His usual bounty, and given you more than you asked.'[19]

His mother taught and prayed over all her children. She explained God's ways to them from Alleine's *Alarm* or Baxter's *Call to the Unconverted* with questions and discussion. She closed these sessions in prayer lifting each child by name to God. This was regularly practiced on Sunday evenings while John was out ministering at the church. One prayer Charles remembers his mother praying was "now, Lord, if my children go on in their sins, it will not be from ignorance that they perish, and my soul must bear a swift witness against them at the day of judgment if they lay not hold of Christ."[20] This pierced young Spurgeon's conscience and stirred his heart.

It seems when Charles moved back from his grandparents to join his siblings, he became a leader to them and a kind of second father. He would pray with them and at times preach to them mini sermons by organizing the younger children into a small congregation to listen to his addresses. He retained his love for reading as well. By the time he left his grandparents he had acquired a small library of books. In fact, he had to put new covers on his books due to the wear and tear of regular usage. He numbered his books, organized them, and put one of his sisters in charge of them as librarian. His love for learning led him to recite the many hymns he had learned at Stambourne to his brothers and sisters. One in particular was a favorite: "Now will I tell to sinners round, what a dear Savior I have found; I'll point to Thy redeeming blood, and say, Behold the way to God," At the words "I'll point" the boy would solemnly raise his finger and point upward (many photographs show Spurgeon in this pose.).[21] Young Charles also wrote a small book called *Passing Events* which contained an article and one of his poems. He also compiled two mission magazines. One he called *Scraps of Missionary News* and the other *Juvenile Magazine*. The latter contained his concern for friends who were weakening in faith and announced prayer meetings he would lead in order to help them to the throne of grace.

John Spurgeon stayed close to his children even though he had a busy schedule. When he came home each evening from work or from preaching, he gathered his children and relayed to them the day's events

---

19. Needham, *Life and Labors of Spurgeon*, 27.
20. Spurgeon, *Autobiography*, vol. 1, 67.
21. Ray, *Spurgeon*, 27.

in a fun and interesting manner. He also played with the children, talked to, and held devotions with them. One instance of instruction Charles received from his dad involved a pencil Charles had secured on credit from a Mrs. Pearson's store. (Charles was often careless about losing and misplacing things.)

> Charles's father . . . got to hear of the transaction, and when the boy arrived home rebuked him severely, likening a debtor to a thief. So vivid was the picture he drew of a boy who, having owed a farthing, might one day owe a hundred pounds, and get into prison disgracing his family, that Charles then and there determined never again to get into debt. After the reproof he was marched off to the shop to pay the farthing, crying bitterly all down the street, because he was so ashamed of himself, and believed everyone he met looked with contempt upon the youthful debtor. The story is told in "John Ploughman's Talk," with many pithy comments thereon, and the parental warnings against debt are repeated. "Ever since that early sickening," wrote C. H. Spurgeon, "I have hated debt as Luther hated the Pope."[22]

This principle guided him in building churches and all other matters of finances, including the houses he and Susannah purchased during their married life. Later in life he said of the experience, "It was a lecture, indeed; I think I can hear it now, and can feel my ears tingling at the recollection of it . . . The farthing was paid amid many solemn warnings, and the poor debtor was set free, like a bird let out of a cage. How sweet it felt to be out of debt! How did my little heart vow and declare that nothing should ever tempt me into debt again! It was a fine lesson, and I have never forgotten it."[23]

A significant event in Charles's childhood took place when he was about ten years old. (This can serve as a lesson to all adults of what being sensitive and spiritually discerning toward children can mean for their futures.) In the summer of 1844 Richard Knill was going through the county of Essex on deputation for the London Missionary Society. On the weekend he preached at Stambourne, he was hosted at James Spurgeon's residence. Charles was visiting at the time and for three consecutive mornings at six o'clock, Knill talked with young Charles. After hearing Charles earnestly read the Scriptures at family prayer time, Knill gave a prophecy that some day Charles would preach the gospel to multitudes

22. Ray, *Spurgeon*, 30.
23. Spurgeon, *Autobiography*, vol. 1, 40.

at Rowland Hill's Surrey Chapel (a huge worship auditorium in London). It came true. Young Spurgeon and Mr. Knill continued a friendship until the elder's death in 1857.

Another childhood practice indicated the future course of Charles Spurgeon. Charles's dad related to a newspaper correspondent that he felt that Charles was destined to be a preacher. Mr. Spurgeon related an experience in Colchester which indicated Charles's direction in life: Charles had climbed up into the hayrack above the stable and having arranged for his younger brother and sisters to congregate below, he proceeded to give them a zealous sermon.[24]

John and Eliza Spurgeon loved their children and made sure they had educational opportunities though it required great sacrifices for them. They taught their children habits of thrift and self-denial. John Spurgeon said of his children's education, "I have frequently worn a shabby coat when I might have possessed a good one, had I cared less for my children's education."[25]

There was no system of free education in England during Spurgeon's youth. Many children remained illiterate. A few charity schools existed in London to educate children; most schooling was conducted as a personal business with parents paying for their children's schooling. Charles Spurgeon continued into adolescence what he had begun in childhood—constantly reading. His father said, "that he did nothing else with his time but to bury himself with books." He further added, "nothing could entice the boy from his studies, and his wonderful memory retained what he read."[26] Pike described Spurgeon's reading abilities:

> The wonder was how, with such demands on his time, Mr. Spurgeon contrived to get through so much reading as he did; but the more you conversed with him in that charming room [Spurgeon's study room at their Helensburgh House, Nightingale Lane] the more clearly did you perceive that the mind of your companion could not only read at lightning speed, but when he had gone through a book the contents became permanently his own.[27]

---

24. Spurgeon, *Autobiography*, vol. 1, 33–39.
25. Conwell, *Spurgeon*, 49.
26. Ray, *Spurgeon*, 20.
27. Pike, *Life and Works of Spurgeon*, vol. 4, 376.

Given Spurgeon's accomplishments in the Lord's service, the impact of reading and the increased skill of doing so is clearly a value to be embraced by the Christian home and by local churches. Howard Hendricks often repeated in our classes at Dallas Seminary, "If you stop reading, you stop leading." For Spurgeon, this helps explain the genius of his abilities in later life regarding his knowledge and reading retention.

PURITANISM

Charles was probably no more than three when he first began pulling books off the shelf and gazing at their content in his grandparent's parsonage. A contemporary of Spurgeon reports that "even when a mere child, before his lips had uttered an articulate word, he would sit patiently for hours, amusing himself with a book of pictures."[28] A small chamber, which led off from one of the upstairs' bedrooms in the parsonage, contained an old Puritan library. This is where Charles immersed himself as a boy in large books of Puritan divinity. It generated a life-long thirst for Puritan works. Spurgeon described these early experiences of reading books in this small library:

> That little room was the minister's study and closet for prayer; and a very nice cozy room, too. In my time, it was a dark den;— but *it contained books,* and this made it a gold mine to me. Therein was fulfilled the promise, "I will give thee the treasures of darkness." Some of these were enormous folios, such as a boy could hardly lift. Here I first struck up acquaintance with the martyrs, and specially with "Old Bonner", who burned them; next, with Bunyan and his "Pilgrim"; and further on, with the great masters of Scriptural theology, with whom no moderns are worthy to be named in the same day. Even the old editions of their works, with their margins and old-fashioned notes, are precious to me . . . I wonder whether some other boy will love them, and live to revive that grand old divinity which will yet be to England her balm and benison.
>
> Out of that darkened room I fetched those old authors when I was yet a youth, and never was I happier than when in their company. Out of the present contempt, into which Puritanism has fallen, many brave hearts and true will fetch it, by the help of God, ere many years have passed.[29]

28. Dallimore, *Spurgeon*, 7.
29. Spurgeon, *Autobiography*, vol. 1, 22–23.

To understand Spurgeon and convictions for the work God ultimately accomplished through his life, knowing the importance and influence of Puritanism on him is key. He valued the writings and ministries of Puritan preachers and prized them most in his library collection. They were his friends and mentors for what he attempted and achieved. The truths of Scripture Spurgeon learned through the Puritans equipped him to believe and obey God with expectation and fervent effort in Great Commission work. Their truths still mean energy and blessings for pastors and churches today.

Puritanism began as a reform movement within the Church of England against Romanish tendencies. In 1572 the Puritans drew up a statement of their position called "The Admonition" which they presented to the government. In it they argued that many ministers did not have a true call from God to minister and urged only those things that issued forth from the Word of God should be placed in churches or used to lead worship meetings. Their protests were discarded.

The Puritans were strongly influenced by Calvin's teachings: they held a high conception of God's sovereignty and His providence and grace. Their movement was loyalty to the Bible and the Bible alone. Following the Act of Uniformity, (three were passed by Parliament during the 1550's and in 1662 another was passed—all had penalties for noncompliance by Nonconformists; in 1668 the Act of Toleration brought limited freedoms to dissenters) nearly two thousand Puritan ministers were expelled from their churches. Penalties varying from petty to vicious were carried out against them. They were branded as fanatics and rebels. This was done in spite of the fact that most of them were graduates of England's leading universities. Puritanism was not stopped. It metamorphosed into the Nonconformists movement. Puritan beliefs and values caught the attention of sixteenth and seventeenth century England. Its sound doctrine and thoroughness of practical application of Scripture to life produced the golden age of evangelical preaching in England.

The Puritans made a great impression on Spurgeon in theology and methodology. They were biblical scholars trained at Oxford and Cambridge in the fifteenth, sixteenth, and seventeenth centuries. Some became exceptional professors at these universities. Spurgeon had a deep love for their writings. He had Susannah read them to him during their engagement; he hunted for Puritan works throughout his lifetime. By the time of his death, he had amassed nearly seven thousand Puritan volumes (his total library contained some twelve thousand books). His mind became steeped in the seventeenth century thinking and language of the Puritans. He always carried Puritan works with him when he traveled or took his annual leaves to Mentone, France (done the last seventeen years of his life because of the gout which was especially inflamed during the cold London winters).

Some of Spurgeon's favorite Puritan volumes he read repeatedly included the following: all the writings of Thomas Brooks, but especially his *Apples of God* and also his *Precious Remedies Against Satan's Devices*; *The Objects and Acts of Justifying Faith* by Thomas Goodwin; John Owen on *The Glories of Christ*, *The Death of Death in the Death of Christ*, *The Holy Spirit, and Hebrews*; Stephen Charnock's massive work on *The Attributes of God*, The *Christian in Complete Armour* by William Gurnall; Thomas Manton's *John 17*, *Mystery of Providence* by John Flavel, *The Body of Divinity* by Thomas Watson, Richard Baxter's *Reformed Pastor* and *Saints' Everlasting Rest*, and John Bunyans' *Pilgrim's Progress* and *The Holy War*.[30]

It is by no means to be understood that Spurgeon read only Puritan authors or solely Christian publications. He had a wide range of literary interests and fields of study which went well beyond the disciplines of theology. But his appreciation and valuing of Puritan works was without question. Spurgeon commented during a sermon preached at the Tabernacle on June 24, 1883, "God gave Elijah forty days' meat at one meal: do you, dear friends, ever get such meals as that? I do when I read certain books;—not modern-thought books. Give me no such fare as that,—a grain of meal to a gallon of water; but let me have one of the good solid Puritan volumes that are so little prized nowadays, and my soul can feed upon such blessed food as that, and be satisfied with it."[31]

The Puritans were prolific writers. One example is that of Richard Baxter who wrote 168 books. Peter Lewis, in his work *Puritans*, defines this body of believers by saying, "essential Puritanism grew out of three great areas: the New Testament pattern of personal piety, sound doctrine and a properly ordered Church-life, and it is the mingling and blending together of all three of these emphases which made English Puritanism the astonishment and the inspiration it was and is still."[32]

Caricatures of Puritanism have made this movement appear harsh, rigid, and closed-minded to the beauty and goodness of the world. But

---

30. Bacon, *Spurgeon: Heir of Puritans*, 108–9.
31. Spurgeon, *Autobiography*, vol. 4, 265.
32. Lewis, *Puritanism*, 11.

Puritanism has always led people at all times to seek a more genuine way of living, one that is simple and good as opposed to the insincere corruptions in the world around them. Puritans obtained their peculiar character through long, unhurried exposure to the Bible on the one hand, and the writings of John Calvin on the other. Spurgeon never placed more value on Puritan authors (or others) over that of the Scriptures, but through his own communing with the Bible and also Puritan authors, he received his baptism of fire. Spurgeon referenced Puritans and his own feelings regarding them and the Scriptures by stating,

> *Oh, that you and I might get into the very heart of the Word of God, and get that Word into ourselves! As I have seen the silkworm eat into the leaf, and consume it, so ought we to do with the Word of the Lord ; . . . it is blessed to eat into the very soul of the Bible until, at last, you come to talk in Scriptural language, and . . . your spirit is flavored with the words of the Lord* [emphasis added]. I would quote John Bunyan as an instance of what I mean. Read anything of his, and you will see that it is almost like reading the Bible itself . . . ; he had read it till his whole being was saturated with Scripture; continually making us feel and say, "Why, this man is a living Bible! . . . He cannot speak without quoting a text, for his soul is full of the Word of God."[33]

It was traditional for Puritans to teach their children so that they could clearly discuss and explain key New Testament doctrines by the age of twelve. They grew up in an atmosphere of strong and confident convictions. Ryken gives us insight of the Puritan's beliefs on the family and the experiences and goals aimed for in the home:

> The Puritans' favorite image for the family was a church. Richard Baxter wrote that "a Christian family . . . is a church . . . a society of Christians combined for the better worshipping and serving of God." William Gouge said that the family is a "little church," while William Perkins wrote, "These families wherein this service of God is performed are, as it were, little churches, yea even a kind of Paradise on earth.". . . Nicholas Byfield advised, Parents should carefully set up the worship of God in the family that from their cradles [children] may see the practice of piety." . . .
>
> The technique that the Puritans found most effective in Christian instruction was catechizing. This question-answer format accorded well both with the Puritans' stress on the

---

33. Spurgeon, *Autobiography*, vol. 4, 268.

intellectual content of the faith and their penchant to have matters well-defined. Richard Baxter devoted a section of the *The Reformed Pastor* to the topic "the duty of personal catechizing and instructing the flock particularly recommended." *The goal of catechizing was not memorization but understanding* [emphasis added]. Cotton Mather cautioned parents not to let "the children patter out by rote the words of the catechism, like parrots; but to be inquisitive how far their understandings do take in the things of God."[34]

Spurgeon learned from the Puritans through preaching the Word as the expected norm of leading people to salvation. And through preaching was spiritual life and holiness maintained among the hearers. John Owen gave this insight on Puritan thinking regarding the work of preaching God's Word: "The Word is like the sun in the firmament . . . it is compared at large in Ps. 19. It hath virtually in it all spiritual light and heat. But the preaching of the Word is as the motion and beams of the sun, which actually and effectually communicate that light and heat unto all creatures, which are virtually (essentially and energetically) in the sun itself."[35]

Puritan sermons placed high demands on the intellect, but they balanced this with appeals to the heart and the will. Puritan authors repeatedly spoke of their preachers aiming at delivering the Word of God into the heart and consciences of their hearers. They purposed to motivate their hearers to apply God's truths to their daily lifestyles. It was a common practice in Puritan church services for note taking. They utilized shorthand to take notes of the sermon. Even the youngest engaged in taking notes. Following the service, the sermon was digested further during the mealtime and throughout the afternoon at home.[36]

Note taking and an active memory were given impetus by yet another Puritan practice, "repeating the sermon" with the family at home. What the Puritans "heard in public" they "repeated in private, to whet it upon himself and family." The practice of Theophilus Eaton's family was in every way typical of Puritan families. He assembled his whole family on Sunday evenings "and in an obliging manner conferred with them about the things with which they had been entertained in the house of God, shutting up all with a prayer for the blessing of God upon them all."[37]

34. Ryken, *Worldly Saints*, 84–86.
35. Lewis, *Puritanism*, 42.
36. Ryken, *Worldly Saints*, 103–4.
37. Ryken, *Worldly Saints*, 104.

This is the great call of every pastor and church: to know and experience the promises and principles of God's Word together in serving Christ. To lead the members to give this kind of attention to the Scriptures in the home life pays great dividends to the health of the church as families are strengthened in their walk with Christ. God's Shema directs this practice in Deut 6:4–9.

The centrality of the pulpit ministry and its applicational practices in the home were key in accomplishing evangelism and maturing believers. This was riveted into Spurgeon's thinking. It was key to seeing churches revitalized and the multiplying of disciples and more churches. These convictions of truth grew and became strongly rooted during Spurgeon's childhood. They would eventually lead him in adulthood to call out believers in his congregation to believe God with conviction and serve Him with passion, seeing lives impacted by the Savior's salvation and life. 2 Tim 2:2 would become a cherished life principal Spurgeon loved fulfilling in seeing leaders raised up for Great Commission work.

3

Schooling, Conversion, and Spurgeon's Foundation for a Ministry of Multiplication

IT IS TRUE THAT young Charles spent much time in reading and less time at playing compared to most children. But he was far from being someone who never had fun; he enjoyed his share of pranks. One of his enjoyments as a child was taking turnips, cutting out the insides and placing candles inside to scare others at night by creating the appearance of ghosts coming out of the woods. Or he would invite boys to his home to come into the kitchen cupboard to take a delicious sniff of the contents of a certain jar which was full of ammonia; the scheme was highly successful until one day a boy fell in a dead faint overcome by the gaseous compound.

He also had a deep love for hunting as a boy and for a time wanted to pursue it as a profession more than anything else. While living at Stambourne he often saw fox hunts complete with dogs and horsemen and the horns blowing. Many townspeople would join in the chase following the hunt. The chase went on through ditches and hedges, farms and fields. For young Spurgeon, it was an adventure rivaling heaven in his imagination for its thrill and excitement. He was enthralled by it. He thought there could be nothing more exciting or rewarding for him to do than to be a professional hunter.[1]

---

1. Ray, *Spurgeon*, 25.

FORMAL SCHOOLING

Having a strong influence of Puritan values from his family background, Spurgeon profited greatly from their commitment to education. University education such as Oxford or Cambridge in the mid-nineteenth century was restricted in England from certain classes of people outside the Church of England. It was out of the question for a Nonconformist. But Puritans worked to provide educational opportunities for young people. Some felt preachers in the church could do as well or better work without being educated, but Puritans believed formal studies were important,

> For the Puritans, zeal was no substitute for knowledge. John Preston declared, "I deny not but *a man may have much knowledge and want grace, but on the other side, . . . you cannot have more grace than you have knowledge* [emphasis added]." Richard Baxter believed that "education is God's ordinary way for the conveyance of his grace, and ought no more to be set in opposition to the Spirit than the preaching of the Word." John Cotton claimed that although "knowledge is no knowledge without zeal," yet "zeal is but a wild-fire without knowledge."[2]

Puritans were active in establishing schools for instruction. The objective of education was to give people ability to read and with that gift to be able to study the teachings of the Bible. They knew the best strategy for precluding Satan's temptations was the study of the Word of God. Their influence marked Emmanuel College at Cambridge University. The statutes of this school stated, "that schools and colleges be founded for the education of young men in all piety and good learning especially in Holy Writ and theology, that being thus instructed they may thereafter teach true and pure religion."[3] Puritans in America helped establish Harvard University. One of the foundational tenets of this college was "Let every student be plainly instructed and earnestly pressed to consider well the main end of his life and studies is to know God and Jesus Christ . . . the only foundation of all sound knowledge and learning."[4]

Charles first entered academic pursuits at Stockwell School in Colchester. This was a middle class classical and commercial school whose principal was Harry Lewis and included a scholarly assistant, Mr. Leeding. Mr. Leeding would teach Spurgeon later at Cambridge—not the

---

2. Ryken, *Worldly Saints*, 159.
3. Ryken, *Worldly Saints*, 162.
4. Ryken, *Worldly Saints*, 161.

University, but another private schooling arrangement located in the same town as the University. Leeding was recognized as a man of faith and firm principle. Regarding the reading of books, Spurgeon described his personal discipline and commitment at this time by saying "at the period of my life, when I ought perhaps to have been in the playground, developing my legs and sinews, which no doubt would have kept me from gout now, I spent my time at my books, studying and working hard, . . . very much to the pleasure of my schoolmaster."[5]

Spurgeon attended the Stockwell School, Colchester, during the ages ten to fourteen. Here he received a good grounding in Latin and mathematics. Charles's first night at the boarding school revealed a slice of his character and personality. When he knelt down to pray before getting into bed he was pelted by a shower of slippers. Charles promptly told the other boys to quit it and knocked several of them down. He then returned to his bedside and on his knees finished his business of praying.[6]

The next schooling effort took place at St. Augustine's College at Maidstone, located a few miles southeast of London. His younger brother, James, accompanied Charles in this schooling venture. They boarded with the school's principal, their uncle. This schooling lasted approximately twelve months. Studies involved agriculture and science. This was a Church of England school and Charles was challenged while attending classes to search the Scriptures regarding repentance and faith as it relates to baptism. From his study, Charles found the Word of God taught baptism was experienced after one had repented and confessed faith in Christ. Spurgeon described his discovery,

> But there was a turning in my life, through being there . . . The Church of England Catechism has in it . . . this question, "What is required of persons to be baptized?" and the answer I was taught to give, and did give, was, "Repentance, whereby they forsake sin; and faith, whereby they steadfastly believe the promises of God made to them in that sacrament." I looked that answer up in the Bible, and I found it to be strictly correct as far as repentance and faith are concerned; and of course, when I afterwards became a Christian, I also became a Baptist; and here I am, and it is due to the Church of England Catechism that I am a Baptist. Having been brought up amongst Congregationalists, I had never looked at the matter in my life. I had thought myself to

---

5. Fullerton, *Spurgeon*, 14

6. Carlile, *Spurgeon*, 56–57.

Schooling, Conversion, and Spurgeon's Foundation

have been baptized as an infant; and so, when I was confronted with the question, "What is required of persons to be baptized?" and I found that repentance and faith were required, I said to myself, "Then I have not been baptized; that infant sprinkling of mine was a mistake; and please God that I ever have repentance and faith [he was yet without the assurance of salvation], I will be properly baptized."[7]

During this year, the young Spurgeon wrote his *Popery Unmasked*, a 295-page treatise on the doctrinal errors and wrongs of the papacy. His seventeen chapters showed a widely developed theological understanding and grasp of spiritual matters from the Scriptures and from history. He wrote this before he was converted, but his reasoning and reflection on the Scriptures were instrumental in bringing about his salvation shortly after completing this paper. The very passage which was used by the Spirit of God to lead him to a firm faith in Christ, Isa 45:22, was dealt with in his paper. He had written the *Popery Unmasked* in November and December 1848; some thirteen months later, his salvation experience occurred on January 6, 1850.

The following words are taken from chapter 3 "Popery, a Spiritual Darkness" and gives a vivid demonstration of his understanding of these subjects at age fourteen:

> In 1824, Pope Leo XII styles the Scriptures in the vulgar tongue, "Poisonous Pastures," and exhorts the clergy to turn the flock away from them. In a Bull of Pope Pius VII, against Bible Societies, in 1816, he says:—"We have been truly shocked by this most crafty device by which the very foundations of religion are undermined. The Bible printed by heretics is to be numbered among other prohibited books, conformably to the rules of the Index; for it is evident, from experience, that the Holy Scriptures, when circulated in the vulgar tongue, have through the temerity of men produced more harm than benefit". . . About the beginning of the sixteenth century, "the ignorance of the priests was extreme." Numbers could not read, most only muttered mass in an unknown tongue, and read a legend on festival days; the very best seldom saw the Bible. It was held by many that the doctrines of religion were so properly expressed by the schoolmen, that there was no need to read Scripture. One of eminence was asked what were the Ten Commandments; he replied, "There is no such book in the library." Many doctors of the

---

7. Spurgeon, *Autobiography*, vol. 1, 52.

Sorbonne declared, and confirmed it by an oath, that, though they were about fifty years of age, yet they had never known what a New Testament was. Luther never saw a Bible till after he was twenty years old, and had taken a degree of arts. Carolstadt had been a doctor of divinity eight years before he read the Scriptures; and yet, when he stood for a degree in the University of Wittemberg, he obtained an honor, and it was entered in the University records that he was "*sufficientissimus.*" Pelican could not procure one Greek Testament in all Germany; the first he got was from Italy.

Who can wonder at the superstitions and errors of the Church of Rome? When sermons were delivered, they were a collection of forced interpretations, legends fabricated on the spot, and base ribaldry. The people would have been better without them, many of these mock sermons were only calculated to excite the audience to laughter, and to furnish them with amusement for the week. Ignorance held its dark reign, with scarcely a spark of light, and must have been of immense service in the establishment of the kingdom of darkness, and the support of the dominion of Antichrist.[8]

Young Charles would often be an irritant to his uncle who was the mathematics instructor at the school. During lectures Charles felt it his duty to correct his uncle when he recognized an error. His uncle soon judged it better to have Charles take his books outside and study under a tree by himself. While at Maidstone, Spurgeon also developed mathematic tables eventually used by a life insurance company in London. These tables were continued in use by the insurance company into the twentieth century.[9]

At this time in his life, he knew so much more than the other pupils he studied with, it meant he had no match when it came to any kind of debate over issues. The only practical way for Spurgeon to participate in discussions, and for varying viewpoints to be ably presented, was to let Spurgeon debate himself. His peers would listen to Charles present one side of an issue, and then listen to him debate himself giving the other side with all facts needing to be considered. He could amuse and amaze classmates with his ability to refute his own answers with logic and reason putting all positions presented upon a solid foundation.[10]

---

8. Spurgeon, *Autobiography*, vol. 1, 64, 66.
9. Spurgeon, *Autobiography*, vol 1, 51.
10. Spurgeon, *Autobiography*, vol. 4, 266.

Schooling, Conversion, and Spurgeon's Foundation

After his year at Maidstone, Charles next entered the school at Newmarket (approximately seventy miles north of London in Suffolk County) on August 17, 1849. He had just turned fifteen and was furthering his education, particularly in the study of Greek. While studying here, Spurgeon taught younger boys as a junior tutor under Mr. Swindell, the principal of the school. Along with Greek studies he pursued French on a daily basis.

At Newmarket Mr. Swindell was assisted by J. D. Everett who would later become a professor at Queen's College in Belfast. Everett was almost eighteen when he joined Swindell to instruct pupils. He and young Spurgeon became fast friends and Everett kept a journal with several entries relating to Charles while at Newmarket. On September 10, 1849, he noted a missionary meeting occurring in which Charles was made chairman. "I believe it was the first time Mr. Spurgeon ever made a speech. He spoke fluently." One other entry on October 9 indicated Spurgeon's character bent, "After dinner, I took Percy [Everett's brother] and four other boys to see the races. We saw the Cesarewitch, the most celebrated race at Newmarket; thirty-one horses ran [Newmarket was the main center for horse racing in Great Britain]. We also saw four other races. I saw quite enough to gratify my curiosity, and did not wish to stop to see any more races. Mr. Spurgeon did not go, as he thought he should be doing wrong if he went."[11]

Mr. Swindell was a devout Christian and was a member of a Baptist church. He employed a woman serving as his housekeeper who was to have a strong impact on young Spurgeon. Mary King, or 'cook' as she was affectionately known, was a member of the Bethesda Baptist church in Ipswich. She was a staunch Calvinist with a wonderful knowledge of the Bible. During the fall of 1849 she and young Spurgeon had many earnest conversations. Spurgeon felt he learned more from her than he did from six teachers of divinity. (This helps us understand Spurgeon's deep valuing of the laity and their potential for kingdom contributions and its advancement.) He was growing in conviction for his own salvation. Following Spurgeon's death, J. D. Everett wrote about this time in Charles's life at Newmarket,

> I can add something to what has been already published. In Mr. Swindell's household there was a faithful old servant—a big, sturdy woman, who was well known to me and all the inmates

11. Spurgeon, *Autobiography*, vol. 1, 55.

> as 'cook.' She was a woman of strong religious feelings, and a devout Calvinist. Spurgeon, when under deep religious conviction, had conversed with her, and been deeply impressed with her views of Divine truth. He explained this to me, and told me, in his own terse fashion, that it was 'cook' who had taught him his theology. I hope I am not violating his confidence in mentioning this fact. It is no discredit to the memory of a great man that he was willing to learn from the humblest sources.[12]

The effect of his parent's instruction and his reading Puritan works eventuated in Spurgeon a strong desire to know his sins were forgiven and that he was in God's favor. Mary King proved very instrumental in helping Charles sort out his theology and better understand the salvation he desired and was convicted for. Spurgeon said he learned more from Mary King than from the minister of the chapel he attended during this time. In his *Autobiography*, Spurgeon described Mary King in the following way: "She was a good old soul, and used to read 'The Gospel Standard.' She liked something very sweet indeed, good strong Calvinistic doctrine; but she lived strongly as well as fed strongly. Many a time we have gone over the covenant of grace together, and talked of personal election of the saints, their union to Christ, their final perseverance, and what vital godliness meant."[13] Spurgeon never forgot her influence. In writing in a volume intended for young Christians he said he was eternally obligated to an old cook "who was despised as an Antinomian, but who in her kitchen taught him many of the deep things of God, and removed many a doubt from his youthful mind."[14]

This story from Spurgeon's life shows the value of every Christian and the investment they can make in the kingdom of God. There are many Mary Kings sitting in our pews today who can be tapped to invest into younger people for Christ's work. Part of Spurgeon's valuing the laity came out of this personal experience with Mary King. The potential of each believer will largely be determined by how the pastor sees his congregants. If pastors can teach these truths from Scripture to their members which impacted Mary King and then Spurgeon, a 2 Tim 2:2 church culture can be created. The how-to of this will be understood more when the farm system developed at the Metropolitan Tabernacle is developed later in the book.

12. Spurgeon, *Autobiography*, vol. 1, 54.
13. Spurgeon, *Autobiography*, vol. 1, 54.
14. Spurgeon, *The Saint and His Saviour*, 131.

THEOLOGICAL CONVICTIONS LEADING TO SPURGEON'S CONVERSION

It is important to understand his conversion experience in order to the properly interpret and apply Spurgeon's principles for leading churches and seeing them multiply disciples and more churches. Out of his own experience would grow his philosophy of ministry based upon his knowledge and understanding of the Word of God. Spurgeon said, "*I know that a man's own experience is one of the very best weapons he can use in fighting with evil in other men's hearts* [emphasis added]."[15]

The fall of 1849 became a time of intense seeking for Spurgeon. It had been building for some time. He described this conviction of his need for the Savior:

> That misery was sent for this reason, that I might then be made to cry to Jesus. Our heavenly Father does not usually cause us to seek the Savior till He has whipped us clean out of all our confidence; he cannot make us in earnest after Heaven till He has made us feel something of the intolerable tortures of an aching conscience, which is a foretaste of hell. I remember, when I used to awake in the morning, the first thing I took up was Alleine's *Alarm*, or Baxter's *Call to the Unconverted*. Oh, those books, those books! I read and devoured them under a sense of guilt, but it was like sitting at the foot of Sinai. For five years, as a child, there was nothing before my eyes but my guilt; and though I do not hesitate to say that those who observed my life would not have seen any extraordinary sin, yet as I looked upon myself, there was not a day in which I did not commit such gross, such outrageous sins against God, that often and often have I wished I had never been born. Sickness is a terrible thing . . . ; but I bear witness that sickness, however agonizing, is nothing like the discovery of the evil of sin. I had rather pass through seven years of the most wearisome pain, and the most languishing sickness, than I would ever again pass through the terrible discovery of the evil of sin. It was my sad lot, at that time, to feel the greatness of my sin, without a discovery of the greatness of God's mercy.[16]

This explained why he taught his College men to preach the law along with grace. Spurgeon's upbringing had made him sensitive to sin. He had been trained to do right and avoid wrong. His childhood training

---

15. Spurgeon, *Autobiography*, vol. 1, 89.
16. Spurgeon, *Autobiography*, vol. 1, 80.

and home-life was a holy influence; he was instructed to have a solid and healthy respect for God. He noted,

> When I was a child, if I had done anything wrong, I did not need anybody to tell me of it; I told myself of it, and I have cried myself to sleep many a time with the consciousness that I had done wrong; and when I came to know the Lord, I felt very grateful to Him because He had given me a tender conscience . . . I am sure that, in my early youth, no teaching ever made such an impression upon my mind as the instruction of my mother; . . . Certainly I have not the powers of speech with which to set forth my valuation of the choice blessing which the Lord bestowed on me in making me *the son of one who prayed for me, and prayed with me. How can I ever forget her tearful eye when she warned me to escape from the wrath to come* [emphasis added]?[17]

But Spurgeon's upbringing also precipitated self-righteous tendencies. Sometimes he would take stock of his situation and believe himself to be quite respectable. He was tempted to think he was better than others because he was not dishonest or disobedient; he didn't swear, he attended church and respected the Sabbath Day. But the law of God became very real to Spurgeon and conviction increased of the reality of sin and God's holiness. Spurgeon affirmed that though this was a terrible time in his life, it was genuinely profitable for him. His assessment: "A spiritual experience . . . which is thoroughly flavored with a deep and bitter sense of sin is of great value to him that had it."[18]

Charles described his pilgrimage during this time "I never can suffer as I suffered when I was seeking Christ . . . whatever staggering doubt . . . ghastly insinuations, even of suicide itself, may assail my feeble heart, they cannot outdo the horror of great darkness through which my spirit passed when I was struggling after a Saviour."[19] But Spurgeon later realized this entire excruciating experience was very, very profitable. He explained the benefits when salvation is accompanied by deep conviction of sin: "Precious is that wine which is pressed in the wine vat of conviction: pure is that gold which is dug from the mines of repentance: and bright are those pearls which are found in the caverns of deep distress . . . He who has stood before God, convicted and condemned with the rope

---

17. Spurgeon, *Autobiography*, vol. 1, 68–69.
18. Ray, *Spurgeon*, 41.
19. Spurgeon, *Autobiography*, vol. 1, 88.

Schooling, Conversion, and Spurgeon's Foundation

about his neck is the man to weep with joy when he is pardoned, and to live to the honor of the Redeemer by whose blood he is cleansed."[20]

Spurgeon gives further insight as to the need and value of experiencing conviction of sin in relation to our salvation by stating, "I do not say that it is desirable that we should have this painful ordeal, much less that we should seek it as an evidence of regeneration; but when we have passed through it victoriously, we may so use it that it may be *a perpetual armory to us* [emphasis added]."[21] This underscores the value and importance of addressing and explaining sin and God's holiness wisely and carefully in our sermons and soul-winning efforts.

Spurgeon confessed he went through a great struggle of soul in giving up trust in his good works and self-sufficiency. This struggle progressed until he felt he could do nothing to secure salvation. But Spurgeon felt God was telling him he needed to 'come down more'—he had too much pride still. Spurgeon was allowed to see his corruption, wickedness, and filthiness before God.

God was orchestrating in Spurgeon's life through his salvation experience what became Spurgeon's soteriology and kerygma. This was not doctrine based on knowledge alone, but convictions from experience based on Scripture—hammered out on the anvil of God's Word and welded into his soul. All that transpired during this time of his life was to be used later in public ministry. Learning his utter sinfulness before his conversion blossomed into his doctrinal understanding of election. In his later pulpit ministry, he was heard to say repeatedly in varied ways, "I love to proclaim these strong old doctrines, that are called by nickname Calvinism, but which are surely and verily the revealed truth of God as it is in Christ Jesus . . . I know of nothing more humbling for us than this doctrine of election."[22] Spurgeon understood his heart was wicked (Jer 17:9) and only God's choosing to redeem him through Christ's blood was the reason for his salvation; this was God's electing love.

What Spurgeon preached later in regard to man's need of a Savior because of his sinfulness came directly out of his own encounter with the Word of God and his salvation experience. He interpreted his own realization of 'total depravity' in the message of grace he preached. The way he expressed it was by explaining, people desire to buy the *bread of*

---

20. Day, *Shadow of Broad Brim*, 58.
21. Spurgeon, *Autobiography*, vol. 1, 88.
22. Spurgeon, *Spurgeon's Sermons*, vol. 2, 69, 84.

life with the money in their sacks when they come hungry and needy to their Egypt: "but it must not be; heaven's bread is given to us freely, and we must accept it freely, without money and without price."[23] Spurgeon understood well there is no price a person can pay for salvation. Individuals are totally dependent and 'owing' to Jesus for it. So, a proper communication and understanding of the gospel makes people fall in love with the Savior and desire to live for the Savior who made this gift and life possible.

The direct relation between the theology of Spurgeon as a teen and the theology of the pastor at the Metropolitan Tabernacle as an adult can be understood by his own confessions. At fifteen, through his conversion encounter with Christ, he declared:

> Out went my supposed merits! What a heap of rubbish! Out went my knowledge, my good resolves, and my self-sufficiency! By-and-by, out went all my strength. When this digging-out was completed, the ditch was so deep that, as I went down into it, it seemed like my grave . . . I know when I first cast my eye to His dear cross, and rested in Him, I had not any merit of my own, it was all demerit. I was not deserving, except that I felt I was hell deserving: I had not even a shade of virtue that I should confide in. It was all over with me . . . I could not have found a farthing's worth of goodness in myself if I had been melted down.[24]

This theology enabled Spurgeon to preach a powerful gospel message. He was convinced we could do nothing without Christ. He had claimed the Apostle Paul as his hero shortly after his conversion—and he agreed with the apostle's spirit in saying "I am the chief of sinners." It was this understanding and conviction that caused Spurgeon to confidently and dogmatically proclaim that without Christ we are naked, poor, and miserable and left with no means to be ransomed. In our need, Christ in His timeliness stepped in the room and became sponsor and representative for us and paid the ransom price "that we might in that hour be delivered from the curse of the law and the vengeance of God, go our way, clean, free, justified by His blood."[25]

Spurgeon's salvation theology gave him a strong and vibrant doctrine of grace. By this he could inspire people to come to Christ for salvation and

---

23. Spurgeon, *Spurgeon's Sermons*, vol. 9, 312.
24. Spurgeon, *Autobiography,* vol. 1, 93.
25. Spurgeon, *Spurgeon's Sermons*, vol. 3, 296.

Schooling, Conversion, and Spurgeon's Foundation

to live for Christ in loving service. Spurgeon's interpretation of God's love for man and Jesus' sacrifice for the sin of man was his constant message:

> "Son of my love," said he [God], "you must stand in the sinner's place; you must suffer what he ought to have suffered; you must be accounted guilty, just as he was accounted guilty; and then I will look upon the sinner in a another light. *I will look at him as if he were Christ; I will accept him as if he were my only-begotten Son, full of grace and truth. I will give him a crown in heaven, and I will take him to my heart forever and ever* [emphasis added]." This is the way we are saved; "Being justified freely by his grace, through the redemption which is in Christ Jesus."
>
> ... Man ceases to be regarded by divine justice as a guilty being; the moment he believes in Christ his guilt is all taken away . . . ; so that, when *God looks upon the sinner who but an hour ago was dead in sins, he looks upon him with as much love and affection as he ever looked upon His Son* [emphasis added].[26]

Spurgeon's soteriology made him see, know, proclaim, and stand on the love of God. He lived on the love of God: "We were not converted because we were already inclined that way, . . . neither were we regenerated because some good thing was in us by nature; but we owe our new birth entirely to his potent love, . . . turning us from death to life, from the alienation of our mind and the enmity of our spirit into that delightful path of love."[27] All this, Spurgeon knew with deep, secure, confident, conviction, was only possible because of the Cross of Christ. This is why he instructed his Pastors' College men to preach Jesus Christ and Him crucified. God's power to change lives is bound up in that doctrine. One of his students said, "whatever text he might take, as a beginning, it led to the cross."[28]

Helmet Thielicke's life and ministry in Germany was greatly impacted and marked by the ministry and teaching of Charles Haddon Spurgeon. Thielicke studied at the University of Marburg, the University of Erlangen, and the University of Bonn earning the Doctor of Theology and Doctor of Philosophy degrees. He was assessed by Fant and Pinson in *20 Centuries of Great Preaching* as one of the greatest preachers in the history of the Christian faith. Thielicke said Spurgeon's preaching appealed to all classes of Christian servants and all regarded Spurgeon as

26. Spurgeon, *Spurgeon's Sermons*, vol. 3, 302–3.
27. Spurgeon, *Spurgeon's Sermons*, vol. 9, 305.
28. Carlile, *Spurgeon*, 99.

one who could help them better find their way. Fundamentalists, Liberals, Conservatives and Reformed all read and are attracted to Spurgeon. Thielicke's description of Spurgeon's preaching is very useful to preachers today in understanding how to apply the theological insights from Scripture which had captured Spurgeon's heart and mind:

> The first thing to strike us is the vigor and even the passion of the language . . . No one should imagine that Spurgeon is just using the loud pedal to try to bring his hearers under the pressure of suggestion or to dominate them psychologically . . . One notes that the emotional element is not deployed here with tactical intentions. It derives from the matter with which Spurgeon deals . . . He pursues the hearer, and accommodates himself to him, in order to bring home to him what a revolution there must be in his life. But he never accommodates himself in order to woo him with guile, or to give the impression that what he is saying is not so bad, that he need not hesitate, that he need not change his life, that it is only a matter of a little edification. *No, Spurgeon leaves him [the congregant] in no doubt that this message will shake his life to its foundation, that it will be like a goad in his flesh* [emphasis added]."[29]

The question and challenge of relevance and faithfulness to the Word of God is always before the servants of Jesus Christ. One writer on the Puritans poses the need of one area of consideration to the modern church: "We may well consider whether . . . with our modern evangelism, we have not stressed enough the fact of sin, . . . the necessity for repentance as well as faith . . . Appeals to 'decide for Christ', without making them thoroughly aware of their sins, . . . and without calling for real repentance, is not the Gospel preaching of the New Testament."[30] Jesus said if we are forgiven little—we will love little. Antithetically, if we are forgiven much—we will love much. This reveals what the proper teaching of sin and grace can produce in Christians' lives for holiness and for earnestness in serving the Savior and His Great Commission call.

Spurgeon's Conversion Experience

Spurgeon communicated the doctrine of repentance to effectively help people to Christ, never to manipulate or guilt them to Him. He said,

---

29. Fant, Jr. and Pinson, *20 Centuries of Great Preaching*, vol. 12, 222–25
30. Bacon, *Spurgeon: Heir of the Puritans*, 21.

"Every man that ever was saved had to come to God not as a lover of God, but as a sinner, and to believe in God's love to him as a sinner."[31] Spurgeon understood we only know this love through recognizing and receiving it by God opening our eyes to its existence and availability.

How did Spurgeon's conversion happen? Spurgeon declared he had wanted to do fifty things until he heard one word: "Look!"[32] Young Spurgeon had been going from church to church during the winter of 1849 to find out how to be saved, "*but never a gospel sentence did I hear* [emphasis added]; but this one text preserved me from what I believe I should have been driven to,—the commission of suicide through grief and sorrow."[33] Spurgeon was desperate to know salvation. His experience helped convince him of the priority of preaching the Cross in his own ministry and the preaching of those he trained in the Pastors' College. The text he referred to as keeping him from possible suicide was Rom 10:13: "Whosoever shall call upon the name of the Lord shall be saved." It comforted Spurgeon, but he did not know how to experience the answer to this promise from the Word of God.

> When I was for many a month in this state, I used to read the Bible through, and the threatenings were all printed in capitals, but the promises were in such small type I could not for a long time make them out; and when I did read them, I did not believe they were mine; . . . I speak what I do know, and not what I have learned by report, when I say that there is a chamber in the experience of some men where the temptations of the devil exceed all belief. Read John Bunyan's *Grace Abounding*, if you would understand what I mean. The devil tempted him, he says, to doubt the existence of God, the truth of Scripture, the manhood of Christ, then His Deity.[34]

On the morning of January 6, 1850, Charles Spurgeon attended a Primitive Methodist worship service in Colchester because a snowstorm prevented his attending the chapel he intended to worship in. The snow prevented the regular minister from being present. Only a dozen or so people were in attendance that day. A layman who was a shoemaker by trade, entered the pulpit to preach. Spurgeon described the man as "really stupid [the term respectively meant *unlearned*]. He was obliged to stick

---

31. Spurgeon, *Spurgeon's Sermons*, vol. 9, 312.
32. Spurgeon, *Autobiography*, vol. 1, 105–6.
33. Spurgeon, *Autobiography*, vol. 1, 95.
34. Spurgeon, *Autobiography*, vol. 1, 85–86.

to his text, for the simple reason that he had little else to say."[35] Because of this, the man stayed close to his text without adding superlatives. After giving out the text from Isa 45: 22 "Look unto Me, and be ye saved, all the ends of the earth," Spurgeon described the situation:

> There was, I thought, a glimpse of hope for me in that text. The preacher began thus: "My dear friends, this is a very simple text indeed. It says, 'Look.' Now lookin' don't take a deal of pain. It ain't liftin' your foot or your finger; it is just, 'Look.' Well, a man needn't go to College to learn to look. You may be the biggest fool, and yet you can look. A man needn't be worth a thousand a year to be able to look. Anyone can look; even a child can look. But then the text says, 'Look unto Me.' 'Ay!' said he, in broad Essex, 'many on ye are lookin' to yourselves, but it's no use lookin there. You'll never find any comfort in yourselves. Some look to God the Father. No, look to Him by-an-by. Jesus Christ says, "Look unto Me." Some on ye say, "We must wait for the Spirit's workin." You have no business with that just now. Look to Christ. The text says, 'Look unto Me.'"[36]

The preacher had gone about ten minutes with his delivery and then paused. He looked directly at Spurgeon and said, "Young man, you look very miserable." The statement arrested Spurgeon's attention. The preacher continued, "Young man, look to Jesus Christ. Look! Look! Look! You have nothing to do but to look and live." Spurgeon's response was "I saw at once the way of salvation."[37] This truth followed him throughout life; he proclaimed it to all he could.

From his conversion experience Spurgeon realized "His Word is true, therefore I am saved . . . By looking to Him, I received all the faith which inspired me with confidence in His grace." The date was January 6, 1850. Spurgeon further commented on this: "To my own humiliation I must confess that I did it because I could not help it; I was shut to it."[38] This was his unquestioned confidence: the gospel, when proclaimed, was effective to make spiritually dead men alive. Spurgeon believed and preached:

> It does not ask your consent; but it gets it. It does not say, will you have it? But it makes you willing in the day of God's power. Not against your will, but it makes you willing. It shows you its

---

35. Spurgeon, *Autobiography*, vol. 1, 105.
36. Spurgeon, *Autobiography*, vol. 1, 106.
37. Spurgeon, *Autobiography*, vol. 1, 106.
38. Spurgeon, *Autobiography*, vol. 1, 112–13.

Schooling, Conversion, and Spurgeon's Foundation

value, and then you fall in love with it; and straightway you run after it and have it . . . The gospel wants not your consent, it gets it. It knocks the enmity out of your heart . . . He makes your will turn round, and then you cry, "Lord, save, or I perish". . . It pleases God by the foolishness of preaching to accomplish his divine purposes, not because of the power of preaching, or the power of the preacher, nor any power in those preached to, but because 'all power' is given unto Christ 'in heaven and in earth,' and he chooses to work by the teaching of the Word.[39]

Spurgeon's confidence in doctrine inspired confidence in his hearers to trust that doctrine. Howard Hendricks of Dallas Theological Seminary (he served there over fifty years serving as their Professor of Applied Theology) was greatly respected and highly regarded by Christian leaders throughout America and around the world. He repeatedly shared his incredible confidence in the Holy Spirit to take the Word of God and apply it to the hearts of people to change their lives. Dr. Hendicks shared this was the reason for his own effectiveness in ministry and the training of students for Christ's service; he knew the Word caused faith in Christ. It is the Holy Spirit's work to lead people into the truths of the Word. This was true for Spurgeon's ministry:

> His appreciation of and reverence for the inspired Word are among the most characteristic and remarkable features of the man. The Word of God is to him a thing of life and power, 'and sharper than any two-edged sword.' He sees God in the very words of the Bible . . . and, to use his own words, 'Hundreds of times have I as surely felt the presence of God, in the page of Scripture, as ever Elijah did when he heard the Lord speaking in a still small voice.' *He seems never to be satisfied, in his study of the Scriptures, till every single verse is thus verified by the Spirit, and becomes to him a living word* [emphasis added].[40]

Spurgeon's conversion had taken place in Colchester while he was temporarily out of school for winter break. The night of his conversion he spent a lengthy visit with his dad discussing the text God had used to bring him to Christ.

Immediately upon returning to Newmarket, Spurgeon became involved in Sunday school work and tract distribution in house-to-house visitation. He would visit seventy people on Saturdays, giving out tracts

---

39. Spurgeon, *Spurgeon's Sermons*, vol. 1, 306.
40. Spurgeon, *Autobiography*, vol. 4, 276.

and leading them in spiritual conversations. "Oh, how I wish that I could do something for Christ! Tract-distribution is so pleasant and easy that it is nothing,—nothing in itself, much less when it is compared with the amazing debt of gratitude I owe."[41]

Conwell reports that Spurgeon began visiting the poor and talking with his classmates about their salvation. He told his teacher, Mr. Swindell, 'It's all settled; I must preach the gospel of Christ!'"[42] He wrote his parents on April 6, 1850 and expressed his desires of preaching like his dad: "Oh, that I could see but one sinner constrained to come to Jesus! How I long for the time when it may please God to make me, like you, my Father [sic], a successful preacher of the gospel!"[43]

Spurgeon began his "secret diary" writing about his spiritual pilgrimage during April 6 to June 20 during 1850. Richard Day's *Shadow of the Broad Brim* reports Spurgeon left this diary with his wife, Susannah, in 1856 with the request it not be opened until after his death. She complied and did not open it until 1896. The entry of May 3, 1850 shows his desire to serve his Lord and the primacy, in his own mind, of the Cross and person of Jesus Christ: "I vow to glory alone in Jesus and His cross, and to spend my life in the extension of His cause, in whatsoever way He pleases. I desire to be sincere in this solemn profession, having but one object in view, and that to glorify God. Help me to honor Thee, and live the life of Christ on earth."[44]

This love relationship with Christ noted in his diary entry was certainly lived out in Spurgeon's life with the Metropolitan Tabernacle and Pastors' College. This became the heart focus and monomania of his life: to multiply effective proclaimers and leaders of the gospel. A vision began to take shape in the next five years of how God wanted him to go about fulfilling his vow: it would be for him to lead a local church and create a farm system for sending out members and pastors into South London and literally around the world. Before this vision matured in Spurgeon's heart and mind, he seriously considered a call to China as a missionary during the early years of his London pastorate. He was focused on extending Christ's cause wherever possible within his means and ability.

---

41. Spurgeon, *Autobiography*, vol. 1, 118.
42. Conwell, *Spurgeon*, 95.
43. Spurgeon, *Early Years*, 116.
44. Day, *Shadow of Broad Brim*, 68.

Susannah gives a glimpse into the contents of the diary revealing the character development God was constructing in young Spurgeon:

> How marked is his *humility*, even though he must have felt within him the stirrings and throes of the wonderful powers which were afterwards developed. "Forgive me, Lord," he says, in one place, "if I have ever had high thoughts of myself,"—so early did the Master implant the precious seeds of that rare grace of meekness, which adorned his after life. After each youthful effort at public exhortation, whether it be engaging in prayer, or addressing Sunday-school children, he seems to be surprised at his own success, and intensely anxious to be kept from pride and self-glory, again and again confessing his own utter weakness, and pleading for God-given strength. What deep foundations were laid in this chosen soul, upon what massive pillars of truth and doctrine did God construct the spiritual consciousness of the man who was to do so great a work in the world for his Master! He was truly a "building fitly framed together," and he grew into "a holy temple in the Lord," "a habitation of God through the Spirit." So young in years, when he wrote these thoughts, yet so old in grace, and possessing an experience in spiritual matters richer and broader than most Christians attain to at an advanced age! How plainly revealed in these pages are the workings and teachings of the Divine Spirit, and how equally clear are the docility, and earnestness, and humility of the pupil! Many of the sentences in the Diary are strangely prophetic of his future position and work,—notably these two,—"Make me Thy faithful servant, O my God; may I honor Thee in my day and generation, and be consecrated for ever to Thy service!" And again, "Make me to be an eminent servant of Thine, and to be blessed with the power to serve Thee, like Thy great servant Paul!"
>
> In these breathings, too, we see where the secret of his great strength lay. He believed and trusted God absolutely, and his faith was honored in a God-like fashion. Deeply realizing his own weakness, he rested with childlike and complete dependence on his Lord. And God carried him, as a father bears his little one in his arms; and God's Spirit dwelt in him, to teach him all things. His whole heart was given to God and His service, God's promises were verities to him; and as "He abideth faithful, He cannot deny Himself," it was with both hands that He heaped gifts and grace upon His dear servant until the time came to receive him into glory. *Perhaps, of greatest price among the precious things which this little book reveals, is the beloved author's personal and intense love to the Lord Jesus* [emphasis added]. He

lived in His embrace; like the apostle John, his head leaned on Jesu's [sic] bosom. The endearing terms used in the Diary, *and never discontinued,* were not empty words; they were the overflowings of the love of God shed abroad in his heart by the Holy Ghost. One of the last things he said to me at Mentone, before unconsciousness had sealed his dear lips, was this, "O wifie, I have had such a blessed time with my Lord!" And it was always so, the Savior was as real to him as if his eyes could look upon Him, and it was his delight to dwell in the very presence of God, in his daily, hourly life.[45]

Charles Spurgeon was baptized by W. W. Cantlow in the Lark River on May 3, 1850—his mother's birthday. Though his parents and grandparents were Congregationalists and believed in infant baptism, Spurgeon knew from Scripture through his St. Augustine's College work, immersion was to follow one's salvation. He asked permission of his dad to be baptized by immersion. It was the first time his father had witnessed a believer's baptism experience. The day after his sixteenth birthday, June 20, 1850, all arrangements were completed for him to matriculate into a small private school at Cambridge. It was here he would continue his education, but also where he would also begin his pulpit ministries.

---

45. Spurgeon, *Autobiography,* vol. 1, 128–29.

4

Early Preaching and Pastoral Experience

AUGUST 1850 FOUND SPURGEON headed to Cambridge to assist his tutor from Colchester, Mr. Leeding. He lodged in a home where all tenants practiced personal devotions each morning at eight o'clock for one-half hour. Charles's parents continued their commitment of seeing their children receive as good an education as they could possibly afford. Mr. Leeding had transferred to Cambridge and had opened a new private school of instruction. Charles's father had written to Mr. Leeding requesting him to take young Charles on as an assistant tutor without salary and in return asking if he could help Charles with further academic preparation. Mr. Leeding responded,

> I hasten to reply to your most welcome letter, which I received this morning. I have more than once wished it possible that an arrangement could be made for securing your son's services in the event of an increase in my school; but my partial success has appeared to me a bar to such an engagement, for I have such an estimate of him, that I could never have started the proposal on such terms as have proceeded from you. I will readily engage to give him all the assistance in my power for the prosecution of his own studies, and his board and washing in return for his assistance. You do me an honor, that I am perhaps unworthy of, in making this proposition when you have a premium at

> your option, but I must say you could not send him to anyone who feels so great an interest in and affection for him, nor to a situation where he could possibly have better opportunities for improving himself. You may, with Mrs. S., rest assured of his domestic comfort, as I am sure he will himself anticipate. I am unwilling to pledge myself at present to an engagement that shall bind me to give a salary hereafter. I am sure we shall not differ in that particular when once it necessarily occurs.[1]

At Cambridge Spurgeon studied general education subjects along with French and Latin. Mr. Leeding was himself a graduate of Cambridge University and this arrangement for Charles continued his education and assured sound instruction.

After arriving in Cambridge, Spurgeon joined the Baptist Church on St. Andrew's Street. Robert Hall served this church from 1791 to 1806 and was instrumental in leading the church into evangelistic ministries. He was a key figure in turning Baptists away from Hyper-Calvinistic views and to preach the gospel to those outside the church. He intentionally sought to help those without a relationship with Christ to come to know Him as Savior and Lord. He was a scholarly and eloquent preacher who practiced thorough preparation of sermons. The church had developed a number of evangelism ministries as a result of Hall's pastoral leadership. One of these, the Lay Preachers' Association, shows how he valued and practiced 2 Timothy 2: 2. Spurgeon commented on the life and fellowship of this church,

> When I joined the Baptist Church at Cambridge,—one of the most respectable churches that can be found in the world, one of the most generous, one of the most intelligent,—this was a good many years ago, when I was young,—nobody spoke to me. On the Lord's-day, I sat at the communion table in a certain pew; there was one gentleman in it, and when the service was over, I said to him, "I hope you are quite well, sir?" He said, "You have the advantage of me." I answered, "I don't think I have, for you and I are brothers." "I don't quite know what you mean," said he. "Well," I replied, "when I took the bread and wine, just now, in token of our being one in Christ, I meant it, did not you?" We were by that time in the street; he put both his hands on my shoulders,—was about sixteen years old then,—and he said, "Oh, sweet simplicity!" Then he added, "You are quite right, my dear brother, you are quite right; come in to tea [refreshments

---

1. Spurgeon, *Autobiography*, vol. 1, 186–87.

often including a meal] with me. I am afraid I should not have spoken to you if you had not first addressed me." I went to tea with him that evening; and when I left, he asked me to go again the next Lord's-day, so I went, and that Sabbath day he said to me, "You will come here every Sunday evening, won't you?" That dear friend used to walk with me into the villages when I afterwards went out to preach, and he remains to this day one of the truest Christian friends I have, and often have we looked back, and laughed at the fact that I should have dared to assume that Christian fellowship was really a truth.[2]

Spurgeon's desire to serve His Savior and Lord continued to grow. It expressed itself in the direction Jesus stated in Matt 4:19 would happen if we would simply and surely follow Him with our lives: "Follow Me, and I will make you fishers of men." There can be no other result with our lives if we are truly following Him. Jesus stated in Luke 19:10, "I am come to seek and to save" and He further explained this in John 20:21: "As the Father has sent Me, I am sending you." Spurgeon knew this Holy Spirit-birthed desire and calling in his life, and he knew it was in the heart of every child of God. Spurgeon wrote at length describing his early months in Christ and how he was inspired by his Lord to reach others for Him:

> In that day when I surrendered myself to my Savior, I gave Him my body, my soul, my spirit; I gave Him all I had, and all I shall have for time and for eternity. I gave Him all my talents, my powers, my faculties, my eyes, my ears, my limbs, my emotions, my judgment, my whole manhood, and all that could come of it, whatever fresh capacity or new capability I might be endowed with. Were I, at this good hour, to change the note of gladness for one of sadness, it would be to wail out my penitent confession of the times and circumstances in which I have failed to observe the strict and unwavering allegiance I promised to my Lord. So far from regretting what I then did, I would fain renew my vows, and make them over again . . .
>
> The very first service which my youthful heart rendered to Christ was the placing of tracts in envelopes, and then sealing them up, that I might send them, with the hope that, by choosing pertinent tracts, applicable to persons I knew, God would bless them. And I well remember taking other tracts, and distributing them in certain districts in the town of Newmarket, going from house to house, and telling, in humble language, the things of the Kingdom of God. *I might have done nothing for Christ if I*

---

2. Spurgeon, *Autobiography*, vol. 1, 185–86.

> had not been encouraged by finding myself able to do a little. Then I sought to do something more, and from that something more, and I do not doubt that many of the servants of God have been led on to higher and nobler labors for their Lord, because they began to serve Him in the right spirit and manner . . . were it not for the first step, we might never reach to the second; but that being attained, we are encouraged to take the next, and so, at the last, God helping us, we may be made extensively useful [emphasis added].
>
> I think I never felt so much earnestness after the souls of my fellow creatures as when I first loved the Savior's name, and though I could not preach, and never thought I should be able to testify to the multitude, I used to write texts on little scraps of paper, and drop them anywhere, that some poor creatures might pick them up, and receive them as messages of mercy to their souls. I could scarcely content myself even for five minutes without trying to do something for Christ. If I walked along the street, I must have a few tracts with me; if I went into a railway carriage, I must drop a tract out of the window; if I had a moment's leisure, I must be upon my knees or at my Bible; if I were in company, I must turn the subject of conversation to Christ, that I might serve my Master. It may be that, in the young dawn of my Christian life, I did imprudent things in order to serve the cause of Christ; but I still say, give me back that time again, with all its imprudence and with all its hastiness, if I may but have the same love to my Master, the same overwhelming influence in my spirit, making me obey my Lord's commands because it was a pleasure to me to do anything to serve my God.[3]

FIRST PREACHING EXPERIENCE

Within a few weeks of arriving in Cambridge and joining the church at St. Andrew's, Spurgeon was teaching Sunday school classes. Various deacons of the church noticed his abilities. They encouraged him to participate in the Lay Preachers' Association, which had been conducted by St. Andrew's for about twenty years.

James Vinter, a deacon who oversaw the Lay Preachers' Association work approached Spurgeon about participating in this ministry. Vinter knew of seventeen villages around Cambridge in need of the gospel and he worked to see all of them have preaching and worship services.

---

3. Spurgeon, *Autobiography*, vol.1, 180–81.

Early Preaching and Pastoral Experience

Interestingly, for his very first assignment, Vinter asked young Spurgeon to accompany an inexperienced preacher to Teversham—a village of about sixty homes, four miles from Cambridge. It was actually Vinter's scheme to get Spurgeon into his first preaching experience because the other young man had no intention of doing the speaking. Spurgeon gives the enlightening story of this first attempt at preaching and how it affected his philosophy of training other preachers in the future:

> There is a Preachers' Association in Cambridge, connected with St. Andrew's Street Chapel, . . . In my day, the presiding genius was the venerable Mr. James Vinter, whom we were wont to address as Bishop Vinter. His genial soul, warm heart, and kindly manner were enough to keep a whole fraternity stocked with love; and, accordingly, a goodly company of zealous workers belonged to the Association, and labored as true yokefellows . . . he was a sort of recruiting sergeant, and drew in young men to keep up the number of the host; at least, I can speak from personal experience as to one case . . . the aforesaid "Bishop" [asked] me to go over to Teversham, the next evening, for a young man was to preach there who was not much used to services, and very likely would be glad of company. That was a cunningly-devised sentence, if I remember it rightly, and I think I do, for, at the time, in the light of that Sunday evening's revelation, I turned it over, and vastly admired its ingenuity. A request to go and preach, would have met with a decided negative; but merely to act as company to a good brother who did not like to be lonely, and perhaps might ask me to give out a hymn or to pray, was not at all a difficult matter, and the request, understood in that fashion, was cheerfully complied with . . . We talked of good things, and at last I expressed my hope that he would feel the presence of God while preaching. He assured me that he had never preached in his life, and could not attempt such a thing; he was looking to his young friend, Mr. Spurgeon, for that . . . He told me that, if I repeated one of my Sunday-school addresses, it would just suit the poor people, and would probably give them more satisfaction than the studied sermon of a learned divine. I felt that I was fairly committed to do my best. I walked along quietly, lifting up my soul to God, and it seemed to me that I could surely tell a few poor cottagers of the sweetness and love of Jesus, for I felt them in my own soul. Praying for Divine help, I resolved to make the attempt. My text should be, "Unto you therefore which believe He is precious," and I would trust the Lord to open my mouth in honor of His dear Son. It seemed a

> great risk and a serious trial; but depending upon the power of the Holy Ghost, I would at least tell out the story of the cross, and not allow the people to go home without a word . . . *Are there not other young men who might begin to speak for Jesus in some such lowly fashion, . . . Our villages and hamlets offer fine opportunities for youthful speakers. Let them not wait till they are invited to a chapel, or have prepared a fine essay, or have secured an intelligent audience. If they will go and tell out from their hearts what the Lord Jesus has done for them, they will find ready listeners* [emphasis added].[4]

This exposure positively impacted Spurgeon and influenced him to do the same for his Pastors' College men years later when he began his work in London. It became a part of Spurgeon's and the Metropolitan Tabernacle's farm system to prepare and send out preachers to plant new churches or go to established churches to see them revived and given renewed vision. The principle holds much counsel and wisdom for pastors and churches today: we need to expose young people to opportunities to share Christ and His amazing grace with those who are unsaved. Whatever manner pastors and churches can creatively involve young people and adults in evangelism ministries, it will pay rich, eternal dividends and prepare more leaders for Christ's work through local churches.

Spurgeon began a Lay Preachers' Association shortly after coming to the London pastorate at New Park Street.[5] In an address to the British and Irish Home Missions meeting of April 23, 1872, Spurgeon shared about his early experiences in the Cambridge Lay Preachers' Association and how it influenced his work in London:

> "Endeavor to maintain in good vigor the Lay Preachers' Association. I might have preached without it, but that Association in Cambridge offered me opportunities of preaching every night in the week, when I first began to open my mouth for Christ, and I found brethren who encouraged me; and I think they were all the greater encouragement to me because I don't think they preached much better than I did, but very much on a par with myself; and we did not mind talking together, because we had not a solitary Doctor of Divinity, or even a Master of Arts, to criticize us, and our pastor did not come to the monthly meetings, which was quite as well, for we there fraternally spoke to each other; and some of my brethren ear-wigged [to jokingly

---

4. Spurgeon, *Autobiography*, vol. 1, 200–202.
5. Carlile, *Spurgeon*, 76.

chide] me about my oddities and eccentricities, and I was able to ear-wig them about their dullness and stupidity. I am sure that the Lay Preachers' Associations assist young men very materially, and help greatly to supply the pulpits with those men who will afterward carry on the work. We ought not to have a single church without a strong back (in proportion to the number of the church) of preaching men. *We must have very many, and indeed we must encourage more to preach. I believe there are a great many men who do very much service by preaching whom you and I would not like to hear, but whom God will bless nevertheless,* [emphasis added] and it is a pity they should have their mouths shut."[6]

With his first experience of preaching, Spurgeon was hooked. His enthusiasm grew for the work. Winds and rains failed to prevent his making rounds in the villages to conduct services. People recognized very soon young Spurgeon evidenced an uncommon power and an intriguing creativity in his preaching practices.

He would walk three to eight miles each evening to conduct the Lord's work. If people didn't come to the meeting place due to weather conditions, he would go to their doorways and tell the people that services would be on as normal and urge them to attend.[7] If there was no meeting place, he would ask if he could conduct services right in the living rooms of their homes. If denied this, he simply went door-to-door and invited people to an open-air meeting if weather permitted. He was effective whether preaching inside or outside. He wrote a friend during this time and shared his heart's ambition: "Souls, souls, souls,—I hope this rings in my ears and hurries me on."[8]

Through his experience with the Lay Preachers' Association, Spurgeon believed this to be an excellent way for young preachers to begin their ministries. He believed it would be better for young ministers to gain experience by beginning with small villages rather than large audiences. This would be wiser training for an enduring ministry. "Let our younger brethren go in for cottage preaching, and plenty of it. If there is no Lay Preachers' Association, let them work by themselves. The expense is not very great for rent, candles, and a few forms: many a young man's own pocket money would cover it all. No isolated group of houses should

6. Pike, *Life and Works of Spurgeon*, vol. 5, 39.
7. Carlile, *Spurgeon*, 73.
8. Ray, *Spurgeon*, 92.

be left without its preaching-room, no hamlet without its evening service. This is the lesson of the thatched cottage at Teversham."[9]

These early ministry experiences gave Spurgeon convictions for the value of exposing young men to preaching and evangelism ministries. He knew God would use missions experiences to shape hearts and heads for a lifetime of service for Jesus. There is much opportunity to creatively apply these principles in modern Christianity. Kingdom expansion can happen through sending out young men to preach and plant works in surrounding communities. House churches can meet in varied settings with little expense.

All the experiences Spurgeon gained in Teversham and Waterbeach contributed to his vision of training young men in revitalizing plateaued churches and planting new ones. During their time of studies at Pastors' College, Spurgeon sent students out to do evangelism work and develop new church plants in south London and the surrounding villages outside London. Ultimately the Pastors' College sent men around the world to plant new churches and help existing churches experience new life and growth. Spurgeon stated his perspective on the work of the college in the early years of its existence, "To refuse aid to rising interests in districts away from home would be far aside from our design, which knows no geographical limit, and is only bounded by our means."[10]

Spurgeon maintained a disciplined schedule while participating in the Lay Preachers' Association during his studies at Cambridge. He rose early each day for prayer and Bible study. He would then teach his students and study theology the balance of the day. At five in the evening, he began his mission travels to preach in the villages. This allowed him to retain and benefit more from his studies by preaching each night to others. Spurgeon described his growth and development during his three years at Cambridge:

> I was up in the morning early, praying and reading the Word; all the day, I was either teaching my scholars or studying theology as much as I could; then, at five in the evening, I became a traveling preacher, and went into the villages around Cambridge, to tell out what I had learned. My quiet meditation during the walk helped me to digest what I had read, and the rehearsal of my lesson in public, by preaching it to the people, fixed it on my memory. I do not mean that I ever repeated a single sentence

---

9. Spurgeon, *Autobiography*, vol. 1, 202.
10. Spurgeon, *Sword and Trowel* 2, 28.

from memory, but I thought my reading over again while on my legs, and thus worked it into my very soul; *and I can bear my testimony that I never learned so much, or learned it so thoroughly, as when I used to tell out, simply and earnestly, what I had first received into my own mind and heart. I found that I derived greater benefit by proclaiming to others what I had learned than if I had kept it all to myself* [emphasis added].[11]

This experience gained Spurgeon the understanding and skill in the application of scriptural truths to both his life and to others. He was effective even in these early years of his preaching. People noted him as being gifted at being able to explain the texts he addressed. His messages utilized points from history, geography, and various parts of science.[12] The experience in the villages developed in him transparent communication abilities and excellent impromptu skills.

Spurgeon shares some interesting stories of lessons learned during his days of itinerant work while at Cambridge. Often, he would encounter stormy weather while making his rounds to various villages around Cambridge to proclaim the gospel. Instead of these experiences frightening him, they turned into times of worship for Spurgeon:

There was real danger, for a stack [haystack] was set on fire a short distance away; but I was as calm as in the sunshine of a summer's day, not because I was naturally courageous, but because I had unshaken confidence in my Lord. I love the lightnings, God's thunder is my delight; I never feel so well as when there is a great thunder and lightning storm. Then I feel as if I could mount up as with the wings of eagles, and my whole heart loves then to sing.[13]

When such weather conditions were encountered, Spurgeon simply went door-to-door to people's homes and invited them to the agreed-on place of worship. The villagers would not expect worship services to occur during such weather, but Spurgeon's perseverance and love for souls resulted in many attending and hearing the gospel.

On one occasion Spurgeon confronted a situation appearing to be the involvement of demons—much as his grandfather had experienced in his own youth. It was an opportunity to learn a principle for life. He relates,

---

11. Spurgeon, *Autobiography*, vol. 1, 204.
12. Shindler, *Life and Labors of Spurgeon*, 52.
13. Spurgeon, *Autobiography*, vol. 1, 205.

> One night, having been preaching the Word in a country village, I was walking home, all by myself, along a lonely footpath. I do not know what it was that ailed me, but I was prepared to be alarmed; when, of a surety, I saw something standing in the hedge,—ghastly, giant-like, and with outstretched arms. Surely, I thought, for once I have come across the supernatural; here is some restless spirit performing its midnight march beneath the moon, or some demon of the pit wandering abroad. I deliberated with myself a moment, and having no faith in ghosts, I plucked up courage, and determined to solve the mystery. The monster stood on the other side of a ditch, right in the hedge. I jumped the ditch, and found myself grasping an old tree, which some waggish body had taken pains to cover with whitewash, with a view to frighten simpletons. *That old tree has served me a good turn full often, for I have learned from it to leap at difficulties, and find them vanish or turn to triumphs* [emphasis added].[14]

After a short time participating in the Lay Preachers' Association, Charles was recognized as the leading preacher of the group. At school he was often overheard by peers reciting whole chapters of the Bible from memory. Companions often compared him with Peter because of his impulsiveness and his strong inclination to berate himself for any failure or seeming sin. In his diary, he challenged himself to be like Paul and committed himself to God to know a power like Paul's for the Great Commission.

Spurgeon's courses under Mr. Leeding included studying through Romans in the Greek New Testament and using Barnes, Doddridge, and Chalmers for commentaries on this Scripture book. Spurgeon also worked in the Septuagint and studied Logic. When Charles taught classes to the students he was assigned, they felt they were reliving the passages he led them through in their Bible courses. He was animated and lively in his delivery. For all of us, we should never bore people with the Word of God: this was Howard Hendrick's constant challenge to us at Dallas Seminary.

Spurgeon's days at Cambridge taught him the rule for life was to serve Christ and carry out His gospel work: "Where I have most opportunity of telling sinners the way of salvation, and of preparation for a future course of labour, I trust I shall always feel most happy."[15] Spurgeon did sound like Paul: "But my life is worth nothing unless I use it to communicate the good news of God's great love in Christ Jesus" (Acts 24: 20 NLT).

---

14. Spurgeon, *Autobiography*, vol. 1, 206.
15. Spurgeon, *Autobiography*, vol. 1, 211.

SPURGEON'S WATERBEACH MINISTRY

Spurgeon went to preach at Waterbeach on October 12, 1851. After one year of preaching experiences, Spurgeon had matured and was ready to take on the charge of pastoring. The church had been without a pastor and soon extended a call to Spurgeon. Under Spurgeon's influence the church soon experienced a reviving movement of God's Spirit. The membership rose from forty to one hundred in a short time. Within a few months the village was turned upside down. Spurgeon said God "showed the power of Jesus' name, and made me a witness of that gospel which can win souls, draw reluctant hearts and mould afresh the life and conduct of sinful men and women."[16]

Young Spurgeon identified himself with Calvinistic tenets from his very first sermon communicating he knew he was chosen of God in Christ Jesus before the foundation of the world. Spurgeon's Calvinism was always marked with intense evangelistic zeal. In his message "Harvest Workers Wanted" based on the text of Matt 9: 37–38; 10:1, Spurgeon said,

> To promulgate a dry creed, and go over certain doctrines, and expound and enforce them logically, but never to deal with men's consciences, never to upbraid them for their sins, never to tell them of their danger, never to invite them to a Saviour with tears and entreaties! What a powerless work is this! What will become of such preachers? God have mercy upon them! We want laborers not loiterers. We need men on fire, and I beseech you ask God to send them. The harvest never can be reaped by men who will not labor . . . *But what kind of laborers are required? First, they must be men who will go down into the wheat. You cannot reap wheat by standing a dozen yards off and beckoning to it: you must go up close to the standing stalk; every reaper knows that . . . Get among the wheat like men in earnest! God's servants ought to feel that they are one with the people; whoever they are they should love them, claim kinship with them, feel glad to see them and look them in the face and say, "brother." Every man is a brother of mine; he may be a very bad one, but for all that I love him, and long to bring him to Jesus. Christ's reapers must get among the wheat* [emphasis added].[17]

---

16. Spurgeon, *Autobiography*, vol. 1, 228.

17. Spurgeon, *Spurgeon's Sermons*, vol. 10, 176–77.

Jesus taught, and modeled, a spiritual physician's mission and work is to get among the spiritually sick. He expects us to 'Go' and be in the world while not being of the world (John 17:15–18).

Waterbeach was a village of some thirteen hundred residents who enjoyed a relative degree of prosperity. But there were many homes in trouble and people with lives in need of Christ. Spurgeon went into these homes and led people to a personal knowledge of the Savior. He had great confidence in the gospel message, and he saw the majority of people in Waterbeach accept Christ and follow Him. There were twenty-one conversions in the first twelve months. The conversion experience and assimilation into church membership was practiced with much higher expectations in Spurgeon's day. What might appear as fewer results had a greater impact in the total numbers reached. (Membership practices exercised by Spurgeon and his Pastors' College men will be explained later in the book.) Spurgeon described the results in Waterbeach:

> It was a pleasant thing to walk through that place, when drunkenness had almost ceased, when debauchery in the case of many was dead, when men and women went forth to labour with joyful hearts, singing the praises of the everliving God; and when, at sunset the humble cottager called his children together, read some portion of the Book of Truth, and then together they bent their knees in prayer to God. I can say, with joy and happiness, that almost from one end of the village to the other, at the hour of eventide, one might have heard the voice of song coming from nearly every roof-tree.[18]

A Deacon Cole in the Waterbeach church described Spurgeon after hearing the young preacher deliver his first sermon: "He talked amazingly, like a man a hundred years old in Christian experience."[19] He gave messages that developed great Scripture doctrines with life application, which had been weighing on his mind since childhood. It brought strong convictions into the Waterbeach members. There were often as many as 450 in attendance during services; many times people stood outside and listened. Sunday after Sunday Spurgeon would lead a group of men and boys into the house of God having gone into the streets and homes earnestly compelling them to attend the services.[20] Spurgeon preached three times on

---

18. Spurgeon, *Early Years*, 193–94.
19. Carlile, *Spurgeon*, 78.
20. Hope, *Spurgeon*, 7.

Sunday and once in the week. His popularity grew and he began to receive invitations to preach in other churches on every night of the week.[21]

What Spurgeon learned about evangelism and Great Commission work at Waterbeach produced a transformed church and community. His devotion to Christ grew. He came to know a total surrender of his person to the will and lordship of Christ. This attitude and practice were consistently sustained in every area of his life.

Shortly after beginning at Waterbeach, Spurgeon was strongly encouraged to attend Regent's Park College in London (at the time called Stepney College). After consulting with his dad, he felt he should pursue college studies. He was to meet with Dr. Angus (who had pastored New Park Street Baptist Church where Spurgeon would go later) of Stepney to discuss plans for beginning college work, but providential circumstances blocked their meeting. The receptionist had asked Spurgeon to wait in a room, but somehow failed to communicate the fact with Dr. Angus, who was waiting in another room. Dr. Angus left for London without ever speaking with young Spurgeon.

Going home from the "missed" meeting with Dr. Angus, Spurgeon had an impression of hearing the words "seekest thou great things for thyself? Seek them not!" (Jer 45:5). From this, Spurgeon believed his life would be spent in smaller spheres of service and "anticipated obscurity and poverty as the result of the resolve." Spurgeon said in reflection, "The Lord guides His people by His wisdom, and orders all their paths in love; and in times of perplexity, by ways mysterious and remarkable, He says to them, 'This is the way; walk ye in it.'"[22] This experience taught Spurgeon a lesson for life:

> From that first day until now, I have acted on no other principle but that of perfect consecration to the work whereunto I am called [being totally committed to the work He has you in now—not waiting to be totally sold out when you obtain the ministry role you think you should have]. I surrendered myself to my Saviour, I gave him by body, my soul, my spirit . . . for eternity! I gave him my talents, my powers, my eyes, my ears . . . my whole manhood! . . . If Christ commands me to hold up my little finger, and I do not obey him, it looks like coolness in my love to him."[23]

---

21. Spurgeon, *Autobiography*, vol. 1,270.
22. Spurgeon, *Autobiography*, vol. 1,242; Shindler, *Life and Labors of Spurgeon*, 59.
23. Day, *Spurgeon*, 80–81.

Waterbeach allowed Spurgeon to understand the role of deacons in the local church work. He had heard a number of antagonistic remarks made by pastors about these church leaders. He concluded, "that, as a rule, they are quite as good men as the pastors, and the bad and good in the ministry and the deaconate are to be found in very much the same proportion."[24]

Spurgeon continued his discipline of study while serving at Waterbeach. He didn't participate in sports and had no attractions to young ladies during this time. He filled his schedule with work by studying, visiting, praying, and preaching. He used his funds from Waterbeach to purchase additional books. He continued working further with the Septuagint to improve his Greek. Spurgeon's philosophy was "I take every opportunity of improving myself, and seize every means of improvement."[25] He realized from his Puritan values if a pastor grows wiser in grace and skills, his church will also grow in the Spirit's anointing and in size of ministry. During his service at Waterbeach, Spurgeon published tracts explaining the gospel which he distributed to the people in the community.

The church at Waterbeach loved their young pastor as he did them. They would host him in their homes each Sunday for lunch. Spurgeon shared that for fifty-two Sundays he had fifty-six homes waiting to take him in. The church initially arranged to pay their minister five to twenty-five pounds per year, but they increased young Spurgeon's pay to an annual figure of fifty pounds. This was just enough for the young pastor to pay his rent in Cambridge and a little left over for expenses. Whenever his Waterbeach members would come to town, they would bring him food from their gardens and trees—even meat at times. Spurgeon shared, "the people, though they had not money, had produce, and I do not think there was a pig killed by any one of the congregation without my having some portion of it, . . . , when coming to the market at Cambridge, would bring me bread, so that I had enough bread and meat to pay my rent with, and I often paid my landlady in that fashion."[26] But the deacons and leaders of the church knew they would not be able to keep their gifted preacher. His strengths and capacities would be needed in other harvest fields.

---

24. Spurgeon, *Autobiography*, vol. 1, 255.

25. Spurgeon, *Autobiography*, vol. 1, 59–60.

26. Spurgeon, *Autobiography*, vol. 1, 253.

Spurgeon's conversion had taught him the crucial need of preaching Jesus Christ and Him crucified. Spurgeon knew by personal experience the gospel was the power of God unto salvation. His preaching experiences in villages and then pastoring at Waterbeach laid deep convictions in Spurgeon's heart and mind that the church's primary reason for existence was to bring lives to Christ, establish them in Christ and send them out to serve Christ. Spurgeon understood proclaiming the gospel through the pulpit and from house-to-house, and any other means effective for bringing lost people into contact with the Savior, was God's methodology for saving souls and changing lives. He once presented a unique and creative idea for doing the church's work to his deacons at Waterbeach. He esteemed these men as dear servants of God, but this experience showed Spurgeon's convictions for the Great Commission and his pastoral leadership. He shared,

> Hard-working men on the week-day, they spared no toil for their Lord on the Sabbath; I loved them sincerely, and do love them still. In my opinion, they were as nearly the perfection of deacons of a country church as the kingdom could afford. Yet, good as my deacons were, they were not perfect in all respects. I proposed to them, on one occasion, that I should preach on the Sunday evening by the river side, and the remark was made by one of them, "Ah! I do not like it, it is imitating the Methodists." To him, as a sound Calvinist, it was a dreadful thing to do anything which Methodists were guilty of; to me, however, *that was rather a recommendation than otherwise, and I was happy to run the risk of being Methodistical. All over England, in our cities, towns, villages, and hamlets, there are tens of thousands who never will hear the gospel while open-air preaching is neglected. I rejoice that God allows us to preach in churches and chapels, but I do not pretend that we have any apostolical precedent for it, certainly none for confining our ministry to such places . . . Our Lord, it is true, preached in the synagogues, but He often spake on the mountainside, or from a boat, or in the court of a house, or in the public thoroughfares. To Him, an audience was the only necessity. He was a Fisher of souls of the true sort, and not like those who sit still in their houses, and expect the fish to come to them to be caught* [emphasis added]. Did our Lord intend a minister to go on preaching from his pulpit to empty pews, when, by standing on a chair or a table outside the meeting-house, he might be heard by hundreds? I believe not, and I held the same opinion at the very beginning of my ministry, so I preached by the river

side, even though my good deacon thought that, by so doing, I was imitating the Methodists.[27]

Spurgeon kept up his outdoors preaching after he went to London. On one occasion he found this method of evangelism allowing him opportunity to preach the gospel to fourteen thousand at King Edwards Road, Hackney. At Abercarne it was reported that twenty thousand heard the gospel from Spurgeon through this open-air strategy.[28]

Spurgeon's Calvinistic theology always drove him to reach people for Christ. His beliefs convinced him no energy should be spared in going after souls—even as his dear Savior had done. Spurgeon knew God had prepared lives who wanted to know His Son's forgiveness and lordship, and it was abhorrent heartlessness and disobedience for Christ followers not to go to work in that harvest prepared by the Father (Matt. 9:36–38). These were God's elect and God had ordained His children to do the harvest work to bring these lives to Him (John 20:21). Spurgeon said he was encouraged early at Stamborne by the example and friendship of a widely known evangelistic missionary:

> It was Richard Knill, that blessed missionary of the cross to whom I am personally so deeply indebted, who said that, if there were only one unconverted person in the whole world, and if that person lived in the wilds of Siberia, and if every Christian minister and every private believer in the world had to make a pilgrimage to that spot before that soul were brought to Christ, the labor would be well expended if that one soul were so saved. This is putting the truth in a striking way, but in a way in which everyone who realizes the value of immortal souls, will heartily concur.[29]

CALL TO LONDON

In the fall of 1853 Spurgeon received a speaking invitation to the anniversary meeting of the Sunday School Union being held in Cambridge. As a result of this engagement Spurgeon was asked to preach at New Park Street Baptist Chapel in London. The speakers at the Cambridge meeting included two respectable, but somewhat dull speakers. The young pastor

---

27. Spurgeon, *Autobiography*, vol. 1, 255–56.
28. Spurgeon, *Autobiography*, vol. 1, 256.
29. Spurgeon, *Autobiography*, vol. 1, 231–32.

from Waterbeach spoke with a unique strength and a dose of imprudence (that wisely matured over time and was quite useful for the Lord's purposes). A deacon from the Loughton Baptist Church, George Gould, was at the meeting and communicated to Deacons James Low and Thomas Olney from the New Park Street Baptist Church that he believed this young man could be the answer to their prayers.

New Park Street has been served and led by respected and revered men of God in its history. The church's worship facility seated twelve hundred people—and it was regularly filled for worship in its former days. By the end of 1853 the church was having one to two hundred worshippers on Sundays. Church life had become somewhat discouraging for the members of New Park Street church.

In November 1853, a letter was sent from Deacon Low and delivered to the Waterbeach church. When Spurgeon arrived the following Sunday and began preparing for the morning service, the letter was handed to him. He read the letter and responded to one of the deacons of the Waterbeach church, "It is, of course, a mistake; they would never think of inviting me; it must be meant for another minister of the same name."[30] Spurgeon put the letter aside and preached as usual. The next day he wrote the London church explaining the pastor at Waterbeach was only nineteen years of age and their letter was evidently intended for someone else. The London church responded back writing they knew his age and that the invitation was, indeed, intended for him.

Spurgeon did not look forward to going to London. But in December 1853, he made his first appearance before the church (it eventually was renamed *Metropolitan Tabernacle* in 1861 following the building completion of their relocation to Newington Butts area of South London). The night before his first pulpit appearance at New Park Street he stayed at a boarding house known as Burr's Hotel. Several of the guests learned of his purpose being there and told Spurgeon he was ridiculous to think he could preach in London where so many other great preachers filled the pulpits in the city. They let him know it was no place for a country parson who had little educational qualifications for such ministries as appropriate for the city's churches.

For Spurgeon's first appearance at the London church on December 11, 1853, the deacons had worked diligently to invite and bring people to attend the service. The first Sunday morning Spurgeon spoke at New

---

30. Wayland, *Spurgeon: Faith and Works*, 30.

Park, about eighty people attended the worship service. Among those present was a Miss Susannah Thompson (who later became Mrs. Charles Spurgeon) whom the deacons had urged to be present for the young minister. She also attended the evening service along with about two hundred other people. Apparently the eighty people in the morning service spent the afternoon spreading word of the morning message and its impact by the nineteen-year-old preacher. Following the evening service of Spurgeon's first appearance before the New Park congregation, the people waited after worship to have assurances from their leadership the young minister would be invited again to speak for them. A deacon escorted him back to the hotel and along the way they stopped to hear a popular London minister. After the service Spurgeon asked, "Do they call that great preaching?" The deacon gave an affirmative response. Spurgeon's reply was "Then I can preach in London."[31]

Spurgeon was asked to speak every other Sunday for the next six weeks. After this, though not unanimous, an invitation was extended to Spurgeon to preach for the London church for the next six months. His feelings and thoughts over the whole initial experience at London were communicated to his father,

> I told them they did not know what they were doing, nor whether they were in the body or out of the body; they were so starved, that a morsel of gospel was a treat to them. The portraits of Gill and Rippon—large as life—hang in the vestry. Lots of them said I was Rippon over again.
>
> "It is God's doing. I do not deserve it;—they are mistaken. I only mention facts. I have not exaggerated; nor am I very exalted by it, for to leave my own dear people makes it a painful pleasure. God wills it. *"The only thing which pleases me is, as you will guess, that I am right about College. I told the deacons that I was not a College man, and they said, 'That is to us a special recommendation, for you would not have much savor or unction if you came from College* [emphasis added]."[32]

This last thought stayed with Spurgeon as he launched the Pastors' College. He wanted scholarship carried out, but he wanted it to be embraced with passion for Christ and souls by his students—nothing less would serve the churches in his thinking.

---

31. Wayland, *Spurgeon: Faith and Works*, 30.
32. Spurgeon, *Autobiography*, vol. 1, 340–41.

A probationary arrangement between prospective pastors and churches was a common practice in Baptist churches of Spurgeon's day. He had entered a similar covenant with the Waterbeach church. They had mutually agreed to a three-month probationary period during which time either party could withdraw their participation in the relationship if things did not progress satisfactorily. The consideration at New Park were similar. When the New Park church offered the six-month probation, Spurgeon's response was "I would engage to supply for three months of that time, and then, should the congregation fail, or the church disagree, I would reserve to myself liberty, without breach of engagement, to retire; and you could, on your part, have the right to dismiss me without seeming to treat me ill." To this he added realizing that popularity is something that can disappear as quickly as it appeared, "but this is the course I should prefer, if it would be agreeable to the church. Enthusiasm and popularity are often the crackling of thorns, and soon expire. I do not wish to be a hindrance if I cannot be a help."[33]

Spurgeon was to be ridiculed by many in London as being audacious and impudent, conceited and self-asserting. But God continued to affirm him and his ministry to more and more hearts. The church did not wait for the six-month probation to be completed as initially arranged. On April 19, 1854, they overwhelmingly voted in favor of inviting young Spurgeon to become their pastor. Fifty male members signed a draft affirming the desire and request of the church. During the probationary period the church had been full during worship services and conversions had been occurring regularly through the ministry of the young country preacher.

The sermons Spurgeon first preached at Waterbeach, and then as the official pastor at New Park, were both from the same text, Matt 1: 21, "She will give birth to a son, and you are to give him the name Jesus, because he will save his people from their sins." It was also the text of his last sermon at Waterbeach: Jesus was always the keynote in all his messages. He never deviated from this as his objective and subject to bring his hearers to throughout his public ministry.[34]

Spurgeon would spend the last thirty-eight years of his life with this London church. During his long pastorate, 14,692 persons were baptized and received into membership of the church. This local ministry was always marked and blessed by the Holy Spirit's desire to see souls come to

---

33. Spurgeon, *Autobiography*, vol. 1, 348.
34. Spurgeon, *Autobiography*, vol. 1, 229.

Jesus. From Spurgeon's first pastorate he never got over the experience of seeing someone come to Christ through his instrumentality. He wrote,

> How my heart leaped for joy when I heard tidings of my first convert! I could never be satisfied with a full congregation, and the kind expressions of friends. I longed to hear that hearts had been broken, that tears had been seen streaming from the eyes of penitents. How I did rejoice, as one that findeth great spoil, one Sunday afternoon, when my good deacon said to me, "God has set His seal on your ministry in this place, sir." Oh, if anybody had said to me, "Someone has left you twenty thousand pounds [a sum which could nearly pay the total construction cost of the Metropolitan Tabernacle]," I should not have given a snap of my fingers for it, compared with the joy which I felt when I was told that God had saved a soul through my ministry! "Who is it?" I asked. "Oh, it is a poor laboring man's wife over at such-and-such a place! She went home broken-hearted by your sermon two or three Sundays ago, and she has been in great trouble of soul, but she has found peace, and she says she would like to speak to you." I said, "Will you drive me over there? I must go to see her;" and early on the Monday morning I was driving down to the village my deacon had mentioned, to see my first spiritual child. I have in my eye now the cottage in which she lived; believe me, it always appears picturesque. I felt like the boy who has earned his first guinea, or like a diver who has been down to the depths of the sea, and brought up a rare pearl. I prize each one whom God has given me, but I prize that woman most. Since then, my Lord has blessed me to see many thousands of souls, who have found the Savior by hearing or reading words which have come from my lips. I have had a great many spiritual children born of the preaching of the Word, but I still think that woman was the best of the lot.[35]

It is of interest to note that Spurgeon was already thinking of opening a school before he had become the pastor at New Park Street. The school he had considered opening at the end of 1853 was somewhat different than what would eventually become the Pastors' College. It appears his motivation involved his being able to pay his bills; the fact of investing himself to help others improve and to gain a valid supplemental income were behind the decision. His gifts had been demonstrated and he was a credible candidate to offer such a school to others. This showed his aptitude and interest in training others which only matured in vision after

---

35. Spurgeon, *Autobiography*, vol. 1, 232–33.

coming to serve the London church at New Park. He had advertised in a Cambridge paper during the latter end of 1853,

> Mr. C. H. Spurgeon begs to inform his numerous friends that, after Christmas, he intends taking six or seven young gentlemen as day pupils. He will endeavor to the utmost to impart a good commercial Education. The ordinary routine will include Arithmetic, Algebra, Geometry, and Mensuration [specific mathematic studies for measuring length, area, and volume]; Grammar and Composition; Ancient and Modern History; Geography, Natural History, Astronomy, Scripture, and Drawing. Latin and the elements of Greek and French, if required. Terms, £5 per annum.[36]

Shortly after settling into the London pastorate Spurgeon would find himself surrounded by young men desirous of serving Christ. It soon became apparent to the young pastor a means of encouraging and equipping these young servants would be necessary. Spurgeon later shared these thoughts of the need and value of his training young men for the ministry during his London pastorate:

> Honorat, in the opening years of the fifth century, retired to the little island, near Cannes, which still bears his name and attracted around him a number of students, many of whom became such famous missionaries that the Romish Church has enrolled them among her "saints." The one best known to us is Patrick, the evangelizer of Ireland. Christianity was then almost as pure as at the first, and we as well imagine the holy quietude in which, among the rocks of this 'sunny isle', hundreds of good men spent the years of their preparation for future ministry. With constant meditation and prayer, it must have been a Patmos to them; and when they left its shores, they went forth, full of zeal, to cry, like John the divine, "The Spirit and the bride say, Come. And let him that heareth say, Come. And let him that is athirst come. And whosoever will, let him take the water of life freely." In all ages, it has seemed good unto the Lord to gather men around some favored instructor, and enable them, under his guidance, to sharpen their swords for the battle of life. Thus did Honorat and Columba, in the olden days, and so did Wycliffe and Luther and Calvin, in the Reformation times, train the armies of the Lord for their mission. Schools of the prophets are a prime necessity if the power of religion is to be kept alive and propagated in the land.[37]

36. Spurgeon, *Autobiography*, vol. 1, 341.
37. Spurgeon, *Autobiography*, vol. 3, 137.

The move to London opened into Spurgeon's life a ministry of intentionally carrying out 2 Tim 2:2. This would mark Spurgeon's ministry for the rest of his life. He would invest into men what God had taught him through St. Andrew's Lay Pastors' Association and his lessons at Waterbeach and then at London.

Confidence and vision for Christ's work comes from participating in the gospel with Him, especially during the years of academic training for ministry. This is always the plan of our Savior—to get us into the field. He practiced this exact training approach with the disciples as He would instruct and then send them out to do it. In our churches, we have great opportunities before us to invest in young people (indeed, in all age groups) recruiting them into studies and evangelism opportunities much as Deacon Vinter did with Spurgeon and others. The rewards of such wise ministry practices for pastors and churches are far reaching and bring observable blessings upon each church as these training systems are developed.

5

The Metropolitan Tabernacle and Growth of the Pastors' College

CHARLES HADDON SPURGEON HAD first preached at New Park Street in London on December 11, 1853. He next preached for the London congregation on January 1, 15, and 29, 1854. Before the last Sunday in January, the New Park Street Baptist Church was taking definite action to secure Spurgeon's permanent services. By April 28, 1854, the decision was made, and Spurgeon accepted the pastorate of the London church.

Spurgeon's impact upon the church was immediate. From the beginning people recognized the young preacher as a prophet for his time, and as time went on this discovery was made by a growing number of people. Spurgeon had come to London with the same zeal and enthusiasm for the gospel and winning people to Christ he had demonstrated at Waterbeach. He used his personality and giftings to minister effectively, and he did so by maintaining his first love with Jesus Christ. Writing in his *Autobiography* he documents the serious reliance on God he and the church had:

> I can never forget how earnestly they prayed ... More than once, we were all so awe-struck with the solemnity of the meeting, that we sat silent for some moments while the Lord's power appeared to overshadow us ... I always give all the glory to God, but I do not forget that He gave me the privilege of ministering

from the first to a praying people . . . and soon the blessing came upon us in such abundance that we had not room to receive it.[1]

With the coming of Spurgeon, the church at New Park Street experienced phenomenal growth, especially the first seven years of his pastorate. The church had huge membership books, which began to be filled quickly, and it became a routine experience. Spurgeon, preaching in May, 1857 said "God gave me souls by hundreds, who were added to my church, and in one year it was my happiness to see not less than a thousand personally who had been converted."[2]

Spurgeon was careful to constantly understand the growth was not from his abilities or gifts. He knew it was God that added to the church, and he wanted to maintain that conviction with the entire church body throughout his ministry. He was careful to assure the messages he preached were clear in presenting who saves and redeems a person from their sins and how He makes them holy. Spurgeon stated,

> Well, but some say, it is the minister they hear who converts men. Ah! That is a grand idea, full sure. No man but a fool would entertain it. I met with a man sometime ago who assured me that he knew a minister who had a very large amount of converting power in him. Speaking of a great Evangelist in America, he said, "That man, sir, has got the greatest quantity of converting power I ever knew a man to have; and Mr. So-and-so in a neighboring town I think is second to him." At that time this converting power was being exhibited, two hundred persons were converted by the converting power of this second best, and joined to the church in a few months. I went to the place some time afterwards—it was in England—and I said, "How do your converts get on?" "Well," said he, "I cannot say much about them." "How many out of those two hundred whom you received in a year ago stand fast?" "Well," he said, "I am afraid not many of them; we have turned seventy of them out for drunkenness already." "Yes," I said, "I thought so: that is the end of the grand experiment of converting power." If I could convert you all, any one else might unconvert you; what any man can do another man can undo; it is only what God does that is abiding.[3]

---

1. Spurgeon, *Autobiography*, vol. 1, 361.
2. Spurgeon, *New Park Street Pulpit*, vol. 3, 197.3.
3. Spurgeon, *New Park Street Pulpit*, vol. 3, 197.

Spurgeon did not look for church growth for any reason other than exalting Jesus Christ in lives and people finding His salvation precious and life changing. The young preacher made it clear early in his ministry he aimed to keep the focus on Jesus Christ and not on anything or anyone else, especially the pastor, at New Park Street Church:

> I would rather be despised and slandered than aught else. This assembly that you think so grand and fine, I would readily part with, if by such a loss I could gain a greater blessing. "God has chosen the base things of the world;" and, therefore I reckon that the more esteemed I may be the worse is my position, so much the less expectation shall I have that God will bless me. He hath put his "treasure in earthen vessels, that the excellency of the power may be of God, and not of man." A poor minister began to preach once, and all the world spoke ill of him, but God blessed him. By-and-by they turned round and petted him. He was the man—a wonder! God left him! It has often been the same. It is for us to recollect, in all times of popularity, that "Crucify him, crucify him" follows fast upon the heels of "Hosanna," and that the crowd today, if dealt faithfully with, may turn into the handful of to-morrow; for men love not plain speaking. We should learn to be despised, learn to be contemned, learn to be slandered, and then we shall learn to be made useful by God. Down on my knees have I often fallen, with the hot sweat rising from my brow, under some fresh slander poured upon me; in an agony of grief my heart has been well-nigh broken, till at last I learned the art of bearing all and caring for none. And now my grief runneth in another line. It is just the opposite. *I fear lest God should forsake me, to prove that he is the author of salvation—that it is not in the preacher, that it is not in the crowd, that it is not in the attention I can attract, but in God, and in God alone* [emphasis added]. And this thing I hope I can say from my heart: if to be made as the mire of the streets again, if to be the laughing stock of fools and the song of the drunkard once more will make me more serviceable to my Master, and more useful to his cause, I will prefer it to all this multitude, or to all the applause that man could give.[4]

Before Spurgeon's arrival, the church at New Park had been recognized as one of the largest, wealthiest and most influential among Baptist congregations in London. In the years prior to his coming the church had decayed and attendance had taken a tremendous decline. The church

---

4. Spurgeon, *New Park Street Pulpit*, vol. 3, 198.

was in a depressed state. A spiritually hungry church at New Park found a spiritually full pastor in C. H. Spurgeon.

It was reported that before Spurgeon had preached three months, there were many young men who were converted by his messages and added to the church's fellowship. Set on fire for Christ through their pastor's example, some of these young men began to work to see others won to Christ. They ministered through open-air preaching and doing Bible studies in the homes of the poor. New Park church was located in a poorer district just south of the Thames River in London.

THE PASTORS' COLLEGE—BEGINNINGS AND DEVELOPMENT

Spurgeon records the fact that within two to three years of coming to New Park he was preaching twelve or thirteen times a week and traveling hundreds of miles by road or rail. He had requests to preach throughout the metropolis of London and throughout the country of England. Through such wide exposure, he attracted young men to his Christ and the same zealous spirit to serve Him as Spurgeon had learned. The vision of the Pastors' College began to take shape in 1856.

The school began when a young man, Thomas William Medhurst, heard Spurgeon preach in 1854 and soon was converted to Christ. He was baptized at New Park Street on September 28, 1854. He began distributing tracts, working in the Sunday School, and preaching in the open air. Medhurst had no intent of entering the ministry when he began doing this service work. But two people were converted under his preaching and became members at New Park. This led Spurgeon to encourage Medhurst to prepare for the ministry and leading a local church.

Spurgeon arranged for Medhurst to reside with C. H. Hosken, pastor of the Baptist Church at Grayford for instruction. This was July 1855. Spurgeon began to personally tutor Medhurst one session per week. Several hours of instruction in theology were given in each of these visits. Medhurst would go to Spurgeon's home for these times of equipping. This had been a practice among pastors in Spurgeon's time to prepare future ministers of the gospel: "The pastor must sympathize with the men God has called to the ministry and must examine them frequently in all that relates to faith, hope, and love. He will instruct them."[5]

---

5. Nicholls, *Baptist Quarterly* 31, 390.

The Metropolitan Tabernacle and Growth of the Pastors' College

Spurgeon valued education for its rightful purpose and he kept his focus on the objective of ministry training with the Pastors' College. The goal was not to attain knowledge. The goal was to gain understanding of God's character and how He blesses and uses His servants to accomplish the Great Commission. He said, "if learning necessarily took men off from dependence upon God we should loathe it, but so far as we can see, ignorance and self-confidence have considerable affinity, while grace makes men humble, however much they know."[6] Some twenty-four years after his experience with Medhurst, the energy and drive to effectively equip and multiply preachers of the gospel was still the passion of Spurgeon's life. He wrote, "*this first work of ours in training men for the ministry still retains the first place in our hearts* [emphasis added]. Nothing can be more important than to fill the pulpits with earnest men who love the gospel of Jesus Christ."[7] By the end of 1856 Medhurst was called to pastor the Baptist church at Kingston-on-Thames. Spurgeon arranged with the church to pay for Medurst's continued training.

On August 5, 1855, Spurgeon delivered a message entitled "Preach the Gospel." It was delivered at New Park in the second year of his pastorate and gives rich insight into the heart and vision of Spurgeon for seeing potential in others for God's purposes. In this message Spurgeon made clear God is always calling some into His service. This gives every pastor a vision of what God intends to do through their ministries regardless the size of their congregation; God is always calling out more men to preach for His kingdom's expansion. L. R. Scarborough, second president of Southwestern Baptist Theological Seminary and their evangelism professor, said "let us do our duty, call out the called and help God supply the mighty demand for more and better preachers." He added to this, "in almost every church where the fires of evangelism burn at all and where God's gospel truths have been faithfully preached, God is calling some young man to preach."[8] At the close of the above-mentioned sermon, Spurgeon said to his church:

> Now, my dear hearers, one word with you. There are some persons in this audience who are verily guilty in the sight of God because *they* do not preach the gospel. I cannot think out of the fifteen hundred or two thousand persons now present, within

---

6. Spurgeon, *Sword and Trowel* 16, 422.
7. Spurgeon, *Sword and Trowel* 16, 422.
8. Scarborough, *Recruits for World Conquests*, 27, 32.

the reach of my voice, there are none who are qualified to preach the gospel besides myself . . . I cannot believe that I have such a congregation that there are not among you many who have gifts and talents that qualify you to preach the Word . . .

But still I say, I cannot conceive but what there are some here this morning who are flowers "wasting their sweetness in the desert air," gems of purest ray serene," lying [sic] in the dark caverns of ocean's oblivion. This is a very serious question. If there be any talent in the church at Park Street, let it be developed. If there be any preachers in my congregation let them preach. Many ministers make it a point to check young men in this respect. There is my hand, such as it is, to help any one of you if you think you can tell to sinners round what a dear Saviour you have found. I would like to find scores of preachers among you; would to God that all the Lord's servants were prophets. There are some here who ought to be prophets, only they are half afraid—well, we must devise some scheme of getting rid of their bashfulness . . . I have preached this sermon especially, because I want to commence a movement from this place which shall reach others. I want to find some in my church, if it be possible who will preach the gospel. And mark you, if you have talent and power, woe is unto you if you preach not the gospel.[9]

Scarborough makes an interesting observation about Spurgeon; "Mr. Spurgeon *prayed, planned, and worked into success* [emphasis added] the Pastors' College"[10]

Spurgeon's own life experience informed and influenced his calling out people to serve Christ. Spurgeon had known the Scriptures since childhood. He understood what was at stake: sin ruins, salvation redeems, people need the Lord; Christ's Good News must be told and proclaimed. To preach the gospel was the passion and conviction of his heart and mind. In fact, Spurgeon stated this in his above referenced sermon, and he made clear a bi-vocational calling can be the faithful way to answer God's call:

> Young man, go home and examine thyself; see what thy capabilities are, and if thou findest that thou hast ability, then try in some humble room to tell to a dozen poor people what they must do to be saved. *You need not aspire to become absolutely and solely dependent* [financially] *upon the ministry* [emphasis

---

9. Spurgeon, *New Park Street Pulpit*, vol. 1, 268.
10. Scarborough, *Recruits for World Conquests*, 30.

added]; but if it should please God, desire even that high honor."
'If a man desire the office of a bishop, he desireth a good work.'
At any rate, seek in some way to proclaim the gospel of God.[11]

Spurgeon set his focus on intentionally calling people out to serve Christ and to challenge young men with the call to become pastors. His aim was to help create a movement which would give renewed life to existing churches and see new churches birthed.

After Spurgeon's training experience with Medhust and seeing him used to minister the gospel, Spurgeon was convinced this would be a promising investment of time and resources. By 1861 the vision had matured. On May 19, 1861, he shared with the Metropolitan Tabernacle congregation how he perceived the strategy of the work:

> There are now seven settled out, all of whom have been eminently successful. They are probably not men who will become great or brilliant, but they have been good and useful preachers. I think there are not other seven in the whole Baptist denomination who have had so many converts during the years that they have been settled. They have been the means, most of them, in the hands of God, of adding many members every year to the churches of which they are pastors; and most of those churches are not in provincial towns, but in villages [i.e., small 'fishing ponds' for evangelism-discipling opportunities]. I have therefore been led still further to increase my number of students, and I have now about sixteen young men wholly to support and train. Beside these, there is a very considerable number of brethren who receive their education in the evening [the Metropolitan Tabernacle Monday night school], though they still remain in their own callings. *With the wider sphere we now occupy as a church, I propose so to enlarge my scheme that all the members of this church and congregation, who happen to be deficient in the plain rudiments of knowledge, can get an education—a common English education—for themselves. Then, if they display any ability for speaking, without giving up their daily avocations, they shall have classes provided for higher branches of instruction. But should they feel that God has called them to the ministry, I am then prepared—after the use of my own judgment, and the judgment of my friends, as to whether they are fit persons—to give them two years' special tutorship, that they may go forth to preach the Word, thoroughly trained so far as we can effect it in so short a time* [emphasis added]. I know I am called to this work, and

---

11. Spurgeon, *New Park Street Pulpit*, vol. 1, 268.

I have had some most singular interpositions of Providence in furnishing funds for it hitherto.[12]

Spurgeon understood an effective and wise life to be one that would establish a vision that would outlive that life. He expressed his views and dream by saying "as long as there is breath in our bodies, let us serve Christ; as long as we can think, as long as we can speak, as long as we can work, let us serve him with our last gasp; and, if it be possible, let us try to set some work going that will glorify him when we are dead and gone."[13]

MOTIVATION FOR THE PASTORS' COLLEGE

There is evidence that Spurgeon had definite convictions and desires for beginning the Pastors' College in how students would be prepared to carry out the Great Commission and communicate the Savior's salvation call. He wanted to be sure they understood solid doctrine and were able to present the gospel. As indicated above, England was feeling the influence of rationalistic thinking from the European continent.

For the Nonconformist segment of England, including Baptists, rationalistic thinking was increasing. More effort was erringly spent on intellectual pursuits to rationally understand miracles, inspiration, and dogmas than had otherwise been previously experienced. Careful study and research giving what Scripture said of its authority and inspiration had not been put in place. Orthodox Christians became troubled by seeming inconsistencies in Scripture because of the inability to explain them rationally. "No longer adequately supported in the traditional doctrine of inerrancy by an overwhelming presupposition in its favour . . . and deprived of miraculous solutions of the most difficult problems, the mid-century nonconformists were much more disturbed by the discrepancies in the Bible than orthodox Christians before them had been."[14]

Spurgeon sensed theological shifting taking place in Nonconformity. He knew strong confidence in Scripture would be pivotal to the work of the Great Commission for seeing disciples and churches multiplied as the Savior instructed. Spurgeon explained the theological alignment of the Pastors' College and its training approach:

---

12. Spurgeon, *Full Harvest*, 97–98.
13. Spurgeon, *Full Harvest*, v.
14. Glover, *Evangelical Nonconformists*, 71, 77.

> The College started with a definite doctrinal basis. I never affected 'to leave great questions as moot points to be discussed in the hall, and believed or not believed, as might be the fashion of the hour. The creed of the College is well known, and we invite none to enter who do not accept it. The doctrines of grace, coupled with a firm belief in human responsibility [Spurgeon said free will (he addressed as free agency) and divine sovereignty were like railroad tracks: both are necessary in the divine work of God—see his sermon "The Lion and the Bear; Trophies Hung Up," September 25, 1884], are held with intense conviction, and those who do not receive them would not find themselves at home within our walls. The Lord has sent us tutors who are lovers of sound doctrine, and zealous for the truth. No uncertain sound has been given forth at any time, and we would sooner close the house than have it so. *Heresy in colleges means false doctrine throughout the churches* [emphasis added]: to defile the fountain is to pollute the streams. Hesitancy which might be tolerated in an ordinary minister would utterly disqualify a teacher of teachers. The experiment of Doddridge ought to satisfy all godly men, that colleges without dogmatic evangelical teaching are more likely to be seminaries of Socinianism than schools of the prophets. Old Puritanic theology has been heartily accepted by those received into our College, and on leaving it they have almost with one consent remained faithful to that which they have received.[15]

Spurgeon wanted to see the gospel proclaimed throughout England and beyond. He wanted to see his world impacted with the message of Jesus Christ he had come to know with deep conviction through the Scriptures. Spurgeon wrote in 1885, "to maintain and spread the gospel of the grace of God by the education of faithful men called of the Holy Ghost . . . was the object which I had in view when I was led to institute the Pastors' College."[16]

Northrop writes that when God began to place in Spurgeon's influence "young men desirous for preaching and service to God, Spurgeon realized the existing colleges would be too expensive and non-selecting of his breed of men."[17] Spurgeon realized the colleges of the time were not suitable for the men God was sending him, and other schools did not quite fit Spurgeon's views of the gospel's work. Spurgeon felt he might be

---

15. Glover, *Evangelical Nonconformists*, 71, 77.
16. Spurgeon, *Sword and Trowel* 21, 307.
17. Northrop, *Life and Works of Spurgeon*, 112.

somewhat harsh, but he "thought the Calvinism of the theology usually taught to be very doubtful, and the fervor of the generality of the students to be far behind their literary attainments."[18]

The principal objective of the Pastors' College compared with Spurgeon's own experience in preparation for the ministry. Having not attended college as many other ministers had experienced and knowing the practical education needed to prepare for the ministry, Spurgeon strategized how this could be accomplished. He stated, "It seemed to me that preachers . . . suitable for the masses, were more likely to be found in an institution where preaching and divinity would be the main objects, and not degrees and other insignia of human learning. I felt that without interfering with the laudable objects of other colleges, I could do good in my own way."[19] His own observations of other churches in London and the educational preparations of their pastors convinced him his own educational preparation had been very effective for the ministry. The Pastors' College strategy is explained in the Sword and Trowel:

> It was expressly designed, moreover, to meet a certain demand which other colleges were unable to supply; and to which they could not well be adapted without interfering with their original constitution and design. Many young men full of zeal to make known to others what they had tasted and felt of the Word of life, and who needed only a certain course of training in order to accomplish their purpose with comfort to themselves and profit to others, were precluded from institutions which had been professedly established for that end, either because they had not the preliminary education required, or because neither they nor their friends were able to contribute to their support.[20]

Spurgeon envisioned a distinct breed of preachers. His success at Waterbeach and New Park encouraged him to train others in the same doctrinal beliefs and convictions for evangelism and disciple making which had blessed others through his ministry. Spurgeon said of the impact made by Luther and Calvin in the days of the Reformation "we must remember that these men became what they were largely through their power to stamp their image and superscriptions upon other men with whom they came into contact."[21] Other Nonconformist colleges were

18. Spurgeon, *Sword and Trowel* 6, 146–50.
19. Spurgeon, *Tabernacle: History and Work*, 96–97.
20. Spurgeon, *Sword and Trowel* 2, 16.
21. Pike, *Life and Works of Spurgeon*, vol. 4, 356.

becoming more information centers for acquiring knowledge rather than equipping centers for fulfilling the Great Commission.

Spurgeon saw a great need for conversion growth and church planting in London and was concerned by the apathy of theological positions held by many. He had been motivated to involve himself with the London Baptist Association to accomplish church extension through partnering with other churches. To effectively reach the world, any church or network of churches (denominations) must make the Great Commission and multiplying disciples and churches their major priority. Engel and Norton stated, "It is a demonstrated principle of church growth that Christianity gains in a society only to the extent that the number of existing churches is multiplied. Multiplication of new congregations of believers, then, is the normal and expected output of a healthy body."[22]

George Rogers became the first principal (dean of the school) of the Pastors' College in 1856 at the age of fifty-seven. He had served as a Congregational pastor of three churches and planted and pastored the last church at Camberwell thirty-six years before coming to the Pastors' College. Spurgeon felt complete unity with Mr. Rogers and esteemed him greatly as a saint and servant of Christ. Students respected and loved him. Spurgeon described him as "a man of Puritanic stamp, deeply learned, orthodox in doctrine, judicious, witty, devout, earnest, liberal in spirit, and withal juvenile in heart to an extent most remarkable in one of his years."[23] Rogers writing in the *Sword and Trowel* in 1866 gave this philosophy and objective of the Pastors' College:

> The men who are the most effective preachers of our day, as a rule, are not the men of high scholastic attainments; but look among them for the rationalistic perverters of the simplicity that is in Christ, and you will not look in vain. This effect, we grant, is not to be attributed to literature itself, but to the undue influence assigned it as a needful and primary element in the Christian teacher, to the undue authority claimed for it in the exposition of divine truth, and consequently to a diminished reliance upon a prayerful and experimental discernment of spiritual things. Such a state of things might well lead us to pause, and to begin to think of retracing our steps, or at least to adopt some new method of collegiate training, better adapted to the real wants of the age. This had been done for us by God himself, in raising up,

---

22. Engel and Norton, *What's Gone Wrong with Harvest?*, 143–44.
23. Spurgeon, *Metropolitan Tabernacle*, 97.

sustaining, and accompanying with many signal tokens of his favour the Metropolitan Tabernacle College.[24]

THE PHILOSOPHY OF PASTORS' COLLEGE

Spurgeon knew God had raised up the Pastors' College. It arose out of his deep desire to communicate the gospel to the multitudes surrounding him in London, particularly south London. Spurgeon said, "to preach efficiently, to get at the hearts of the masses, to evangelize the poor,—this is the College ambition, this and nothing else."[25] The motto of the College was the Cross of Christ: "*Our desire is that every man may both hold the TRUTH, and be held by it, especially the truth of CHRIST CRUCIFIED* [emphases added]."[26] The College anthem was "Hallelujah for the Cross!"[27]

This was the one object of the College—the preaching (teaching) of the gospel, to send gospel proclaimers out of the College. The Pastors' College was predicted by many to accomplish vast good for the church through the evangelistic enterprising of the students. The training developed enthusiasm for that end.[28] In fact Spurgeon later declared his hope was to send preachers to every town in England.

The atmosphere of the Pastors' College was decidedly toward accomplishing the Great Commission with emphases on seeing new churches planted. When Spurgeon gave his annual report of the Pastors' College in the 1878 edition of the *Sword and Trowel* reviewing fifty-three churches planted by students from the college, he stated, "Only one other fact requires to be mentioned, namely, that *from the commencement our plan was not only to train students, but to found churches* [emphasis added]."[29] A comment in the *Sword and Trowel* represented the spirit of all churches planted in connection with the Pastors' College: "Although Baptists, we love all who love our Lord Jesus Christ in sincerity, and rejoice in the work of the Lord among any people. Our great object is not to spread a sect, but to extend the Kingdom of Jesus, by bringing souls to him."[30]

24. Spurgeon, *Sword and Trowel* 2, 42.
25. Spurgeon, *Autobiography*, 2, 149.
26. Skinner, *Lamplighter and Son*, 212.
27. Spurgeon, *Autobiography*, vol. 4, 55.
28. Pike, *Life and Works of Spurgeon*, vol. 3, 39.
29. Spurgeon, *Sword and Trowel* 23, 240.
30. Spurgeon, *Sword and Trowel* 2, 28.

Spurgeon desired to provide the opportunity of training for the ministry to those who would not be academically acceptable at other colleges. Scholarship for its own sake was never sought. It was solely used to make preachers more efficient and effective in their calling. What Spurgeon deprecated was not education, but not fitting it to the work anticipated and what that work would require. This is a matter needing careful consideration in our ministry schools today.

In his last book, *Effective Evangelism: A Theological Mandate*, Donald McGavran (the father of the modern church growth movement served as a missionary for over twenty years in India experiencing disciple-making movements and later he founded the School of World Missions at Fuller Seminary) argued all seminaries should require five courses in Great Commission work which would practically prepare church leaders to help churches multiply disciples and churches. He explained how a maintenance mentality had dominated most seminary training. Due to the focus of training being to avoid aberrant theology, passion for Christ and souls had ebbed. Students need training in both ends of this spectrum. The need is for graduates of Bible colleges and seminaries to have the understanding and skill sets of how to lead churches in conversion growth and church multiplication due to sound theological footing.

The Pastors' College did prepare men to enter their fields of service with a capacity for continued personal and professional growth through personal readings in subjects related to the ministry. The pulpit ministry was the chief focal point of the Pastors' College training. This is where vision casting to help church members have the convictions for participating in Great Commission work, and motivation to do it, is best afforded the pastor. Spurgeon told the students, "The visitation of the sick, private visitation among his people, organization of useful and benevolent institutions, platform speaking, occasional contributions to magazines and reviews—these are all good and important; but the work of the pulpit is more important than any of them."[31] Experiencing Christ changing lives through personally sharing the gospel during the week allows the preacher to effectively call his members to be proclaimers of the gospel. This is the call of God upon all believers as given in 1 Pet 2:9: "But you are a chosen people, a royal priesthood, a holy nation, God's special possession, that you may declare the praises of him who called you out of darkness into his wonderful light." The sheep need shepherds to help them

---

31. Pike, *Life and Works of Spurgeon*, vol. 3, 184.

understand and to encourage them to embrace their calling. The Pastors' College teachers modeled what they taught. James Spurgeon, the younger brother of Charles, was already teaching in the Pastors' College when he became co-pastor with his brother at the Metropolitan Tabernacle in January 1868. James had planted a new church in 1864 and the church had grown to sixty-two members within two years.

Though Spurgeon and the Pastors' College faculty stressed solid doctrinal understanding, they deeply impressed upon students that all ministry efforts and endeavors must be anointed by the Holy Spirit. Spurgeon's challenge was: "A preacher ought to know that he really possesses the Spirit of God, and that when he speaks there is an influence upon him, otherwise out of the pulpit he should go directly; he has not been called to preach God's truth."[32] This anointing is best learned through living daily with the Savior and following Him in His service (John 15). Spurgeon throughout his life was held by the conviction that all evangelization and multiplying of disciples and churches was the work of God's Spirit. Spurgeon wrote his Pastors' College men in 1875:

> I feel sure that you have all stuck to your studies diligently; and my prayer is, that the Holy Spirit may sanctify your human acquirements by a double measure of His anointing. Your power lies in His grace rather than in natural gifts or scholastic acquisitions. Without the Spirit, you will be failures, and worse; therefore, pray much, and see to it that your whole selves are in such a condition that the Spirit of God can dwell in you; for in some men He cannot reside, and with some men He cannot work. Let the channel through which the living water is to flow be both dear and clean.[33]

APPLICATION REQUIREMENTS AND ADMISSIONS

Spurgeon was convinced that most churches needed a particular type of minister—men who would not aim for scholarship, but for the winning of souls. Spurgeon neither undervalued nor overvalued education, but always kept the end goal of the training in mind—that which makes men effective in leading churches to help their members reach lost friends and acquaintances for Christ.

32. Bacon, *Spurgeon*, 84.
33. Spurgeon, *Autobiography*, vol. 3, 129.

Surgeon wrote, "We laid down, as a basis, the condition that a man must, during about two years, have been engaged in preaching, and must have had some seals to his ministry, before we could entertain his application."[34] No matter what amount of talent or scholarship a young man might possess, he had to evidence some sense of a divine call and conviction for preaching the gospel. Sometimes men were accepted who could not read so long as they evidenced a call of God to preach; the College would teach them how to read. These students later became productive in ministry. Spurgeon shared,

> When the Pastors' College was fairly molded into shape, we had before us but one object, and that was, the glory of God, by the preaching of the gospel. To preach with acceptance, men, lacking in education, need to be instructed; and therefore our Institution set itself further to instruct those whom God had evidently called to preach the gospel, but who labored under early disadvantages... This became a main point with us, for we wanted, *not men whom our tutors could make into scholars, but men whom the Lord had ordained to be preachers* [emphasis added].
>
> Firmly fixing this landmark, we proceeded to sweep away every hindrance to the admission of fit men. We determined never to refuse a man on account of absolute poverty, but rather to provide him with needful lodging, board, and raiment, that he might not be hindered on that account. We also placed the literary qualifications of admission so low that even brethren who could not read have been able to enter, and have been among the most useful of our students in after days.[35]

Spurgeon made it clear the Pastors' College was not intended for everyone who wanted theological instruction. It asked for men who were proven—who demonstrated a passion for the ministry of the gospel. These were the student candidates who were encouraged to seek admission. Spurgeon said, "No matter how talented or promising he might appear to be, the College could not act upon mere hopes, but must have evident marks of a Divine call, so far as human judgment can discover them."[36]

Spurgeon said any man who had any doubt regarding the great truths of free grace, the atonement, and the deity of Christ need not apply to the Pastors' College. He made a very practical first inquiry of

---

34. Spurgeon, *Autobiography*, vol. 2, 148.
35. Spurgeon, *Autobiography*, vol. 2, 148–49.
36. Spurgeon, *Autobiography*, vol. 2, 148.

those seeking admittance. His question to an applicant was "have you won souls for Jesus?"[37] Evidence of spirituality, a teachable spirit, zeal for evangelism, along with effectiveness in ministry were ascertained. Much weight was placed on the sending church references provided by those who knew the applicant best.

From time-to-time Spurgeon would issue invitations in his *Sword and Trowel* for men to come and study at the Pastors' College. He used this communication tool to inform his world of the Pastors' College and the work of the Metropolitan Tabernacle. Writing in July 1871, Spurgeon gave this notice:

> We have need of more students at the College. Many have gone to pastorates . . . We are waiting for the Lord to send us really gracious earnest young men, no matter how poor, nor how many. They should apply at once, for a new session begins in August, and we require a few weeks in which to investigate the character and fitness of the applicants. Only devout, hardworking, studious, holy men need apply. A life of toil and probable poverty lies before them; and if they are not called of God to the work, woe unto them. Whosoever is truly called, we shall be glad to take as Aquila did Apollos, and show him the way of God more perfectly.[38]

Spurgeon felt a responsibility to the churches as well as to the young men seeking admission for training. If he believed a young man was not qualified to minister, he turned him down. After personally hearing what an applicant had to say, reading his testimonials, and hearing his responses to questions—if Spurgeon did not feel convinced God had called the young man, he simply told him this. Spurgeon's aim was to "send away none who might ultimately become qualified, and yet to retain none who would be a burden rather than a service to the churches."[39] He explained more by saying,

> Of course, I do not set myself up to judge whether a man shall enter the ministry or not, but my examination merely aims at answering the question whether the Pastors' College shall help him or leave him to his own resources. Certain of our charitable neighbors accuse me of having "a parson manufactory," but the charge is not true at all. I never tried to make a minister, and

---

37. Spurgeon, *Autobiography*, vol. 2, 149.
38. Spurgeon, *Sword and Trowel* 7, 333.
39. Spurgeon, *Sword and Trowel* 6, 146–50.

should fail if I did; I receive none into the College but those who profess to be ministers already. It would be nearer the truth if they called me "a parson-killer," for a goodly number of beginners have received their quietus from me; and I have the fullest ease of conscience in reflecting upon what I have so done. It has often been a hard task for me to discourage a hopeful young brother who has applied for admission to the College. My heart has always leaned to the kindest side, but duty to the churches has compelled me to judge with severe discrimination. After hearing what the candidate has had to say, having read his testimonials and seen his replies to questions, when I have felt convinced that the Lord has not called him, I have been obliged to tell him so.[40]

The Pastors' College had applicants from men from various backgrounds of vocational experiences other than ministry related responsibilities. If an applicant had not been faithful and effective in other fields, this presented a red flag to Spurgeon. He felt those applying for ministry training should be capable of having success in several fields. If this was not evident and yet an applicant was enthusiastic that he should be admitted, Spurgeon stated:

My answer generally is, *Yes,* I see; you have failed in everything else, and therefore 'you think the Lord has especially endowed you for His service; but I fear you have forgotten that the ministry needs the very best of men, and not those who cannot do anything else.". . . A really valuable minister would have excelled in any occupation. There is scarcely anything impossible to a man who can keep a congregation together for years, and be the means of edifying them for hundreds of consecutive Sabbaths; he must be possessed of some abilities, and be by no means a fool or a ne'er-do-well. Jesus Christ deserves the best men to preach His gospel, and not the empty-headed and the shiftless.[41]

Some students had to be asked to leave after having been admitted into the school. This was a rarity and was due either to a lack of study skills or scholastic ability. "Young men who come to us loaded with testimonials, are occasionally found after a while to be lacking in application . . . and after due admonishment and trial they have to be sent back . . . others are as good as gold, but their heads ache, and their health

---

40. Spurgeon, *Autobiography,* vol. 3, 143.
41. Spurgeon, *Autobiography,* vol. 3, 145.

fails under hard study . . . these must be kindly, but firmly, set aside: but I always dread the task."[42]

The kind of men the Pastors' College appealed to included a wide age range. Men already in the pastorate were drawn to the school. The Pastors' College was unique in comparison to other ministry institutions in that it accepted married men as students. As to cost of the education, Spurgeon believed if a student had the ability to pay for their schooling, this was only right. But if a student was unable to pay, Spurgeon wanted to make it possible for his training. "We determined never to refuse a man on account of absolute poverty, but rather to provide him with needful lodging, board, and raiment, that he might not be hindered on that account."[43]

Spurgeon cast the challenge and vision of church planting and for men to come and study for this work regularly through his monthly *Sword and the Trowel*. In 1881 he wrote, "If growing London is not provided with the means of grace coming generations will blame us."[44] Students of the Pastors' College came primarily from the Metropolitan Tabernacle. Because of the worldwide circulation of the *Sword and Trowel*, students applied from France, Germany, America, as well as Scotland. Those students who were received from other countries were encouraged to go back home and plant new churches.

There were no records kept on the graduates of the Pastors' College until 1865. By the time of Spurgeon's death in 1892, nearly nine hundred men had been educated through the College programs. The student body never surpassed one hundred and ten; normally eighty to one hundred studied in the Pastors' College after the school had become established and known throughout London and England.

CURRICULUM AND COLLEGE LIFE AT THE PASTORS' COLLEGE

Spurgeon was the presiding genius and the driving force behind the school. He insured the doctrines of grace and clear teachings of the Cross were studied and understood throughout the curriculum of the College. The students were taught by instructors who were under the direction and supervision of Spurgeon himself.

42. Spurgeon, *Sword and Trowel* 17, 304.
43. Spurgeon, *Autobiography*, vol. 2, 148.
44. Spurgeon, *Sword and Trowel* 6, 146–50.

The curriculum involved studies of whole books of Scripture and making use of expositional commentaries. There was a thorough study of doctrine, the study of church history (including the history of nations) and the administration of church work. Studies also included astronomy, chemistry, zoology, geology and botany, mental and moral science, metaphysics, mathematics, homiletics, Latin, Greek, and Hebrew. There were classes in composition and style, and poetry to prepare students' communications skills.[45] Spurgeon said he included astronomy and other sciences for the students' personal enlargement and also for communicating the gospel better and more effectively. "I arranged for a regular course of lectures on physical science; and many of the brethren have thanked me, not only for the knowledge thus imparted, but also for the wide field of illustration which was thereby thrown open to them. The study of astronomy, as illustrative of Scriptural truth, proved especially interesting."[46]

By 1867 the College had added David Gracey, Archibald Fergusson, and James Spurgeon to the faculty. Pastors of churches in the metropolis served as part-time lecturers in the College and guest lecturers came to the College to offer instruction in specialized subject-matter. David Gracy described course work in the classes he taught; it defines how the practical application of all course work was pursued:

> In my own separate classes there has been most gratifying progress. The seniors have been working very hard at Plato and Homer, Horace and Virgil. Of the three divisions of Hebrew, the first has carefully read through thirteen chapters of Genesis, and from the first to the eighteenth Psalm. In the Greek Testament we have been critically reading the Epistles of Peter, the Epistle to the Romans, and the Acts of the Apostles. In the lectures on Theology which I have been delivering to the whole College, I have been much encouraged by the close attention with which they have been received. And as at the end of each section of the lectures examinations have followed, I have had good evidence that the subjects have been thoughtfully considered. *My general plan has been to exhibit, as far as possible, every question under a Biblical light. My effort has been, instead of avoiding difficulties, to render help in overcoming them, and to show that in presence of a skeptical and denying age, we have the very best grounds for maintaining a fearless front. In these respects it is assuredly believed among us that the gospel committed to our charge is the only truth*

---

45. Nicholls, *Baptist Quarterly* 32, 78.
46. Spurgeon, *Autobiography*, vol. 3, 146.

that can give real rest to the heart of the world, that it is supported by the strongest of reasons, and that it supplies the most effectual incentives to Christian life and work [emphasis added].[47]

Each fall the classes began with Charles Spurgeon's Friday afternoon class. The Friday afternoon lecture began at three o'clock. The students regarded this time as the most profitable experience in their Pastors' College studies. In fact, the students always cheered as their president entered the classroom. Spurgeon was very open and intimate with the men and gave relevant, practical instruction in these sessions.

In these Friday sessions different students would preach and Spurgeon critiqued them. He was able to make his greatest impact upon the students in these experiences. One student wrote "how gently he corrected faults, and encouraged genuine diffidence! What withering sarcasm for all fops and pretenders."[48]

Through his lectures to the students on Fridays, Spurgeon dealt with practical concerns of the minister for preaching the gospel and serving the church. The lectures were eventually published under the title, *Lecture to My Students*, containing lectures given before 1879. Spurgeon's primary teaching concern was the minister's spirituality. He realized then what pastors must realize now—*people give out what they've got in*; there are no shortcuts on this one. People must see in their pastors a selfless, Christ-centered agenda and His passion for souls in order for them to buy into the vision their pastor is casting. Then members will invest their time, talents, and treasures in helping bring the vision to reality. Spurgeon covered all details of a pastor's ministry.

One of the most noted features of Spurgeon was his voice—often being referred to as being like "a silver bell." James Douglas wrote in *Prince of Preachers*, "To himself modulation of voice and appropriate emphasis seemed as natural as it was to breathe."[49] Spurgeon had trained himself in the appropriate use of tone, pitch, volume, and rate in his speaking: he knew the impact of communication beyond the words expressed. Spurgeon worked hard to develop his skills and he continually emphasized to his students to be industrious in self-development.

Even when he began taking his annual trips to Mentone, France for health reasons, Spurgeon would write to the students encouraging

---

47. Spurgeon, *Sword and Trowel* 17, 371.
48. Spurgeon, *Autobiography*, vol. 3, 142–43.
49. Douglas, *Prince of Preachers*, 85.

them to be diligent in their studies and service to the Lord. (Spurgeon had developed the muscular disease called *gout* early in his adult life and was forced to spend his last seventeen winters of his life in this warm Mediterranean climate.) Spurgeon urged his men to read and keep their minds sharp and prepared. First, they must know God's Word, and then he suggested their careful study of Puritan authors. He told the students to master the books they owned.

> The next rule I shall lay down is, *master those books you have. Read them thoroughly. Bathe in them until they saturate you. Read and re-read them, masticate them, and digest them. Let them go into your very self. Peruse a good book several times, and make notes and analyses of it. A student will find that his mental constitution is more affected by one book thoroughly mastered than by twenty books which he has merely skimmed, lapping at them, as the classic proverb puts it; "As the dogs drink of Nilus." Little learning and much pride come of hasty reading. Books may be piled on the brain till it cannot work. Some men are disabled from thinking by their putting meditation away for the sake of much reading. They gorge themselves with book-matter, and become mentally dyspeptic. Books on the brain cause disease. Get the book into the brain, and you will grow . . . In reading books let your motto be, "Much, not many." Think as well as read, and keep the thinking always proportionate to the reading,* [emphasis added]. *and your small library will not be a great misfortune.*[50]

By the time of his death, Spurgeon had amassed a library of twelve thousand volumes, including Puritan works dating back to 1525. Spurgeon said, "the old Puritans have more sense in one line than there is in a page of our new books, and more in one page than there is in a whole volume of our modern divinity."[51] Spurgeon encouraged his men to value what he himself had received great profit from—reading the right kinds of books and much of them. His wife and secretary said of his reading abilities, "He could read from cover to cover of a large octavo or folio volume in the course of a very short space of time, and he would thus become perfectly familiar with all that it contained."[52]

Spurgeon made it a practice to read five to six difficult books each week. He said "he wished to rub his mind against the strongest;" he

---

50. Spurgeon, *Lectures to My Students*, 177–78.
51. Spurgeon, *Spurgeon's Sermons*, vol. 3, 258.
52. Spurgeon, *Autobiography*, vol. 4, 273.

would also read magazines and journals treating the fields of medicine and science. (A doctor and an architect on different occasions discussed their fields with Spurgeon and walked away feeling he knew more of their disciplines than they.)[53] This reading practice was in addition to Puritan and other biblical studies. For Spurgeon, once he read it, the contents became permanently his.[54] His value of reading was passed on to the Pastors' College students.

The Pastors' College was indeed distinct in its approach for training pastors, but ever practical in its aim. Pike says, "The institution may have shown some shortcomings; it might not be the place for such young men as had enjoyed exceptional advantages, and had set themselves to attain to a high standard of scholarship, but it was nevertheless such a training-school as the age required."[55] George C. Lorimer, pastor of Tremont Temple in Boston described the work and educational training in 1892,

> "The curriculum of the Pastors' College has been criticized as too meagre, and as not affording the student an education sufficiently comprehensive for the times; but it ought always to be remembered that the plan of study adopted by this institution was never designed to be a substitute for university training, and its President never under-estimated the value of higher and ampler advantages. Nor should it be forgotten that until within a recent period it has not been an easy thing for Nonconformists to obtain the privileges of Oxford or of Cambridge . . . It was devised and inaugurated as an institution for practical equipment, and as such it has unquestionably justified its existence . . . They have likewise obtained a complete knowledge of Holy Scripture; and have listened to sagacious suggestions regarding pastoral duties."[56]

Dr. John Campbell, editor of the *British Banner*, (himself a Congregationalist minister and Paedobaptist thereby not completely aligned with Spurgeon's beliefs) described Spurgeon's approach with the Pastors' College as being practical and suited to the needs of churches. He wrote, "Spurgeon has the true ideas of the wants of the Church and of the times, and he has fully provided for them. He is not the foe of learning by any means, but he is more the friend of souls. *What he deprecates is, not*

---

53. Spurgeon, *Autobiography*, vol. 4, 284.
54. Spurgeon, *Autobiography*, vol. 4, 265; Carlile, *Spurgeon*, 179.
55. Pike, *Life and Work of Spurgeon*, vol. 3, 39.
56. Pike, *Life and Work of Spurgeon*, vol. 2, 234.

education, but non-adaptation to the work contemplated, and every man of sense and reflection will join him* [emphasis added]."⁵⁷

STUDENT LIFE AT THE PASTORS' COLLEGE

Throughout their studies, the primacy of active ministry and missions work was held before the students. Speaking on soul winning, Spurgeon told his students "*Let this be your choice work while studying, and let it be the one object of your lives when you go forth from us* [emphasis added]."⁵⁸ There was clear scriptural accountability support for his exhortation: "Follow Me and I will make you fishers of men" (Matt 4:19). Spurgeon and the leadership of the Pastors' College knew a genuine atmosphere of love for the Savior and souls was needed in the school, or the students would miss their main preparation for ministry. Spurgeon shared how this was focused on: "Foremost among our aims is the promotion of a vigorous spiritual life among those who are preparing to be undershepherds of Christ's flock. By frequent meetings for prayer, and by other means, we labor to maintain a high tone of spirituality. I have endeavored in my lectures and addresses to stir up the holy fire; for well I know that if the heavenly flame burns low nothing else will avail."⁵⁹

Student housing was provided in the homes of church members who lived nearby the Metropolitan Tabernacle. Spurgeon saw the strategy of housing students in the homes of Tabernacle families during their studies to better prepare them for the ministry:

> The young brethren are boarded generally in twos and threes, in the houses of our friends around the Tabernacle, for which the College pays a moderate weekly amount. The plan of separate lodging we believe to be far preferable to having all under one roof; for, by the latter mode, men are isolated from general family habits, and are too apt to fall into superabundant levity. The circumstances of the families who entertain our young friends are generally such that they are not elevated above the social position which in all probability they will have to occupy in future years, but are kept in connection with the struggles and conditions of every-day life.⁶⁰

57. Pike, *Life and Work of Spurgeon*, vol. 3, 78.
58. Spurgeon, *Soul-Winner*, 225.
59. Spurgeon, *Sword and Trowel* 17, 304.
60. Spurgeon, *Metropolitan Tabernacle*, 100.

Spurgeon controlled the atmosphere of the College so the end product resulted in effective preachers for Christ's kingdom's extension. He made sure the culture of the College encouraged every student to grow in Christ-centered character and commitment. Devotional habits were cultivated into the students' daily schedules, in and out of the classroom. Spurgeon encouraged the men to pray for each other by name. Additionally, the value of discipline and punctuality were stressed, and hard work was emphasized to the students upon entering the Pastors' College. Spurgeon said, "I am always afraid of their learning the ways of the idle, and am very watchful to nip anything of the sort in the bud; for you know it is best to kill the lion while it is a cub."[61]

The men were challenged to do as much evangelistic work as they could while carrying out their studies at the College. The arrangement of free tuition and books along with room and board elevated the opportunity to call students to practical ministries during their academic programs. Students were given opportunities to preach in churches, mission halls, and the open-air. House-to-house visitation was carried out in the south London area—the poorer sections of the London metropolis. This gave them an education in ministering to those who were depressed and suffering.

In spite of all challenges, the classes at the Pastors' College were filled with hard work and a hearty attitude. Spurgeon's spirit of joy and genuine love influenced the atmosphere of the Pastors' College. Having the occasion of speaking before a group of students at Bristol College for a breakfast meeting during the 1868 autumn Baptist Union meeting, Spurgeon evidenced why his students desired to imitate him. The Bristol meeting was filled with humor and a caring informality—spontaneous laughter and tears were prevalent. Students were naturally attracted to Spurgeon's enthusiasm and mannerisms. They sought to emulate his delivery and voice style which were impactful and arrested the attention of hearers. They learned to practice preaching without notes as Spurgeon modeled; this was not the norm for preachers in their day.

James Sheridan Knowles (1784–1862) was trained as a medical doctor but became a prominent actor and playwright. He was later invited to become a homiletics teacher at Stepney College following his conversion. He told his students at Stepney in 1854 to go and study the young pastor just beginning in London. A Pastor G. H. Davies, of Lisbon, North

---

61. Spurgeon, *John Ploughman's Pictures*, 10–11.

Dakota, who had studied under Knowles at Stepney gave a vivid picture of what Knowles told them about Spurgeon:

> I was a student at Stepney, now Regent's Park College. Sheridan Knowles, the celebrated actor and play-writer, had just been baptized by Dr. Brock, and appointed our tutor in elocution. We had collected funds to give the grand old man a handsome Bible. The presentation was made one Wednesday afternoon. It was an occasion never to be forgotten, not only for the sake of Sheridan Knowles himself, but because of his prophecy concerning one of whom till then we knew nothing. Immediately on entering, Mr. Knowles exclaimed, 'Boys, have you heard the Cambridgeshire lad?' None of us had heard him. 'Then, boys,' he continued, 'go and hear him at once.' This was after Mr. Spurgeon had been preaching at New Park Street Chapel two Sundays. 'Go and hear him at once if you want to know how to preach. His name is Charles Spurgeon. He is only a boy, but he is the most wonderful preacher in the world. He is absolutely perfect in his oratory; and, beside that, a master in the art of acting. He has nothing to learn from me, or anyone else. He is simply perfect. He knows everything. He can do anything. I was once lessee of Drury Lane Theater; and were I still in that position, I would offer him a fortune to play for one season on the boards of that house. Why, boys, he can do anything he pleases with his audience! He can make them laugh, and cry, and laugh again, in five minutes. His power was never equaled. Now, mark my word, boys, *that young man will live to be the greatest preacher of this or any other age. He will bring more souls to Christ than any man who ever proclaimed the gospel, not excepting the apostle Paul. His name will be known everywhere, and his Sermons* [sic] *will be translated into many of the languages of the world* [emphasis added].[62]

Knowles' prophecy of Spurgeon became fulfilled: at the time of Spurgeon's death, his sermons were published weekly into over forty different languages and circulated around the world. Five years after his death, they were selling 500,000 weekly. What Knowles told his students is an encouragement to all aspiring ministers to develop their communication gifts for Christ's service; it can mean more lives coming to know His saving grace. We must ever understand effective communication comes from the heart: what is lodged the well of the heart comes out of the bucket of the mouth. Spurgeon points us to this value and need.

---

62. Spurgeon, *Autobiography*, vol. 3, 353–54.

THE PASTORS' COLLEGE CONFERENCE

Spurgeon wanted a way to continue encouraging his Pastors' College men after they had finished their schooling and entered into their ministry callings. The annual meetings of the Pastors' College Conference began in 1865. The meetings were purposed to provide fellowship, inspiration, and prayer. This was Spurgeon's strategy of helping the graduates of the Pastors' College to gain fresh vision and strength for dreaming bigger in their present labors. The graduates testified that the conference was a means of saving many men from despair. Spurgeon described the benefit of the Conference:

> Each year the brethren at the Pastors' College are invited to meet in conference at the Tabernacle, and they are generously entertained by our friends. The week is spent in holy fellowship, prayer, and intercourse. By this means men in remote villages, labouring under discouraging circumstances, and ready to sink from loneliness of spirit [it's always easier for Satan to defeat pastors who are loners from their peers in ministry], are encouraged and strengthened: indeed, all the men confess that a stimulus is thus given which no other means could confer. The Conference of 1870 was regarded by all as a visitation of the Holy Spirit, and the brethren returned to their labour full of zeal and hope.[63]

The conference meetings were conducted each spring. Spurgeon always spoke to the conference and devoted much time to prepare the addresses he delivered to these pastors. Other noted denominational preachers were brought in to speak to the men as well. The conference met from Monday through Friday. Meetings were daily at different church locations throughout London with the finale taking place at the Tabernacle. Spurgeon asked for prayer for the annual Conference through the *Sword and Trowel*.

A fellowship supper was held at the Metropolitan Tabernacle and the occasion always included an offering being received for the Pastors' College. During most of Spurgeon's pastorate at the Tabernacle, a deacon of the Tabernacle, T. R. Phillips, provided this supper which made possible an effective fund-raising opportunity for the Pastors' College. The conference operated on the basis of a Constitution with members being admitted by the nomination of a Standing Committee. The Constitutional

---

63. Spurgeon, *Metropolitan Tabernacle*, 102.

agreement held beliefs in (1) the doctrines of grace, (2) believer's baptism, and (3) the winning of souls for Jesus Christ.

The Annual Pastors' College Conference was dissolved by Spurgeon in 1888; a new conference, the "Pastors' College Evangelical Association," was formed immediately. This action was eventuated by the course of events in the Downgrade Controversy. Many of the former Pastors' College students had accepted various forms of modern thought and teachings departing away from absolute belief in the teachings of Scriptures. Spurgeon felt he must withdraw fellowship from them in the annual Pastors' College Conferences. The influence of Darwinism and German rationalism was influencing some Baptist ministers to let go of fundamental doctrines of Scripture.

The new Pastors' College Evangelical Association was a realignment of the old annual conference along more specific doctrinal statements. It was comprised of former and present students and other ministers sympathetic to these doctrines. At the 1890 Conference meeting Spurgeon commented "men are down-grade in doctrine, because they were never put up-grade by the renewal of their minds."[64]

In addition to the annual conference for the graduates, the College also sponsored the work of the Society of Evangelists. This ministry was begun in 1874 and centered its efforts in local churches. The most notable evangelists of the Society were W. Y. Fullerton and Menton Smith. They served together all over the British Isles until 1893. They labored for conversions and looked for 'instant decisions' because of their concentrated evangelism efforts through meetings held in local churches.[65] Distinct and definite preparation was carried out ahead of time. They made sure the seed had been sown, soil prepared, and a harvest prepared for prior to their meetings.

A foreign missions ministry was also conducted and was known as the Pastors' College Missionary Association. Never achieving wide dimensions due to limited funding, it did, however, send missionaries to Africa, France, and South America. The majority of students who became foreign missionaries went under the auspices of the Baptist Missionary Society, the American Baptist Missionary Union, or the China Inland Missions. Hudson Taylor and Spurgeon were friends in Christ's work and

---

64. Cook, *Wit and Wisdom of Spurgeon*, 148.

65. Spurgeon, *Sword and Trowel* 27, 272.

Taylor made many speeches on behalf of the China Inland Mission at the Metropolitan Tabernacle.

THE TABERNACLES FUNDING AND SUPPORTING THE PASTORS' COLLEGE

The initial funding of the College was primarily carried by Spurgeon's own support through the sale of his sermons—and the additional support coming from the two New Park Street Baptist deacons. Due to Spurgeon's denouncing slavery, the sales of his sermons in America were reduced decisively and available revenues for funding the College began to shrink quickly. Spurgeon always held the position that the College was begun in faith, and "trust in Jesus became the financial basis of the Pastors' College. The very essence of its existence is simple reliance on the Redeemer."[66] Spurgeon's upbringing and the development of his temperament had developed him to be straightforward and intentionally upright. His responded when censured in America because of his anti-slavery position reveals his perspective toward matters of life:

> It is frequently objected that the preacher is censorious: he is not desirous of defending himself from the charge. He is confident that many are conscious that his charges are true, and if true, Christian love requires us to warn those who err; nor will candid men condemn the minister who is bold enough to point out the faults of the Church and the age, even when all classes are moved to anger by his faithful rebukes, and pour on his head the full vials of their anger. IF THIS BE VILE, WE PURPOSE TO BE VILER STILL.[67]

After the loss of support from America because of his slavery comments, Spurgeon shared with his church the need of the Pastors' College. Spurgeon was committed to seeing the Pastors' College vision survive. Before he had gone to his people with the need, he thought of selling off material items of his own to fund the project.

> I am firmly persuaded that we ought under no pretense to go into debt. On one occasion, I proposed the sale of my horse and carriage, although these were almost absolute necessaries to me on account of my continual journeys in preaching the Word.

---

66. Harte, *Historical Tablets of the College*, 19.
67. Spurgeon, *Autobiography*, vol. 2, 259.

This my friend Mr. Rogers would not hear of, and actually offered to be the loser rather than this should be done. Then 'it was that I told my difficulties to my people, and the *weekly offering* commenced.[68]

The church officially adopted the Pastors' College on July 1, 1861. The church committed to praying for and financially helping the College through weekly offerings and praying for the school. Regarding this action Spurgeon said,

> It is a grand assistance to our College that it is connected with an active and vigorous Christian church. If union to such a church does not quicken the student's spiritual pulse, it is his own fault. It is a serious strain upon a man's spirituality to be dissociated, during his student-life, from actual Christian work, and from fellowship with more experienced believers. At the Pastors' College, our brethren can not only meet, as they do every day, for prayer by themselves, but they can unite daily in the prayer-meetings of the church, and can assist in earnest efforts of all sorts. Through living in the midst of a church which, despite its faults, is a truly living, intensely zealous, working organization, they gain enlarged ideas, and form practical habits. Even to see church-management and church-work upon an extensive scale, and to share in the prayers and sympathies of a large community of Christian people, must be a stimulus to rightminded men. It has often done me good to hear the students say that they had been warned against losing their spirituality during their College course; but they had, on the contrary, approved that their piety had been deepened and increased through association with their brethren and the many godly men and women with whom they were constantly brought into contact. Our circumstances are peculiarly helpful to growth in grace, and we are grateful to have our Institution so happily surrounded by them. The College is recognized by the church at the Tabernacle as an integral part of its operations, and is supported and loved as such[69]

The church gave about 2,000 pounds annually to the College from the special weekly offerings collected for this school's work. Expenses ran about 5,000 pounds per year. The additional revenues needed came from various other donations in addition to the annual College Conference

---

68. Spurgeon, *Metropolitan Tabernacle*, 99.
69. Spurgeon, *Autobiography*, vol. 3, 125.

dinner made available by T. R. Phillips. (The dinner in 1877 raised over 2,000 pounds for the College.)

Throughout Spurgeon's lifetime he gave better than half of his salary from the church to the College expenses. Spurgeon noted, "The large sale of my sermons in America, together with my dear wife's economy, enabled me to spend from 1600 to 1800 a year on my own favorite work."[70] They devoted the profits from the sale of the *Sword and Trowel* to pay insurance premiums on behalf of the graduates. The Pastors' College Assurance Community was formed in 1868 to provide life insurance for the ministers.

As to asking financial assistance from the Christian community at large, Spurgeon followed a policy of first asking for prayer before finances:

> But it would be, to my own soul, an inexpressible source of joy if believers would afford this Institution a place in their fervent prayers. All of us engaged in the enterprise feel our entire dependence upon the Holy Spirit; and, hence, we value, beyond all price, the prayers of the saints. We cannot teach efficiently, our men cannot study to any purpose, and their labours cannot avail to win souls, except as the Lord our God shall pour out His blessing upon us. Oh, that we could win the hearts of some of the King's intercessors, so that they would plead with our Lord to remember us in mercy! Moreover, if the Christian Church should be moved to take an interest in our affairs, many of God's people would feel stirred up to give of their substance for the support of the Lord's young prophets. While we look up to the treasury in the skies for the supply of every need, we know that the means must come through the channel of the saints. It is not consistent with our plan to ask anyone personally, or to request regular pledged subscriptions; yet we think it meet to remind believers of their stewardship, and of their obligation to extend their Master's Kingdom; and we do not hesitate to declare that no work more deserves their aid than that which the Lord has laid upon us; there is not one more likely to bless the Church, and to gather together the wandering sheep. Of this, however, each one must judge for himself; and, according to the verdict of his conscience, each one must act. None but those who thoroughly appreciate our work will be likely to send assistance. This is as it should be, and as we believe the Lord would have it.[71]

---

70. Spurgeon, *Autobiography*, vol. 2, 110.
71. Spurgeon, *Autobiography*, vol. 3, 128

Spurgeon knew God had called the Pastors' College into existence. He knew he had to continually rely upon God for the needs and provisions of the school. Spurgeon utilized his influence and communication opportunities via the *Sword and Trowel* to ask and implore people of the church at large to pray for the Pastors' College. He wrote:

> We need the daily prayer of God's people that much grace may be with all concerned in this important business; for what can we do without the Holy Spirit? How few ever pray for students! If ministers do not come up to the desired standard, may not the members of the churches rebuke themselves for having restrained prayer on their account? When does a Christian worker more need prayer than in his early days, when his character is forming and his heart is tenderly susceptible both of good and evil influences? I would beseech all who have power with God to remember our Colleges in their intercessions. The solemn interests involved in the condition of these schools of the prophets compel me to entreat, even unto tears, that the hopeful youth of our ministry may not be forgotten in the supplications of the saints. For us also, who have the responsible duty of guiding the minds of these young men, much prayer is requested, that we may have wisdom, love, gentleness, firmness, and abounding spiritual power. It is not every man who can usefully influence students, nor can the same men have equal power at all times. The divine Spirit is needed, and He is given to them that ask for his sacred teaching.[72]

Spurgeon and the Metropolitan Tabernacle created an internal "farm system" so that a continuous flow of harvesters and harvest leaders were developed. This is what he argued should be the work of every church—creating their own farm system for the work of the Savior and what He has called the church to be and do. This is discussed further in the last two chapters of this book.

---

72. Spurgeon, *Sword and Trowel* 17, 305.

6

The Applied Theology of Spurgeon and the Tabernacle which Multiplied Disciples and Churches

IN THIS CHAPTER PARTICULAR Scripture truths and their applications used by Spurgeon and the Metropolitan Tabernacle will be carefully considered. How these doctrines effected the ability to win people to Christ and develop them into leaders for His kingdom work will be studied. The areas of grace, election, faith, preaching Christ and the Cross (salvation and repentance), the Holy Spirit, love, and faith (for doing evangelism and discipleship) will be studied. Quotations on these by Spurgeon in his sermons will be highlighted. These truths which transformed Spurgeon's life and the lives of his members as well those trained in the Pastors' College, are invaluable for modern church work.

Charles Spurgeon believed and understood the only reason to enter into the ministry was to bring glory to God and win souls to Jesus Christ. He learned with the people in his church the value and joy of multiplying disciples and leaders so that more lives could be impacted by the gospel. The Metropolitan Tabernacle played a strategic role in the training of the Pastors' College students who became primary instruments in their farm system. Spurgeon utilized the testimony and modeling of evangelism and discipleship ministries done by the Metropolitan church to help students be called into ministry service and subsequent training. Spurgeon stated, "To be in union with a living church is a great part of a young minister's training."[1] Pastors and churches have more potential to shape and send workers out for Christ in their communities than is often realized. Through such calling out and sending, churches inspire their own "Timothies" into a life of ministry service and leadership resulting in a functional farm system for Christ's work. The Tabernacle church expanded the vision of the future pastors coming out of the Pastors' College. Spurgeon had a clear grasp of necessary core values and ideologies: he knew what he believed, and why, and constantly gave a vivid picture of this to the church to fulfill the Great Commission.

THE GREAT COMMISSION EXERCISED THROUGH LOVING GOD AND OTHERS

Spurgeon clearly and continually placed before his congregation the call of the Savior to follow Him and make disciples. This was his conviction from Scripture that every child of God is called to be both a minister and a missionary (Eph 4:11–16; Matt 4;19). In his 1879 sermon Spurgeon stated: "Yes, my young friends, ye young men and maidens, ye are not too young to be recruits in the King's service. If the kingdom is ever to come to our Lord,—and come it will,—*it never will come through a few ministers, missionaries, or evangelists preaching the gospel. It must come through every one of you preaching it* [emphasis added]."[2] Spurgeon knew by leading his people to become directly involved in making new disciples of Christ, it would bring the Savior's blessings upon their lives and upon the church. In his message, "Soul-Winning," Spurgeon said,

> Wisdom is justified in all her children. Only children wrangle about incidental methods: men look at sublime results. Do these workers of many sorts and divers manners win souls? Then they are wise; and you who criticize them, being yourselves unfruitful, cannot be wise, even though you affect to be their judges. God proclaims soul-winners to be wise, dispute it who dare. This degree from the College of Heaven may surely stand them in good stead, let their fellow mortals say what they will of them. "He that winneth souls is wise," and this can be seen very clearly. He must be a wise man in even ordinary

1. Spurgeon, *Sword and Trowel* 14, 188.
2. Spurgeon, *Soul Winner*, 264.

respects who can by grace achieve so divine a marvel. Great soul-winners never have been fools. *A man whom God qualifies to win souls could probably do anything else which providence might allot him* [emphasis added].³

Spurgeon taught the call of the Great Commission out of his own life change by the gospel. Of his early experiences with Christ, Spurgeon said of Matt 4:19,

> I know another man, not named "Matthew," but "Charles," and the Lord said to him, "Follow Me;" and he also arose, and followed Him. I do not know all that He saw when He looked upon me, I fear that He saw nothing in me but sin, and evil, and vanity; but I believe that He did say to Himself concerning me, "I see one to whom I can teach My truth, and who, when He gets a hold of it, will grip it fast, and never let it go, and one who will not be afraid to speak it wherever he is." So the Lord saw what use He could make of me . . . *I do not see how our sense of oneness to Christ could ever have been perfected if we had not been permitted to work for Him. If He had been pleased to save us by His precious blood, and then leave us with nothing to do, we should have had fellowship with Christ up to a certain point, but (I speak from experience) there is no fellowship with Christ that seems to me to be so vivid, so real to the soul, as when I try to win a soul for Him* [emphasis added]. Oh, when I come to battle with that soul's difficulties, to weep over that soul's hardness; when I begin to set the arguments of Divine mercy before it, and find myself foiled; when I am in a very agony of spirit, and feel that I could die sooner than that soul should perish; then I get to read the heart of Him whose flowing tears, and bloody sweat, and dying wounds showed how much He loved poor fallen mankind.⁴

For Spurgeon, there was no distinction in Scripture between clergy and laity. Again, in his history of the Metropolitan Tabernacle he stated, "*As our church recognizes no distinction of clergy and laity* [emphasis added], it is not meet that its history should consider entirely of the lives and labours of its pastors."⁵ This understanding of Spurgeon factors huge in understanding how God brought about the revitalization of the New Park Street Baptist Church and what ultimately was achieved in multiplying disciples and churches in the farm system they developed.

3. Spurgeon, *Metropolitan Tabernacle Pulpit*, Vol 15, 28.
4. Spurgeon, *Autobiography*, vol. 1, 179.
5. Spurgeon, *Metropolitan Tabernacle*, 55.

If the words "called," "calling," and "call" are studied in the Word of God, one can agree with Spurgeon's sentiments about the laity in the church. Rom 10:14–15 gives definite instruction to the laity to be preaching Christ in their sphere of influence: "How, then, can they call on the one they have not believed in? And how can they believe in the one of whom they have not heard? And how can they hear without someone preaching to them? And how can anyone preach unless they are sent? As it is written: 'How beautiful are the feet of those who bring good news!'" The members of our churches are to be sent into Christ's harvest fields. The Savior states in John 20:21, "Again Jesus said, 'Peace be with you! As the Father has sent me, I am sending you.'" He prayed in 17:18, "As you sent me into the world, I have sent them into the world."

CHURCH VALUES AND ATMOSPHERE

The Metropolitan Tabernacle had a history of missions-mindedness. They possessed a rich legacy of proclaiming the gospel in the south London area dating back to the 1600's. While Keach served as pastor for thirty-six years, he was physically persecuted for his preaching Christ. He said "The cross is the way to the crown . . . Oh! Did you but experience . . . the great love of God, and the excellencies that are in Him, it would make you willing to go through any suffering for his sake."[6] God's bringing together this people and Charles Spurgeon enabled their passion to increase for the gospel and the multiplying of souls as Kingdom participants. Spurgeon talked about *atmosphere* in a church:

> It is hard when you are rowing against wind and tide, but it is worse even than that if you have a horse on the bank pulling a rope, and dragging your boat the other way. Well, never mind, brethren, if that is your case, but work away all the harder, and pull the horse into the water. Still, *remember that when once a favourable atmosphere is created, then the difficulty is to maintain it.* You notice that I said, "When the atmosphere is created," and that expression reminds us how little we can do, or rather that we can do nothing without God, for it is He who has to do with atmospheres, He alone can create them and maintain them; therefore, our eyes must be continually lifted up to Him, whence cometh all our help [emphasis added].[7]

6. Spurgeon, *Metropolitan Tabernacle*, 22–23.
7. Spurgeon, *Soul-Winner*, 139.

The right kind of atmosphere (culture) in any organization encourages and helps its members to perform at a higher level. (How to lead as a pastor in seeing the right atmosphere in a church developed will be addressed in the book's final chapter.) It is what Jesus explained and gave value to and prayed for in John 17:11, 21–23; He asked the Father four times to grant this to His local churches. When a church understands its mission with a passion derived from the Spirit of God, God's power as described in Acts can be upon such a church and miracles of changed lives will take place as they proclaim the gospel.

One of the most outstanding examples of a Tabernacle member contributing to this atmosphere and culture was a member, Mrs. Bartlett. Her life epitomized the values and vision communicated by Spurgeon. She possessed the monomania which had captured her pastor. Her example influenced others in the church (especially the Pastors' College students exposed to such Christ-focused character and ministry service).

A Sunday School teacher was to be absent for a month and the church needed to find a substitute to guide and care for her class. Mrs. Bartlett was asked to fill in and she reluctantly accepted the responsibility of leading three high school ladies in Bible study and growth in Jesus Christ. The impact of God using this lay person is explained:

> Mr. Spurgeon used often to say that his best deacon was a woman [they did not have women deacons, but Spurgeon acknowledged Mrs. Bartlett's worth and impact comparable to any deacon],—alluding to Mrs. Bartlett. In the summer of 1859, one of the teachers of New Park Street Sunday-school was going away for a month, and asked Mrs. Bartlett to take charge of her class during her absence; but, on presenting herself at the school, the superintendent (Mr. Thomas Olney, Junr., as he was then called,) directed her to the senior class. There were only three young women in attendance that afternoon, but in the course of the month the number had so increased that she was asked to continue as teacher. She did so, and before long the class had outgrown its accommodation, an experience which was again and again repeated until it was finally settled in the lecture-hall of the new Tabernacle, where there were some 600 or 700 regularly present. When Mrs. Bartlett was "called home," in 1875, it was estimated that between 900 and 1000 members of her class had joined the church at the Tabernacle.[8]

---

8. Spurgeon, *Autobiography*, vol. 3, 36

Mrs. Bartlett was a model and reflection of the atmosphere at the Metropolitan Tabernacle. She was an example of God's blessings upon the church in response to her work and her pastor's vision: for Christ to be exalted through Great Commission work. Her convictions and commitment contributed to the farm system taking place in this local church. Spurgeon gives this insight into Mrs. Bartlett's life and character:

> Mrs. Bartlett was a choice gift from God to the church at the Tabernacle, and the influence of her life was far-reaching, stimulating many others besides those who by her means were actually led to the Savior ... *She believed with all her heart, and therefore acted with decision and power. Hence, she did not constantly look to the Pastor for help in her appointed service; but, beginning in a small and quiet way, toiled on till everything grew around her to large proportions. She took small account of difficulty or discouragement, but trusted in God, and went on as calmly sure of success as if she saw it with her eyes. When anything flagged, she only seemed to throw out more energy, waited upon God with more fervency, and pushed forward with the resolve to conquer* ... such expressions as 'I know God will help us. It must be done; it shall be done; sisters, you will do it!' were just the sort of speeches that we expected of her. She flamed in determined earnestness at times when only fire could clear a path, and then there was no withstanding her, as her class very well knew ... She kept close to the cross, extolled her Savior, pleaded with sinners to believe, and stirred up saints to holy living. Of her theme she never tired, nor would she allow others to tire. She looked as if it was treason to grow cold; her glance indicated that, to be indifferent about the Redeemer's Kingdom, was a shameful crime. From first to last of her long leadership of her class, she appeared to be almost equally energetic and intense.
>
> It pleased God to make our sister an eminently practical woman. *She was no dreamer of dreams, but a steady, plodding worker* [emphasis added] ... Her addresses were always practical; never speculative, or merely entertaining. She aimed at soul winning every time she met the class, and that in the most direct and personal manner. In pursuing this object, she was very downright, and treated things in a matter-of-fact style. The follies, weaknesses, and temptations of her sex were dealt with very pointedly; and the griefs, trials, and sins of her class were on her heart, and she spoke of them as real burdens.[9]

---

9. Spurgeon, *Autobiography*, vol. 3, 37–38.

Pike describes Spurgeon and the Metropolitan Tabernacle as a working hive with ceaseless ordered activity in carrying out the Great Commandment and Great Commission work of the Savior. Every ministry answered this focus and passion of the church and pastor. The church conducted an almhouse ministry providing care for those widows over sixty years of age; it ran an orphanage with some of these children eventually entering ministry training in the Pastors' College later; it also conducted a colportage association which engaged young men going door-to-door distributing tracts, conducting prayer with households and offering Christian resources for a minimum cost. Pike described Spurgeon's leadership at Metropolitan by saying "Spurgeon was recognized as a great preacher, but his oratorical powers were thought to be less striking than his great personal influence and the various beneficent agencies which had the Tabernacle for their head-quarters."[10] A journalist described the church: "Thence I passed to the Tabernacle itself. Now, I fancy most persons have the idea that this is simply a 'preaching shop' closed, and doing nothing from Sunday to Sunday. Never was there a greater mistake. It is a perfect hive of busy workers from seven every morning until night."[11]

TIMOTHIES AND DISCIPLE MAKING

On September 28, 1854, Thomas Medhurst was baptized by Spurgeon at New Park and began preaching in open air ministries. Further training for ministry was arranged. Spurgeon wrote to Medhurst and shared, "I have been meditating upon the pleasure of being the means of sending you to so excellent a scene of preparation for the ministry, . . . for I love you very much. Oh, how I desire to see you a holy and successful minister of Jesus! . . . I must find another to be *my dearly-beloved Timothy* [emphasis added], just as you are."[12]

Spurgeon taught his congregation from Matt 9:37–38: "Then he said to his disciples, 'The harvest is plentiful but the workers are few. Ask the Lord of the harvest, therefore, to send out workers into his harvest field.'" In this message Spurgeon stated,

---

10. Pike, *Life and Works of Spurgeon*, vol. 4, 342.
11. Pike, *Life and Works of Spurgeon*, vol. 4, 342.
12. Spurgeon, *Autobiography*, vol. 2, 146.

> Will ye pray it, my brethren? *This text is laid on my heart; it lies more on my heart than any other in the Bible; it is one that haunts me perpetually, and has done [so] for many years* [emphasis added]. What can one voice, one tongue do! Therefore it is that we instituted the College, that men might be instructed in the way of God more perfectly, and you, my beloved people, have helped me these many years, for which I thank you, thank you lovingly, and with all my heart. You have never ceased from that best of works [their Great Commission farm system via the Pastors' College], and therefore you, as a church, can honestly pray, because you work as well as pray[13]

He commented during this message "If there is one thing noticeable in this church it is our continual prayer that God may be pleased to raise up among us men who will work for him, and he has done it, and he will do it if we continue to pray for it."[14] Spurgeon went on to say in applying this message to his members:

> Should not a Christian man say, "I shall try and find a trade for myself which will bring me into contact with a class of persons that need the gospel, and I will use my trade as the stalking-horse for Christ; since hypocrites use religion as a stalling-horse for gain, I will make my trading subservient to my religion. "Oh," says one, "we can leave that to the society." God bless the society, and, I was going to say, smother the society, rather than allow it to smother personal effort. We want our godly merchants, working men, soldiers, and sailors everywhere to feel "I cannot go and get a proxy in the shape of a society to do this for me; in the name of God, I will do it myself, and have a share in this great battle." If you cannot labor yourself, the society is the grandest thing conceivable, for you may help others thereby; but still the main cry from Christ is that you yourself should go into the highways and hedges, and as many as you find compel them to come in to the gospel feast. *The world is dying, the grave is filling, hell is boasting, and yet you have the gospel; can it be that you do not care to win souls, do not care whether men are damned or saved! The Lord wake us from this stony-hearted barbarity to our fellow-men, and make us yearn over them, care about them, and pray about them, and work for them, till the Lord shall arise and send forth laborers into his harvest* [emphasis added]![15]

13. Spurgeon, *Treasury of the Bible*, vol. 5, 159.
14. Spurgeon, *Treasury of the Bible*, vol. 5, 158.
15. Spurgeon, *Treasury of the Bible*, vol. 5, 160.

The healthiest churches are characterized by all its members having a concern for souls in response to Christ's love and work in their hearts. When members are led by their pastors to think the thoughts of Christ about the lost around them and are taught they can win others to Him, their excitement and fervor in Christ explodes. Their hunger for more of Christ and His Word and His Holy Spirit becomes dominant in the lives. The fellowship of the church begins to rival that of Acts 2:42–47.

Spurgeon was consistent in his living out and encouraging the Great Commission call to his members. In his message "Soul-Saving Our One Business," Spurgeon introduced the subject by saying,

> It is a grand thing to see a man thoroughly possessed with one master-passion. Such a man is sure to be strong, and if the master-principle be excellent, he is sure to be excellent, too. The man of one object is a man indeed. *Lives with many aims are like water trickling through innumerable streams, none of which are wide enough or deep enough to float the merest cockleshell of a boat; but a life with one object is like a mighty river flowing between its banks, bearing to the ocean a multitude of ships, and spreading fertility on either side* [emphasis added]. Give me a man not only with a great object in his soul, but thoroughly possessed by it, his powers all concentrated, and himself on fire with vehement zeal for his supreme object, and you have put before me one of the greatest sources of power which the world can produce. Give me a man engrossed with holy love as to his heart, and filled with some masterly celestial thought as to his brain, and such a man will be known wherever his lot may be cast.[16]

Spurgeon believed this to be the calling and work for every church, i.e., to somehow multiply harvest leaders for the Great Commission. This work would come from truly loving and following the Lord Jesus as a pastor and people: "But remember this is the Lord's word, 'Follow Me, and I will make you fishers of men.' *Keep close to Jesus, and do as Jesus did, in His spirit and He will make you fishers of men* [emphasis added]."[17] He saw this as following the example and pattern of Jesus in His investing in a few the work of making disciples in order to multiply again and again the same. "It was very important that, during the short active lifetime of our Saviour,—a little more than three years,—He should confine His operation to a comparatively small district, so as to produce a permanent

---

16. Spurgeon, *The Soul Winner*, 249.
17. Spurgeon, *The Soul Winner*, 295.

result there which would afterwards radiate over the whole world. He knew what was best for men, and therefore He restricted Himself."[18] The same example and pattern of work became the Great Commission strategy of the apostle Paul. He states this in 2 Tim 2:2, "You then, my son, be strong in the grace that is in Christ Jesus. And the things you have heard me say in the presence of many witnesses entrust to reliable people who will also be qualified to teach others."

Spurgeon explained his belief of every church seeking to develop a farm system of multiplying workers and leaders for the Savior's harvest work:

> It appears to us that the maintenance of a truly spiritual College is probably the readiest way in which to bless the church.
>
> We are not singular in this opinion, for to be successful workers in all times the same method had occurred. Without citing the abundant incidents of early times, let us remember the importance which John Calvin attached to the College at Geneva. Not by any one of the Reformers personally could the Reformation have been achieved, but *they multiplied themselves* [emphasis added] in their students, and so fresh centres [sic] of light were created . . .
>
> Wherever a great principle is to be advanced, prudence suggests the necessity of training men who are to become the advancers of it. Our Lord and Saviour did just the same thing when he elected twelve to be always with him, in order that, by superior instruction, they might become leaders of the church.[19]

Again, Spurgeon explained this in his referencing Luther (who was also a hero to Spurgeon). "We talk of Luther and Calvin in the days of the Reformation, but we must remember that these men became what they were largely through their power to stamp their image and superscriptions upon other men with whom they came in contact."[20] Spurgeon saw in the lives of Luther and Calvin the valuing and the practical working out of 2 Tim 2:2. This is God's intent for every pastor—to be able to pass on to others what God has put into his heart. The potential and impact of a life set on fire for Jesus Christ and in love with fellow servants of Christ was pointed out by Spurgeon is stating, "How much have other nations derived from the little republic of Switzerland on account of Calvin

---

18. Spurgeon, *Autobiography*, vol. 3, 27.
19. Harte, *Historical Tablets of College*, 14.
20. Pike, *Life and Works of Spurgeon*, vol. 4, 356.

having the clear common-sense to perceive that one man could not hope to affect a whole nation except by multiplying himself, and spreading his views by writing them upon the fleshly tablets of the hearts of young and earnest men!"[21]

The existence of the Pastors' College was to help further Christ's work by providing the churches with men who could preach the gospel and lead in such a manner that disciples could be multiplied. Spurgeon described its purpose:

> Our College began by inviting men of God to her bosom, whether they were poor and illiterate, or wealthy and educated. We sought for earnest preachers, not for readers of sermons, or makers of philosophical essays. "Have you won souls for Jesus?" was and is our leading enquiry of all applicants. "If so, come thou with us, and we will do thee good." If the brother has any pecuniary means, we feel that he should bear his own charges, and many have done so; but if he cannot contribute a sixpence, he is equally welcome, and is received upon the same footing in all respects. *If we can but find men who love Jesus, and love the people, and will seek to bring Jesus and the people together, the College will receive two hundred of such as readily as one*, and trust in God for their food; but if men of learning and wealth should come, the College will not accept them unless they prove their calling by power to deliver the truth, and by the blessing of God upon their labors. *Our men seek no Collegiate degrees, or classical honors,—though many of them could readily attain them; but to preach efficiently, to get at the hearts of the masses, to evangelize the poor, this is the College ambition, this and nothing else* [emphasis added].[22]

The character needed for multiplying disciples and churches can only come from God. Character, competence, and chemistry are needed to be effective in ministry. Competence (as a pastor is knowing your role and responsibilities from Scripture and developing the skills and wisdom to do it) and chemistry (knowing how to bring people under your influence to be able to lead them further with Christ and teaming with you to accomplish the vision God has called you as pastor and people to fulfill) are of unquestionable importance, but character always trumps them both. A pastor or church leader lacking in character will himself implode and lead to the weakening and downfall of those he or she has influence

---

21. Pike, *Life and Works of Spurgeon*, vol. 4, 356.
22. Pike, *Life and Works of Spurgeon*, vol 2, 149.

upon. The challenge and value of helping develop this in ministerial students is huge. How did Spurgeon and the Metropolitan Tabernacle do this?

APPLIED THEOLOGY

In life, our behavior is always guided by our thinking which is shaped by our beliefs. Errant thinking leads to errant living. What I believe determines how I feel determines how I behave. This is what Jesus was helping us see when He stated in Matt 22:29, "You are in error because you do not know the Scriptures or the power of God." Ps 119 gives 176 verses of instruction and encouragement for our knowing and following the Word of God. The first three verses alone state this fact: "Blessed are those whose ways are blameless, who walk according to the law of the Lord. Blessed are those who keep his statutes and seek him with all their heart—they do no wrong but follow his ways." Blessed living comes from holy thinking.

Spurgeon had been raised up in his childhood being explained and taught the value and application of the Scriptures. Because of his Puritan upbringing, he could quote the Scriptures extensively by age twelve. Spurgeon's theology was gained through deep conviction and personal experience. He believed the doctrines of grace would bring about the character and conduct for what Christ needed in ministers for leading churches to do His work.

Doctrines of Grace

Spurgeon understood what the Pastors' College men believed would determine their work. "To be effective preachers you must be sound theologians" was his constant maxim to the students in the College.[23] He stated the buildings they would preach in "were erected as monuments to the power of the doctrines of grace. Mind you preach these doctrines in them. The doctrines some now preach could not build a mousetrap."[24]

He understood and was confident in the fact that if the men were grounded in a good understanding of the gospel message and equipped to communicate it effectively, there would be a harvest of souls reaped for Christ, and disciples and churches multiplied. The primary influence on

---

23. Williams, *Personal Reminiscences of Spurgeon*, 138.
24. Williams, *Personal Reminiscences of Spurgeon*, 170.

Spurgeon's theological understanding and convictions was Puritanism: "We endeavor to teach the Scriptures, but, as everybody else claims to do the same, and we wish to be known and read of all men, we say distinctly that the theology of the Pastors' College is Puritanic."[25] He went on to say "Believing that the Puritanic school embodied more for gospel truth in it than any other since the days of the apostles, we continue in the same line of things; and, by God's help, hope to have a share in that revival of Evangelical doctrine which is as sure to come as the Lord himself."[26]

Spurgeon's conviction was the simple and dynamic message of grace would change lives and produce disciple-making disciples. Spurgeon knew it was the gospel that saved lives from sin and for the service of the Savior. What Spurgeon understood as the "doctrine of grace," the "doctrine of substitution," and the "doctrine of Christ crucified" created in him a confident and bold gospel to preach to lost and saved people. Scripture's teaching on grace gave understanding for other doctrines. The essential doctrines and their place in preaching the gospel for Spurgeon was this:

> I am sure, my beloved brother, that your growing experience must have endeared to you the gospel of the grace of God. I feel more and more every day that nothing but salvation by grace will ever bring me to Heaven, and therefore I desire more and more explicitly to teach *the grand truths of electing love, covenant security, justification by faith, effectual calling, and immutable faithfulness* [emphasis added]. Love to souls, as it burns in our hearts, will also lead us to preach a free as well as a full salvation; and so we shall be saved at once from the leanness of those who have no doctrine, and from the bitterness of those to whom creed is everything. We have aimed at the happy via media of a balanced ministry, and succeeding years confirm us in the correctness of our views.[27]

For Spurgeon grace represented the fact man can do nothing for his salvation. Jesus, through the ransom price of his blood, paid for all mankind's sin debt. Therefore, man must come to Christ with nothing to offer Him and receive from Jesus only what Jesus can give him. Spurgeon's understanding and preaching of the gospel caused people to see their

---

25. Spurgeon, *Autobiography*, vol. 3, 149.
26. Spurgeon, *Autobiography*, vol. 3, 150.
27. Spurgeon, *Autobiography*, vol. 3, 150.

sinfulness, their total depravity, and their utter dependency upon Christ for grace. Spurgeon explained the value of the preaching of this grace:

> A spiritual experience which is thoroughly flavored with a deep and bitter sense of sin is of great value to him that hath had it. It is terrible in the drinking, but it is most wholesome in the bowels, and in the whole of the *after-life. Possibly, much of the flimsy piety of the present day arises from the ease with which men attain to peace and joy in these evangelistic days. We would not judge modern converts, but we certainly prefer that form of spiritual exercise which leads the soul by the way of Weeping-cross, and makes it see its blackness before assuring it that it is "clean every whit." Too many think lightly of sin, and therefore think lightly of the Savior. He who has stood before his God, convicted and condemned, with the rope about his neck, is the man to weep for joy when he is pardoned, to hate the evil which has been forgiven him, and to live to the honor of the Redeemer by whose blood he has been cleansed* [emphasis added].[28]

The Puritans believed the aim of preaching was "influencing the will, animating the emotions and reforming the life . . . They regarded proclamation of the Word and instruction from the Word, accompanied by the power of the Holy Spirit, as the principal mediating instrument of the power of God unto salvation and sanctification."[29] Spurgeon, along with the teachers at the Pastors' College, inspired and instructed the students to be committed to the Word's proclamation and the grace of God it presented.

Grace was rich in the mind of Spurgeon. He knew it forgives all sin and fixes all affections upon Jesus and His service. Spurgeon's sermon "Love's Logic" is based on the text of 1 John 4:19: "We love Him because He first loved us." His opening remark was "This is a great doctrinal truth, and I might with much propriety preach a doctrinal sermon from it, of which the sum and substance would be the sovereign grace of God."[30] In this message Spurgeon presents his understanding of grace by stating, "Oh what an encouraging truth this is. I, a sinner, do not believe that God loves me because I feel I love him; but I first believe that he loves me, sinner as I am, and then having believed that gracious fact, I come to love my Benefactor in return." He then shares,

28. Spurgeon, *Autobiography*, vol. 1, 76.
29. Lewis, *Genius of Puritanism*, 50, 53.
30. Spurgeon, *Spurgeon's Sermons*, vol. 3, 304.

> Your first step is to believe that God loves you, and when that truth is fully fixed in your soul by the Holy Spirit, a fervent love to God will spontaneously issue from your soul, even as flowers willingly pour forth their fragrance under the influence of the dew and the sun. Every man that ever was saved had to come to God not as a lover of God, but as a sinner, and to believe in God's love to him as a sinner. We all wish to take money in our sacks when we go down hungry to this Egypt to buy the bread of life; but it must not be, heaven's bread is given to us freely, and we must accept it freely, without money and without price.[31]

Spurgeon wanted his hearer to know there was nothing the sinner could do for God or offer God which could gain God's favor and grace. This grace was all wrapped up in Jesus and every sinner owes all these mercies, love, and grace in God—to Jesus. Spurgeon said,

> Go to Christ himself at once. If you go to the law and begin to judge yourself, if you get the notion that you are to undergo a sort of spiritual quarantine, that you must pass through a mental purgatory before you may renew your faith in the Savior, you are mistaken. Come just as you are, bad as you are, hardened, cold, dead as you feel yourselves to be, come even so, and believe in the boundless love of God in Christ Jesus. Then shall come the deep repentance; then shall come the brokenness of heart; then shall come the holy jealousy, the sacred hatred of sin, and the refining of the soul from all her dross; then, indeed, all good things shall come to restore your soul [Spurgeon was directing this portion of his message to Christians who had left their first love, but the truths presented were based upon the gospel of grace for whosoever will], and lead you in the paths of righteousness. Do not look for these first; that would be looking for the effects before the cause. The great cause of love in the restored backslider must still be the love of God to him, to whom he clings with a faith that dares not let go its hold.[32]

Scripture states this encouragement in 2 Chr 15:1-2, "The Spirit of God came on Azariah son of Oded. He went out to meet Asa and said to him, 'Listen to me, Asa and all Judah and Benjamin. The Lord is with you when you are with him. If you seek him, he will be found by you, but if you forsake him, he will forsake you.'" Spurgeon had been mastered by these truths and so he preached the doctrine of grace.

---

31. Spurgeon, *Spurgeon's Sermons*, vol. 3, 311-12.
32. Spurgeon, *Spurgeon's Sermons*, vol. 3, 318.

Election

For Spurgeon there was no dissonance in believing sovereign grace, i.e., election, and human responsibility. He explained this by saying,

> But there are some who say, "It is hard for God to choose some and leave others."
>
> Now, I will ask you one question. Is there any of you here this morning who wishes to be holy, who wishes to be regenerate, to leave off sin and walk in holiness? "Yes, there is," says some one, "I do." Then God has elected you. But another says, "No; I don't want to be holy; I don't want to give up my lusts and my vices." Why should you grumble, then, that God has not elected you to it? For if you were elected you would not like it, according to your own confession. If God this morning had chosen you to holiness, you say you would not care for it. Do you not acknowledge that you prefer drunkenness to sobriety, dishonesty to honesty? You love this world's pleasures better than religion [an intimate relationship with Christ]; then why should you grumble that God has not chosen you to religion? If you love religion, he *has* chosen you to it. If you desire it, he has chosen you to it. If you do not, what right have you to say that God ought to have given you what you do not wish for? . . ."Ah, but," say some, "I thought it meant that God elected some to heaven and some to hell. "That is a very different matter from the gospel doctrine. He has elected men to holiness and to righteousness and through that to heaven. You must not say that he has elected these simply to heaven, and others only to hell. He has elected you to holiness, if you love holiness. If any of you love to be saved by Jesus Christ, Jesus Christ elected you to be saved. If any of you desire to have salvation, you are elected to have it, if you desire it sincerely and earnestly. But, if you don't desire it, why on earth should you be so preposterously foolish as to grumble because God gives that which you do not like to other people?[33]

Election in Spurgeon's mind meant God wanted people to know His Son in salvation. They were elected by God to have a life of faith and holiness through such a wonderful Savior. "I know nothing, nothing, again, that is more humbling for us than this doctrine of election."[34] God does not save a person because of his or her faith; if so, then a

---

33. Spurgeon, *Spurgeon's Sermons*, vol. 2, 75–76.
34. Spurgeon, *Spurgeon's Sermons*, vol. 2, 84.

person would play a part in producing their salvation. But it is Christ and Christ alone that saves.

The fact that one's election, all one's freedom from guilt of sin, all one's aspiring to growth in godly character was due to grace and through grace alone—this creates a ceaseless, grateful heart to God. Regarding a person's having confidence in their faith to save them or to keep them right with God, Spurgeon said, "what we want to do is to kill it once and for all, to show him that he is lost and ruined, and that his activities are not now at all equal to the work of conversion; that he must look upward."[35]

In his sermon on the "The Comer's Conflict with Satan," Spurgeon gives one of the clearest explanations as to the basis of election. He explains election's benefit to the saved and how it sustains an increasing walk with the Savior:

> Satan brings the carcass of self and pulls it about, and because that is corrupt, tells us that most assuredly we cannot be saved. But remember, sinner, *it is not thy hold of Christ that saves thee— it is Christ; it is not thy joy in Christ that saves thee—it is Christ; it is not even faith in Christ, though that is the instrument—it is Christ's blood and merits; therefore, look not so much to thy hand with which thou art grasping Christ, as to Christ; look not to thy hope, but to Christ, the source of thy hope; look not to thy faith, but to Christ, the author and finisher of thy faith; and if thou dost that, ten thousand devils cannot throw thee down, but as long as thou lookest at thyself, the meanest of those evil spirits may tread thee beneath his feet* [emphasis added].[36]

Spurgeon's understanding of the teachings of election, atonement, and faith when accurately and effectively communicated from Scripture were all parts of the gospel which riveted people to the Savior and His cross. "Don't fancy election excuses sin—don't dream of it—don't rock yourself in sweet complacency in the thought of your irresponsibility. You are responsible."[37] Spurgeon preached a strong and confident gospel because he knew Christ was what every heart needs. He knew a person was never nearer grace than when he or she felt they could do nothing at all except simply trust in Jesus. He wanted his students to know and communicate in their preaching the gospel—to leave no doubt a person's only hope in this life and in eternity is solely trusting in Jesus.

35. Spurgeon, *New Park Street Pulpit*, vol. 6, 259.
36. Spurgeon, *Spurgeon's Sermons*, vol. 2, 307.
37. Spurgeon, *Spurgeon's Sermons*, vol. 2, 83.

When the individual is presented with the clear doctrines of grace and understands what the blood of Jesus means and their being elected by God, it helps them know they stand on the Rock of Ages with their life and eternity. Such knowledge and confidence, such conviction and faith give the believer a sure confidence with God and with men.

> The man who knows he is elect will be too proud to sin; he will not humble himself to commit the acts of common people. The believer in this truth will say "*I* compromise my principles? *I* change my doctrines? *I* lay aside my views? *I* hide what I believe to be true? No! since I know I am one of God's elect, in the very teeth of all men I shall speak God's truth, whatever man may say." Nothing makes a man so truly bold as to feel that he is God's elect. He shall not quiver, he shall not shake, who knows that God has chosen him. Moreover, election will make us *holy*. Nothing under the gracious influence of the Holy Spirit can make a Christian more holy than the thought that he is chosen. "Shall I sin," he says, "after God hath chosen me? Shall I transgress after such love? Shall I go astray after so much loving kindness and tender mercy? Nay, my God; since thou hast chosen me, I will love thee; I will live to thee . . . I will give myself to thee to be thine forever, by election and by redemption, casting myself on thee, and solemnly consecrating myself to thy service."[38]

Preaching Christ and the Cross

Spurgeon trained his men to preach a compelling gospel of Jesus Christ and only aim to keep their messages centered on Him and His cross. When people come to know Christ, they are put into a personal relation with the Lord and Savior Jesus Christ. Regarding Christ being Lord of our lives and not just Savior, the Granville Sharp rule in Greek applies to this title understanding for Jesus: "When two nouns are in the same case, connected by the word *kai* (and), the first noun having the definite article, the second noun without the article, the second noun refers to the same person or thing to which the first noun refers and is a further description of it."[39] This means we cannot take one title without the other. He is embraced as both Lord and Savior in our lives—or not at all. This is the same Greek arrangement in Eph 4:11–12 for the pastor-teacher office;

---

38. Spurgeon, *Spurgeon's Sermons*, vol. 2, 85.
39. Wuest, *Word Studies*, vol. 2, 195.

the role and responsibility of the pastor is do both: feed and lead, build and equip saints for fruitful service to Jesus Christ.

In preaching Christ and His cross, Spurgeon taught the Pastors' College men to present Jesus as the Savior from sin and self. He taught them to present this *whole* gospel and nothing else or less. His sermon on the "Comforter" gives ample insight into what he meant:

> If you have received one blessing from God, you will receive all other blessings too. Let me explain myself: If I could come here as an auctioneer, and sell the gospel off in lots, I should dispose of it all. If I could say here is justification through the blood of Christ—free; giving away, gratis; many a one would say, "I will have justification: give it me; I wish to be justified, I wish to be pardoned." Suppose I took sanctification, the giving up of all sin, a thorough change of heart, leaving off drunkenness and swearing; many would say, "I don't want that; I should like to go to heaven, but I do not want that holiness; I should like to be saved at last, but I should like to have my drink still; I should like to enter glory, but then I must have an oath or two on the road." Nay, but sinner, if thou hast one blessing, thou shalt have all. God will never divide the gospel. He will not give justification to that man, and sanctification to another; pardon to one and holiness to another. No, it all goes together. Whom he calls them he justifies; whom he justifies, them he sanctifies; and whom he sanctifies, them he also glorifies. O! if I could lay down nothing but the *comforts* of the gospel, ye would fly to them as flies do to honey. When ye come to be ill, ye send for the clergyman. Ah! you all want your minister then to come and give you consoling words. But if he be an honest man, he will not give some of you a particle of consolation. He will not commence pouring oil when the knife would be better. I want to make a man feel his sins before I dare tell him anything about Christ. I want to probe into his soul and make him feel that he is lost before I tell him anything about the purchased blessing. *It is the ruin of many to tell them, "Now just believe on Christ, and that is all you have to do* [emphasis added]." If, instead of dying they get better, they rise up whitewashed hypocrites—that is all . . . May these people ever be kept from having comfort when they have no right to it! Have you the other blessings? Have you had conviction of sin? Have you ever felt your guilt before God? Have your souls been humbled at Jesus' feet? And have you been made to look to Calvary alone for your refuge? If not, you have no right to consolation. Do not take an atom of it. The Spirit is a convincer before

he is a Comforter; and you must have the other operations of the Holy Spirit before you can derive anything from this.[40]

Spurgeon's confidence was the gospel changes lives; he taught his men to preach and look for radical change in lives. This is what the gospel had meant in Spurgeon's own life, and he had witnessed it do the same in thousands through the work of God's Spirit in and through the Metropolitan Tabernacle. There were over two thousand in attendance by the time the College was started. Spurgeon came to a church of approximately 100 attenders and God had wonderfully proved the power of the gospel to change lives.

In his training message to the students entitled "Sermons Likely to Win Souls," Spurgeon explained to his students: "we preach Jesus Christ to those who want Him, and we also preach Him to those who do not want Him, and we keep on preaching Christ until we make them feel that they do want Him, and cannot do without Him."[41] Spurgeon explained the challenge and priority of preaching the Christ presented in Scripture:

> The production of faith is the very centre [sic] of the target at which you aim. The proof to you that you have won the man's soul for Jesus is never before you till he has done with himself and his own merits, and has closed in with Christ. Great care must be taken that this faith is exercised upon Christ for a complete salvation, and not for a part of it. Numbers of persons think that the Lord Jesus is available for the pardon of past sin, but they cannot trust Him for their preservation in the future. They trust for years past, but not for years to come; whereas no such sub-division of salvation is ever spoken of in Scripture as the work of Christ. Either He bore all our sins, or none; and He either saves us once for all, or not at all. His death can never be repeated, and it must have made expiation for the future sin of believers, or they are lost, since no further atonement can be supposed, and future sin is certain to be committed. Blessed be His name, "by Him all that believe are justified from all things." Salvation by grace is eternal salvation. Sinners must commit their souls to the keeping of Christ to all eternity; how else are they saved men? Alas! according to the teaching of some, believers are only saved in part, and for the rest must depend upon their future endeavours. Is this the gospel? I trow not. Genuine faith trusts a whole Christ for the whole of salvation. Is it any

40. Spurgeon, *Spurgeon's Sermons*, vol. 1, 81–83.
41. Spurgeon, *Soul-Winner*, 107.

wonder that many converts fall away, when, in fact, they were never taught to exercise faith in Jesus for eternal salvation, but only for temporary conversion? A faulty exhibition of Christ begets a faulty faith; and when this pines away in its own imbecility, who is to blame for it? According to their faith so is it unto them: the preacher and possessor of a partial faith must unitedly bear the blame of the failure when their poor mutilated trust comes to a break-down. I would the more earnestly insist upon this because a semi-legal way of believing is so common. We must urge the trembling sinner to trust wholly and alone upon the Lord Jesus for ever, . . . True faith in Jesus receives *eternal* life, and sees perfect salvation in Him, whose one sacrifice hath sanctified the people of God once for all. The sense of being saved, completely saved in Christ Jesus, is not, as some suppose, the source of carnal security and the enemy of holy zeal, but the very reverse. Delivered from the fear which makes the salvation *of* self a more immediate object than salvation *from* self; and inspired by holy gratitude to his Redeemer, the regenerated man becomes capable of virtue, and is filled with an enthusiasm for God's glory . . . but planted firmly on the Rock of ages, he has time and heart to utter the new song which the Lord has put into his mouth, and then is his moral salvation complete, for self is no longer the lord of his being. Rest not content till you see clear evidence in your converts of a simple, sincere, and decided faith in the Lord Jesus.[42]

Spurgeon's theological beliefs from Scripture were the reason for the blessings of God upon his ministry and also those on the Pastors' College students. Scriptural convictions issued forth the preaching, praying, spirituality, and earnestness which marked his life. The beliefs he held shaped all he undertook in Christian ministry. Spurgeon stated at his Jubilee celebration service for his fiftieth birthday, "Next to that [having referenced dependence upon the Holy Spirit's ministry], it behooves me to say that I owe the prosperity I have had in preaching the gospel to the gospel which I have preached. I wish everybody thought as much, but there are some who will have it that there is something very particular and special about the preacher."[43]

He held continually before his students in the Pastors' College what he unceasingly preached at the Metropolitan Tabernacle: Christ, Christ alone and Him crucified. Spurgeon taught them Christ must be the

42. Spurgeon, *Soul-Winner*, 34–35.
43. Spurgeon, *Autobiography*, vol. 4, 243.

centerpiece of their own lives and the clear focus of all their messages. He told the students:

> Let your sermons be full of Christ, from beginning to end crammed full of the gospel. As for myself, brethren, I cannot preach anything else but Christ and His cross, for I know nothing else, and long ago, like the apostle Paul, I determined not to know anything else save Jesus Christ and Him crucified. People have often asked me, "What is the secret of your success?" I always answer that I have no other secret but this, that I have preached the gospel,—not about the gospel, but the gospel,—the full, free, glorious gospel of the living Christ who is the incarnation of the good news. Preach Jesus Christ, brethren, always and everywhere; and every time you preach be sure to have much of Jesus Christ in the sermon.[44]

Spurgeon did not preach at people; he preached them up to Christ. His preaching paved the way for lost people to want to come and hear this gospel. He attracted all classes of people but made his message so the least educated could fully understand. His expression was described as "hearty, open, English frankness, which has no hesitation in giving full and free utterance to its opinions, loves, and dislikes. Then there is the ready, acute perception which never fails to bring out fresh and striking illustrations from any text . . . There was an earnestness, an unction . . . too seldom imitated."[45] This was the kind of transparent delivery of the Word of God in proclaiming Christ which Spurgeon instilled into his Pastors' College men. He wanted them to present Christ as Christ presented Himself and His message—full of grace and truth.

Spurgeon made clear the preaching of the Cross of Christ was always to hold center stage in every message delivered by those he trained. It was what he had practiced throughout his ministry. It was the motto of the Pastors' College. Spurgeon held the apostle Paul as his hero and said of Paul's words in Gal 6:14 "There had not been in all his ministry any doctrine that he extolled more highly than this of 'Christ crucified.'"[46] Spurgeon lived at the Cross with Christ and trained his students in this most blessed discipline for the believer. To live this way, a preacher and pastor will be led and used by Christ to fulfill the Great Commission and multiply disciples and churches for His Kingdom. Spurgeon said of 2 Tim

---

44. Spurgeon, *Soul-Winner*, 106.
45. Spurgeon, *Autobiography*, vol. 2, 113.
46. Spurgeon, *Treasury of the Bible*, vol. 7, 333.

2:3 "With a good soldier of Christ the master passion is to spread the gospel, to save souls from perishing, and he would sooner do this and be poor than be rich and neglect it; he would sooner to be useful and live unknown than rank among the great ones of the earth and be useless to his Lord."[47]

Spurgeon taught and preached these truths of Scripture throughout his entire ministry. The Metropolitan Tabernacle recognized their pastor in a special manner when he turned fifty years of age. This Jubilee ceremony was prepared over a six-month period of time (January until his birthday in June 1979). During this time, Spurgeon cooperated to give an interview to the editor of the *Pall Mall Gazette*, W. T. Stead. In one of his responses, Spurgeon made the statement " 'In theology,' said Mr Spurgeon, 'I stand where I did when I began preaching, and I stand almost alone. If I ever did such a thing, I could preach my earliest sermons now without change so far as the essential doctrines are concerned. I stand almost exactly where Calvin stood in his maturer years;—not where, he stood in his Institutes.'"[48]

The Holy Spirit

Spurgeon gave his final lecture to the annual Pastors' College Conference in April 1891. It was published under the title of *The Greatest Fight in the World*. In this volume of just over sixty pages, he spends the first half addressing the value and necessity of complete faith and integrity in handling and obeying the Word of God; the second half addresses the Holy Spirit.

Spurgeon knew the presence and power of the Holy Spirit must be upon every effort attempted for Jesus Christ. He wrote to his College students in 1875,

> I feel in an agony when I imagine any one of you going forth to preach unendowed by the Spirit. The Lord alone knows how I have the work of the College on my heart, and what exercises it has cost me; and, verily, if souls are not won, churches are not built up, and Christ is not glorified by you, I have lived in vain as to the master-work of my life. I am not able to discover any motive in my heart for originating and carrying on the College, but a desire to glorify God, and to bless this generation by the promulgation of the pure gospel. *For this end you came into the*

---

47. Spurgeon, *Treasury of the Bible*, vol. 7, 843.
48. Spurgeon, *Autobiography*, vol. 4, 240.

> College; do not miss it, any one of you; and yet you will do so if the Spirit rests not upon you. Be not content till Pentecost is repeated among you [emphasis added].[49]

Spurgeon was a very rational *Pentecostal* used of God to multiply disciples and churches. He believed all of Scripture and his heart for souls caused his firm dependency upon the Holy Spirit as instructed in Acts 1:8. He stated without any uncertainty to the 1891 Pastors' Conference,

> Granted that we preach the Word alone; granted that we are surrounded by a model church, which, alas, is not always the case; but, granted that it is so, OUR STRENGTH is the next consideration. This must come from THE SPIRIT OF GOD. We believe in the Holy Ghost, and in our absolute dependence upon him. We believe; but do we believe practically? Brethren, as to ourselves and our own work, do we believe in the Holy Ghost? Do we believe because we habitually prove the truth of the doctrine?[50]

Spurgeon realized all true church growth, all true conversions, all true service to Jesus Christ would only be done if the Holy Spirit anointed, guided, and controlled all. If we are to see the multiplying of disciples and churches, we must believe and practice Christianity so. Spurgeon genuinely believed this and so lived and taught and trained. In the 1891 meeting he explained to the pastors,

> Furthermore, *we must depend upon the Spirit of God as to our results*. No man among us really thinks that he could regenerate a soul. We are not so foolish as to claim power to change a heart of stone. We may not dare to presume quite so far as this, and yet we may come to think that, by our experience, we can help people over spiritual difficulties. Can we? We may be hopeful that our enthusiasm will drive the living church before us, and drag the dead world after us. Will it be so? Perhaps we imagine that if we could only *get up* a revival, we should easily secure large additions to the church? Is it worth while to *get up* a revival? Are not all true revivals to be *got down*? We may persuade ourselves that drums and trumpets and shouting will do a great deal. But, my brethren, "the Lord is not in the wind." Results worth having come from that silent but omnipotent Worker whose name is the Spirit of God: in him, and in him only, must we trust for

---

49. Spurgeon, *Autobiography*, vol. 3, 159.
50. Spurgeon, *Greatest Fight in World*, 33.

the conversion of a single Sunday-school child, and for every genuine revival. For the keeping of our people together, and for the building of them up into a holy temple, we must look to him. The Spirit might say, even as our Lord did, "Without me ye can do nothing."[51]

He honestly committed himself to knowing the Holy Spirit's presence and power in his ministry. All ministry, all evangelism, all preaching without Him guiding the labor he knew was fruitless. Without the Holy Spirit Spurgeon knew there would be no life change, no conviction for loving and obeying Jesus, and no passion for spreading His gospel. Spurgeon stated, "You know that arctic cold; and it may occasionally be felt even where the doctrine is sound. When the Spirit of God is gone, even truth itself becomes an iceberg. How wretched is religion frozen and lifeless!"[52]

He told his congregation on June 12, 1861, shortly after entering their new building at the Metropolitan Tabernacle, "The one thing then which we want, is the Spirit of God . . . If there were only one prayer which I might pray before I died, it should be this: Lord, send thy Church men filled with the Holy Ghost, and with fire . . . Courage then, brethren, we have only to seek for that which God has promised to give, and we can do wonders. He will give the Holy Spirit to them that ask him."[53]

His counsel to the College men was direct and to the point as he taught them in his Friday afternoon lectures: "*If we have not the Spirit which Jesus promised, we cannot perform the commission which Jesus gave* [emphasis added]."[54] He shared further,

> Miracles of grace must be the seals of our ministry; who can bestow them but the Spirit of God? Convert a soul without the Spirit of' God! Why, you cannot even make a *fly*, much less create a new heart and a right spirit. Lead the children of God to a higher life without the Holy Ghost! You are inexpressibly more likely to conduct them into carnal security, if you attempt their elevation by any method of your own. Our ends can never be gained if we miss the cooperation of the Spirit of the Lord. Therefore, with strong crying and tears, wait upon him from day to day.[55]

---

51. Spurgeon, *Greatest Fight in World*, 34.
52. Spurgeon, *Greatest Fight in World*, 37.
53. Spurgeon, *Metropolitan Tabernacle Pulpit*, vol. 10, 337, 339.
54. Spurgeon, *Lectures to My Students*, 187.
55. Spurgeon, *Lectures to My Students*, 195.

Spurgeon knew for any believer, and especially pastors and church leaders, to know by experience the Holy Spirit's anointing on their lives, they must learn His holiness and love. Our character must be marked by Christ's character or we will not enjoy His Spirit's presence and power.

Love

Spurgeon's theology arrested his heart and life on the love of God. This was what kept him going in the ministry. He defined and explained to the pastors and students at the annual Conference of his own leadership effectiveness as a pastor: "I have no power but that which gentleness and love have brought me."[56]

Theology for Spurgeon wasn't something just believed; it was lived. This is what Spurgeon understood from Scripture about love and its practice in life for the believer:

> And in proportion as I am thus scripturally confident, and rest in my Lord, will my love to him engross all my heart, and consecrate my life to the Redeemer's glory. Beloved, I desire to make this very clear; that to feel love to God we must tread along the road of faith. Truly, this is not a hard or perilous way, but one prepared by infinite wisdom. It is a road suitable for sinners, and indeed saints must come that way too. If thou wouldst love God, do not look within thee to see whether this grace or that be as it ought to be, but look to thy God, and read his eternal love, his boundless love, his costly love, which gave Christ for thee; then shall thy love drink in fresh life and vigor.[57]

He knew pastors were called to do careful work in shepherding the flock. Love must mark them as it characteristically marked and colored all the Savior did. Spurgeon said all believers were obligated to demonstrate this character in their lives. He admonished if a believer did not love, it meant he did not really know Christ and have a meaningful relationship with Him. For pastors Spurgeon's admonition was "if we were better [in expressing the Spirit's fruit of love], our church-members would be better."[58]

Spurgeon knew if his Pastors' College men did not love their people, they as pastors would never have their members' confidence nor their

---

56. Spurgeon, *All-Round*, 277.
57. Spurgeon, *Spurgeon's Sermons*, vol. 9, 315.
58. Spurgeon, *All-Round*, 246.

hands joining them in the work of the harvest. He understood leadership and knew the spirit and attitude of the pastor will produce the spirit and attitude of the church. If the churches were to be effective in leading lost people to fall in love with and follow Jesus, it would have to be demonstrated at the top, i.e., from the bottom—the leader being the servant of all in the spirit and love of Christ. One of the best words I ever heard on this truth was "Christ will forgive a lot of things, but he will not forgive self-serving." This was shared an annual meeting of Southern Baptist field ministry teachers and the theme of our speaker from John 13 was "Jesus was known for His towel; where's your towel?"[59]

For Spurgeon, the biblical doctrine of love was alive, and it was his source of strength for the journey and his cue in relating with all peoples. It was a doctrinal truth which refereed his forceful temperament and conditioned his heart for the entirety of his life in ministry and service to Jesus Christ. In his first sermon in London when New Park Street had invited him to come in consideration of pastoring them, he proclaimed:

> But reminding you that there is no change in His power, justice, knowledge, oath, threatening, or decree, I will confine myself to the fact that His love to us knows no variation. How often it is called *unchangeable*, everlasting love! He loves me now as much as He did when first He inscribed my name in His eternal book of election. He has not repented of His choice. He has not blotted out one of His chosen; there are no erasures in that book; all whose names are written in it are safe for ever. Nor does God love me less now than when He gave that grand proof of love, His Son, Jesus Christ, to die for me. Even now, He loves me with the same intensity as when He poured out the vials of justice on His darling to save rebel worms. We have all had times which we considered times of special love, when His candle shone round about us, and we basked in the light of His smiling face; but let us not suppose that He really loved us more then than now. Oh, no! He then discovered His love in a way pleasing to flesh and blood; but trials are equally proofs of His love. In the fight with Apollyon in the Valley of Humiliation, in the Valley of the Shadow of Death, or in Vanity Fair, He will be ever the same, and will love us neither more nor less than when we sing with seraphic voices the songs of Heaven.[60]

---

59. McCarty, *Ministry Guidance Professionals*, 2011.

60. Spurgeon, *Autobiography*, vol. 1, 325.

George Rogers reported the law of love was dominant in the Pastors' College. The school had a rare spirit of teamship and the fraternity between tutors and students was observable. This is what Spurgeon modeled in the church at Metropolitan Tabernacle and what he wanted the students to understand and practice in their churches. He told them in the Friday lectures, "Sound judgment and solid experience must instruct you; gentle manners and loving affections must sway you; firmness and courage must be manifest; and tenderness and sympathy must not be lacking . . . If such gifts and graces be not in you and abound, it may be possible for you to succeed as an evangelist, but as a pastor you will be of no account."[61]

Faith

Spurgeon knew faith was the means of God's blessings. He learned and taught the College students God was the source of answers and the provider of every need. Faith was the means to knowing Christ as Savior and Lord. Faith was also the means of receiving all God's blessings in Christian living. "We are altogether saved by faith . . . our claim to privileges of the covenant is of faith, and our life in its beginning and continuance is all of faith, so may I boldly say that our ministry is of faith, too" were his words to pastors and students at the annual Pastors' Conference.[62] The truth of Col 2:6, "So then, just as you received Christ Jesus as Lord, continue to live your lives in him," was fully embraced and practiced by Spurgeon and he taught this to his students.

He understood the success of the students would be measured by their faith in God. As Jesus established with His disciples that their faith would determine their blessings from God, so Spurgeon established with his College men and all pastors,

> Our work especially requires faith. If we fail in faith, we had better not have undertaken it; and unless we obtain faith commensurate with the service, we shall soon grow weary of it. It is proven by all observations that success in the Lord's service is very generally in proportion to faith. It certainly is not in proportion to ability, nor does it always run parallel with a display of zeal; but it is invariably according to the measure of faith,

---

61. Spurgeon, *Lectures to My Students*, 30–31.
62. Spurgeon, *All-Round*, 2.

for this is a law of the Kingdom without exception, "According to your faith be it unto you." It is essential then, that we should have faith if we are to be useful, and that we should have great faith if we are to be greatly useful.[63]

Spurgeon taught his students they must walk sure of their calling in the ministry. He counseled the best assurance they could know for their calling to be preachers was seeing God use them to win souls to Jesus. "His commission is without seals until souls are won by his instrumentality to the knowledge of Jesus . . . There must be some measure of conversion-work in your irregular labours before you can believe that preaching is to be your life-work."[64]

Through faith in God and what he learned in his journey in following Christ, Spurgeon committed the Metropolitan Tabernacle would plant one hundred churches at the foundation stone-laying ceremony for their new building. "God sparing my life, I will not rest till the dark country of Surrey be filled with places of worship. It is only within the last six months we have started two churches, one Wandsworth and the other in Greenwich, and we will do so the one hundredth time, God being our helper."[65]

The students at the Pastors' College were continuously encouraged in their exercise of and growth in faith. Spurgeon held this before them in their studies and their observing the faith of the people of the Tabernacle. They often heard words like,

> Oh, that we were altogether rid of unbelief, that we believed great things of God, and with heart and soul so preached that men were likely to be converted by such discourses, proclaiming truths likely to convert them, and declaring them in a manner that would be likely to be blessed to the conversion of our hearers. Of course, all the while we must be trusting to the Holy Spirit to make the work effectual, for we are but the instruments in His hands.[66]

Spurgeon knew faith was key to experiencing the miracles of changed lives by the gospel as the Lord's work was carried out by human hearts and hands. Short of faith, the Christian looks at the harvest work and reasons how lives can be won by human agency? With faith,

---

63. Spurgeon, *All-Round*, 3–4.
64. Spurgeon, *Lectures*, 31.
65. Pike, *Life and Works of Spurgeon*, vol. 2, 316.
66. Spurgeon, *Soul-Winner*, 93.

the Christian knows his/her Savior is with them and will lead and be with them showing them the way to go, what to do and the manner by which to express the gospel word and work. Spurgeon stated, "Does it not rather direct us to our true power by shutting us out from our own fancied might? I trust we are all of us already aware that the man who lives in the region of faith dwells in the realm of miracles."[67]

The work of Christ is always the work of miracles. To go into the world and see spiritually dead men and women, boys and girls made alive by Jesus Christ is the work of the miraculous. It is an impossible task the church is commissioned to perform; it can only be done through Christ. "Faith, mighty faith, the promise sees, And looks to that alone; Laughs at impossibilities, And cries, 'It shall be done.'"[68] The joy of the Lord is our strength and it is found as we walk with Him by faith into the harvest fields of souls He has placed us among. Nothing is more important than loving Him and participating in the gospel. This is the theology He taught us in John 15.

Studying at Liberty University were rich years of watching faith in action in the 1970's. Jerry Falwell practiced living in the realm of faith in order to see the Great Commission carried out. He constantly said to us "You do not determine a person's greatness by what they possess or how much they know or what they have accomplished, but you determine a person's greatness by what it takes to discourage them." He always wanted to believe God for more lives to be impacted and changed by the gospel. Much like Spurgeon, he had a vision of a farm system to produce preachers and leaders for the gospel. He knew if he could multiply harvest leaders for Christ, the spread of the gospel would be without limit. Another faith principle Dr. Falwell gave us regularly was "The difference between mediocrity and greatness is vision."

Both of the above quotes were based on knowing Jesus Christ intimately and committing to what the Master instructs us to be and do. Spurgeon said in relation to faith and obedience, "We usually get what we expect, and if we expect 50 or 100 conversions a month [this was after being at the Tabernacle some years], the Lord will not disappoint us."[69] Writing to his students about leading churches to grow by conversions, Spurgeon said "Believe what you do, or else you will never persuade

---

67. Spurgeon, *Soul-Winner*, 146.
68. Spurgeon, *Soul-Winner*, 146.
69. Lorimer, *Spurgeon*, 83.

anybody else to believe it." And he then added, "God uses the faith of His ministers to breed faith in other people. You may depend upon it that souls are not saved by a minster who doubts; and the preaching of your doubts and your questions can never possibly decide a soul for Christ. You must have great faith in the Word of God if you are to be winners of souls to those who hear it."[70]

Our Savior invites each pastor and church to go with Him on this journey of watching Him bear His fruit through us. Spurgeon and the Metropolitan Tabernacle did so. In the next two chapters we will look at how they did this and what we in our current generation can learn from them.

---

70. Spurgeon, *Soul-Winner*, 36.

7

A Farm System for Local Churches Using Spurgeonic Principles

THIS CHAPTER ADDRESSES HOW the local church (or a group of churches) can form its own farm system in raising up leaders for Christ's harvest work to make and multiply disciples. Spurgeon and the Metropolitan Tabernacle provide a template to work off of to form a fruitful farm system. American baseball has utilized the farm system to find aspiring talent to develop and direct for the organization's objectives and success. Local churches need to intentionally create farm systems to successfully achieve their objective: the Great Commandment accomplished through the Great Commission. Such farm systems fulfill the instructions in 2 Tim 2:2.

A farm system can benefit greatly from developing five components: calling out the called, internships, mentor-coaching, formal studies, and wise sending practices. These five 'values' or 'disciplines' were practiced by the Metropolitan Tabernacle and their work through the Pastors' College. Calling out the called is the ongoing prayer for workers and continually discerning those God is giving passion for service and leadership in His Son's work. Internships give guided ministry experiences to those evidencing a call to ministry. Mentor-coaching is investing sustained encouragement and accountability to these in discovering, developing, and deploying their giftings and leadership to greater levels of effectiveness. Formal studies engage them in needful research in Scripture and applied theology studies which provide the mental framework affording wise perspectives and confidence in the Savior's work. Sending is the work of local churches (or groups of churches) giving validation and ongoing support to these sent out in order for them to go serve existing churches or start new ones.

We will look at seven principles drawn from Spurgeon and the Metropolitan Tabernacle's experience which, if wisely applied to each church's context, will allow a church to develop and implement a fruitful farm system. Before looking at these seven principles we will look at the culture needed in a local church family for a successful farm system to occur. In considering these principles, it's important to further understand the ecclesiology Spurgeon led his church to believe and practice.

A CHURCH CULTURE FOR MAKING AND MULTIPLYING DISCIPLES

To have a farm system come to life and be effective in a church (or group of churches), there must be the clear and constant encouragement of God's calling on each believer. Spurgeon's Scripture messages to his church, Sunday School workers, and Pastors' College gave them confidence and conviction God wanted to use them. His hero, Paul, had done this in Ephesus. By making use of Tyranneus' lecture hall and through his personal modeling and coaching, he helped build the farm system work of the Ephesus church identified in Acts 19:9-10. Spurgeon saw the local church from Scripture as being the program and tool of God to best accomplish the Great Commission. This, he understood, was to be the character bent of every church. In 1865, ten years after being at Metropolitan Tabernacle, he wrote in his *Sword and Trowel* magazine,

> Such a Church [the Metropolitan Tabernacle], with its many agencies in incessant operation, becomes a power, not in this country merely, but in the world. Such were the first Churches in Corinth, in Philippi, in Ephesus, and in Rome. Most of these arose, as in the case before us, almost entirely from the labors of one man. Is not this then, we ask, as we appeal to its efficiency, as we appeal to its spirituality, as we appeal to its internal harmony, as we appeal to its development of all Christian gifts and graces, and as we appeal to its freedom from all the evils of secular ecclesiasticism,—Is not this the fashion after which the Gospel was originally designed to spread, and in which it can best be

> extended in any country and in any age? The combination of many churches in one system of organization for the support of missions, both at home and abroad, may be the best thing when Churches are small and feeble in themselves; but it is second-best only to the primitive plan. It is more costly, and it creates a power unknown to the apostles, and detrimental to the liberty of individual Churches. We admit its great utility in a transition state from false to genuine Christianity, and are thankful for its results, but, at the same time, we are persuaded it has its limits, and is chiefly valuable, as it restores to the Church, and multiplies its own centers of illumination.[1]

Spurgeon believed Scripture to teach that every follower of Christ is a minister, missionary, and disciple-maker. This is what a New Testament church is to be characterized as and structured for, i.e., to be a disciple-making Christ united team. He explained,

> The Christian Church was designed from the first to be aggressive. It was not intended to remain stationary at any period, but to advance onward until its boundaries became commensurate with those of the world. It was to spread from Jerusalem to all Judea, from Judea to Samaria, and from Samaria unto the uttermost part of the earth. It was not intended to radiate from one central point only; but to form numerous centers from which its influence might spread to the surrounding parts . . . The influence of the past had established a deep-rooted conviction that the officials were the only authorized agents for Church extension; but gradually the cooperation of the whole Church was required, and was found to be the appropriate and healthful exercise of all its gifts and graces. [This was Spurgeon's understanding and application of the "priesthood of the believer" doctrine in ecclesiology]. *A Church, in which each member has something to do towards its increase, is in its proper and normal state. In proportion as it grows, it must seek to grow more, because growth is necessary to the most healthy state of life* [emphases added]; and in proportion as it blesses others, it is itself blessed.[2]

Spurgeon believed in the priesthood of the believer. This is a doctrine and foundational truth in Scripture which cannot be overlooked or given light attention if a church is to realize a 2 Tim 2:2 farm system. Darrell Robinson published a very helpful book in 1985 called *Total Church Life* in

---

1. Spurgeon, *Sword and Trowel* 1, 176.
2. Spurgeon, *Sword and Trowel* 1, 174–75

which he gave the essence of this teaching in Scripture that every believer is a minister and a missionary. In the Foreword of the book, Billy Graham wrote, "The situation in the organized and institutional church today is in danger . . . One of the problems is that the average person [member] has little concept of what the true church really is."[3] Spurgeon continuously taught this Scripture understanding to his church members what Paul communicated to all believers in Rom 10:14–15 and 1 Cor 9: 19–27,

> Seek that *some* may be there in glory. Behold your Master. He is your pattern. He left heaven to save some. He went to the cross, to the grave, to "save some": this was the great object of His life, to lay down His life for His sheep. He loved His Church, and gave Himself for her, that He might redeem her unto Himself. Imitate your Master. Learn His self-denial and His blessed consecration, if by any means you may save some.
>
> My soul yearneth that I personally may "save some", *but broader is my desire than that. I would have every one of you, my beloved friends, associated here in church-fellowship, to become spiritual parents of children for God. Oh, that every one of you might "save some"*! [emphasis added] . . . I would enlist you all afresh to-night, and bind anew the King's colours upon you. I would that you would fall in love with my Master over anew, and enter a second time upon the love of your espousals. There is a hymn of Cowper's which we sometimes sing,—"Oh, for a closer walk with God!" May we get to have a closer walk with Him; and if we do so, we shall also feel a more vehement desire to magnify Christ in the salvation of sinners."[4]

He knew fear was the key hurdle for his members to overcome in being engaged in the art and discipline of personally winning people to Christ:

> Timidity often prevents our being useful in this direction, but we must not give way to it; it must not be tolerated that Christ should be unknown through our silence, and sinners unwarned through our negligence. We must school and train ourselves to deal personally with the unconverted. We must not excuse ourselves, but force ourselves to the irksome task till it becomes easy. This is one of the most honourable modes of soul-winning; and if it requires more than ordinary zeal and courage, so much the more reason for our resolving to master it. Beloved, we must

---

3. Robinson, *Total Church Life*, xiii.
4. Spurgeon, *Soul-Winner*, 263–64.

win souls, we cannot live and see men damned; we must have them brought to Jesus. Oh! then, be up and doing, and let none around you die unwarned, unwept, uncared-for. A tract is a useful thing, but a living word is better. Your eye, and face, and voice will all help. Do not be so cowardly as to give a piece of paper where your own speech would be so much better. I charge you, attend to this, for Jesus' sake.[5]

A fruitful church is comprised of faithful followers of Jesus Christ. As Jesus taught in John 15:1–16, this all hinges on abiding in Him. There is no abiding in Him while sin is abiding in us. Holiness is simply heaven on earth—just what Jesus taught us to pray for in the Sermon on the Mount (Matt 6:9–13). If there can be more of Christ's saving power experienced in the church, there will be more of His converting power expressed through the church. Spurgeon said "the worldly Christian will not convert the world."[6] For Spurgeon, his most cherished strategy for helping his people become participants in the gospel was by helping them know and love Christ better. In addressing his membership from Matt 4:19, Spurgeon declared,

> When Christ calls us by His grace, we ought not only to remember what we are, but we ought also to *think of what He can make us*. It is "Follow Me, and I *will make you*." We should repent of what we have been, but rejoice in what we may be. It is not, "Follow Me, because of what you are already." It is not, "Follow Me, because you may make something of yourselves;" but, "Follow Me, because of what I will make you.". . . It did not seem a likely thing that lowly fishermen would develop into apostles, that men so handy with the net would be quite as much at home in preaching sermons and in instructing converts. One would have said, "How can these things be? You cannot make founders of churches out of peasants of Galilee." That is exactly what Christ did; and when we are brought low in the sight of God by a sense of our own unworthiness, we may feel encouraged to follow Jesus because of what He can make us.[7]

Spurgeon preached and taught God's Word so that his people could understand and follow their Savior better. He knew this was the path to their overcoming fear and unbelief for being used of God to win others

---

5. Spurgeon, *Soul-Winner*, 244–45.
6. Spurgeon, *Soul-Winner*, 278.
7. Spurgeon, *Soul-Winner*, 273.

to His dear Son. This is the life business of every believer: to truly know Christ as one's Lord. Spurgeon implanted this understanding and conviction into the hearts of his people:

> We are like the fishes, making sin to be our element, as they live in the sea; and the good Lord comes, and with the gospel net He takes us, and He delivers us from the life and love of sin. But He has not wrought for us all that He can do, nor all that we should wish Him to do, when He has done this; for it is another and a higher miracle to make us who were fish to become fishers,—to make the saved ones saviours,—to make the convert into a converter,—the receiver of the gospel into an imparter of that same gospel to other people. *I think I may say to every person whom I am addressing,—If you are yourself saved, the work is but half done until you are employed to bring others to Christ. You are as yet but half formed in the image of your Lord. You have not attained to the full development of the Christ-life in you unless you have commenced in some feeble way to tell others of the grace of God* [emphasis added]; and I trust that you will find no rest to the sole of your foot till you have been the means of leading many to that blessed Saviour who is your confidence and your hope. His word is, "Follow Me, not merely that you may be saved, nor even that you may be sanctified; but, 'Follow Me, and I will make you fishers of men.'" Be following Christ with that intent and aim; and fear that you are not perfectly following Him unless in some degree He is making use of you to be fishers of men.[8]

Spurgeon held before his church family this call on their lives from the Savior. He wanted a church which God could bless and use for the ultimate goal of life—enjoying God and bringing glory to Him through seeing lives changed through His Son. Jesus' statement in Luke 19:10 was embraced by Spurgeon: "Jesus Christ came . . . to seek and to save that which was lost; *and on the same errand has He sent His Church, . . . to preach Christ and Him crucified is the only object for which she exists among the sons of men* [emphasis added]. The business of the Church is salvation."[9] His words to his people were, "Settle it that this is the top and bottom of the business, and throw your whole strength, in the name of Christ, and by the power of the Eternal Spirit, into this object—if by

---

8. Spurgeon, *Soul-Winner*, 275.
9. Spurgeon, *Soul-Winner*, 252.

any means you may save some, and bring some to Jesus that they may be delivered from the wrath to come."[10]

This was the desire and ecclesiological conviction Spurgeon had for his church, the Pastors' College graduates and their churches, and all churches in Christendom: "Oh, that all our places of worship were soul-traps, and every Christian a fisher of men, each one doing his best, as the fisherman does, by every art and artifice, to catch those he fishes for! . . . Rouse yourselves, my brethren, for this God-like work, and may the Lord bless you in it!"[11] Paul states in Acts 20:24 the only life practice that makes sense for a Christian is to be making disciples in response to his/her Savior's calling: "But my life is worth nothing to me unless I use it for finishing the work assigned me by the Lord Jesus—the work of telling others the Good News about the wonderful grace of God (NLT)." Spurgeon expressed this same conviction for his life: "As for us, we hope during the rest of our lives to follow Him who is *The* Soul-Winner, and to put ourselves in His hands who maketh us soul-winners, so that our life may not be a long folly, but may be proved by results to have been directed by wisdom."[12]

SEVEN SPURGEONIC PRINCIPLES FOR TODAY

Charles Spurgeon labored with Christ to create a culture and atmosphere at Metropolitan Tabernacle of believing, working, and expecting people of all ages be brought to a personal knowledge of and relationship with the Lord Jesus Christ. He engrained into the hearts and minds of the Metropolitan Tabernacle members they were ministers and missionaries of the Savior. Spurgeon gave motivation and provided venues of training and participation in the gospel for the members.

During his time at Metropolitan Tabernacle, the church eventually saw 1462 "preaching stations" operated by the members under the direction of the elders of the church. These were in principle the same mission practices Spurgeon had participated in as a teenager at St. Andrews Baptist. This provided strategic places of evangelism and disciple making work in and around London. Many of these became permanent churches. The Monday Evening School conducted at the Tabernacle provided training in

---

10. Spurgeon, *Soul-Winner*, 255.
11. Spurgeon, *Soul-Winner*, 271.
12. Spurgeon, *Soul-Winner*, 225.

evangelism and an array of other subjects and became a 'feeder' for the Pastors' College. By the time of Spurgeon's death nearly 900 young men had been educated, trained, and sent out by the Pastors' College (approximately one-half started new churches). The challenge given all of them was: "Usefulness is the law of the moral universe. This, in relation to the Christian ministry, means the moral renovation, the saving conversion of human souls. Nothing short of this can satisfy the desires of any 'godly minister of Christ's gospel, and, therefore, all such will estimate the amount of their success by the number of well-sustained instances of conversion, which are the fruit, under God's blessing, of their ministerial labours."[13]

There are seven principles from what God taught Spurgeon and the Metropolitan Tabernacle which can be applied in churches today to help create a farm system to make new disciples and new churches. These principles are taught and modeled in Scripture. They were lived out through the London congregation and serve as encouragement to what God can work in a church if the church body and pastor will intentionally apply them under His power and purposes.

Pulpit Ministry

We begin with preaching as the first principle of study for a disciple making-multiplying farm system. Why this? Because it was the truths of Scripture which gripped and guided Spurgeon's heart and mind which eventuated the faithful and fruitful work of ministry through him and the Metropolitan Tabernacle. The belief in and practice of doing what the Scriptures taught inspired the strength and enduring work and growth of Christ's cause through the Tabernacle. Spurgeon's confession on this was,

> We desire so thoroughly to know, and so heartily to love the truth, as to declare the whole counsel of God, and to speak it as we ought to speak it. This is no small labour. To proclaim the whole system of truth, and to deal out each part in due proportion, is by no means a simple matter. To bring out each doctrine according to the analogy of faith, and set each truth in its proper place, is no easy task. It is easy to make a caricature of the beautiful face of truth by omitting one doctrine and exaggerating another. We may dishonour the most lovely countenance by giving to its most striking

---

13. Spurgeon, *Autobiography*, vol. 2, 79.

feature an importance which puts it out of proportion with the rest; for beauty greatly consists in balance and harmony.[14]

The principle here is to understand the pulpit ministry in the larger context of the church's work. Through preaching the Cross in the Spirit's power, lives can be radically transformed by Jesus and churches vitalized for multiplying disciples and producing more kingdom leaders. He taught his Pastors' College men "the main business of the minister is his pulpit."[15] Carlisle, one of Spurgeon's Pastors' College men, said of Spurgeon's preaching, "'We preach Christ crucified' was his proud boast. He knew that such preaching had in it the power of God unto salvation. The death on the Cross is wondrously linked with moral regeneration as well as justifying grace."[16]

Preaching the message of Jesus Christ and Him crucified as Spurgeon did enabled and equipped saints for holy living. Through this they were led into works of ministry and missions. The church who understands this message and whose leaders are molded by it, is capable of being an effective army for Christ. The Holy Spirit controls its desires and disciplines, rather than the flesh. Such a church doesn't experience internal dissensions. When the flesh is being crucified at the Cross, there's no attacking each other as believers. The fellowship stays healthy, and its unity gives impetus and power for Great Commission accomplishment. A church committed to Christ and His cross cannot be without passion for Jesus and His work—the only thing giving it life is Jesus and His calling. Crucified with Christ, members are impotent to be a cause or impetus to disunity in the church. They understand Eph 4:3, "Make every effort to keep the unity of the Spirit through the bond of peace" and they know this is crucial to their Great Commission work, as the Puritan theologian Thomas Manton made popular the understanding that disunity in the church breeds atheism out in the world.

Preaching is the one event that strategically climatizes the church for effectively pursuing the purposes and passion of Jesus, enabling the church to do so as a team (John 17:21, 23). The principle for every local church and pastor to follow is to fill the pulpit with the life and message of Jesus Christ and Him crucified. This is communicated by one who knows Jesus and daily lives at His cross. Then it must be discipled into the

---

14. Spurgeon, *All-Round*, 320.
15. Pike, *Life and Works of Spurgeon*, vol. 3, 184.
16. Carlisle, *Spurgeon*, 49.

church leaders' lives so they can model (teach) the same truth. Preaching is truth through personality; the preacher is the conduit of the message. You cannot divorce the message from the messenger; both must be offered fully to God if His message is to impact lives. Spurgeon said,

> You will never properly indulge your emotions in preaching, so as to feel at home with the people, until you are at home with your subject. When you know what you are at, you will have your mind free for earnestness. Unless you open-air preachers know the gospel from beginning to end, and know where you are in preaching it, you cannot preach with due emotion; but when you feel at home with your doctrine, stand up and be as bold, and earnest, and importunate as you please. Face the people feeling that you are going to tell them something worth hearing, about which you are quite sure, *which to you is your very life* [emphasis added].[17]

Preaching is where vision is cast, and people are challenged and inspired to carry out the purposes of God. Spurgeon is a sure encouragement to the potential of the pulpit ministry. God launched the church through the pulpit ministry (Acts 2:18ff) and He continues to revitalize and multiply disciples and churches through the pulpit ministry. This is required for an effective farm system to be grown. Donald McGavran, stated in his last published work, *Effective Evangelism: A Theological Mandate,*

> In our preaching let us make sure that this aspect of the Christian faith is repeatedly held up before our congregations, Sunday school meetings, and other assemblies of the saints. To be a true church we must become a reproductive church. Let us remember that full biblical soundness and spiritual renewal *cannot* limit themselves to existing congregations. They must multiply congregations. They must win non-Christian men and women in many locations. This teaching must become an essential part of all theological instruction.[18]

Prayer

Although Spurgeon taught his men their main business was their pulpit ministries, he modeled and taught that all blessings accomplished

---

17. Spurgeon, *Soul-Winner,* 170–71.
18. McGavran, *Effective Evangelism,* 45.

through pulpit ministrations (and all else) were received through prayer. Spurgeon viewed prayer as a priority to be lived by or a church would be impotent to its task. "But, brethren, only a living church—holy, prayerful, active—can make the old truth victorious."[19] He knew prayer was the means to power with God in seeing the Great Commission fulfilled by Jesus changing lives. "We should be crying, praying, and pleading that the church may continually grow."[20]

Spurgeon shared prayer was always valued in the Metropolitan Tabernacle during his pastorate. "Our reliance upon prayer has been very conspicuous; at least, I think so. We have not begun, we have not continued, we have not ended anything without prayer."[21] The church maintained a Monday night prayer meeting in which two to three thousand regularly participated. Spurgeon realized the prayer meetings were the thermometer of the church's spiritual vitality. He led these meetings to be interesting and focused on Christ through varied practices, never allowing staleness to seep life out of them. There was also on Thursday evenings "The Pastor's prayer-meeting" specifically requesting power from God upon the preaching of the Word.[22]

Prayer meetings in Spurgeon's day were as challenging to motivate members to participate in as they are in our present day. He taught his Pastors' College men when they went out to serve churches, they would have to begin the movement alone for the most part: "Wait a while, work on, plod on, plead on, and in due time the blessing will be given, and you shall find that you have the church after your own ideal, but it will not come to you all at once."[23] But he made clear the pastor is responsible to establish the practice of prayer in the church. He taught pastors "Your work, brethren, is to set your church on fire somehow. You may do it by speaking to the whole of the members, or you may do it by speaking to the few choice spirits, but you must do it somehow."[24]

Spurgeon taught and modeled this with his life and church leadership until the final months of his life. Nine months before he graduated to heaven, he addressed the Pastors' College Conference one last time. His instructions were:

19. Spurgeon, *Autobiography*, vol. 4, 230.
20. Spurgeon, *All-Round*, 43; *Greatest Fight*, 42.
21. Spurgeon, *Autobiography*, vol. 4, 243.
22. Spurgeon, *Autobiography*, vol. 4, 81, 88.
23. Spurgeon, *Soul-Winner*, 128.
24. Spurgeon, *Soul-Winner*, 131.

> If a church is to be what it ought to be for the purposes of God, *we must train it in the holy art of prayer* [emphasis added] . . . There is no interest, no power, in connection with the meeting. Oh, my brothers, let it not be so with you! Do train the people to continually meet together for prayer. Rouse them to incessant supplication. There is a holy art in it. Study to show yourselves approved by the prayerfulness of your people. If you pray yourself, you will want them to pray with you; and when they begin to pray with you, and for you, and for the work of the Lord, they will want more prayer themselves, and the appetite will grow. Believe me, if a church does not pray, it is dead. Instead of putting united prayer last, put it first. Everything will hinge upon the power of prayer in the church.[25]

As Spurgeon taught his men, the movement of prayer will not come overnight, but with zealous and careful consistency practiced in the pastor's life, God will begin to mark the members with an understanding of its value. The culture of dependency upon God expressed through concerted prayer by pastor and people is non-negotiable for a farm system to multiply disciples and churches. Only as we pray continuously can we stay focused upon our Lord. Through this life practice we are kept wise to the reality that all victories come from Him and not from our strength and wisdom.

Spurgeon made clear any ministry leader's effectiveness in following Jesus Christ and leading others to seek and serve Him all pivoted upon the prayer practice of the leader. He taught pastors and those desiring to enter the ministry in his Pastors' College,

> To you, as the ambassadors of God, the mercy-seat has a virtue beyond all estimate; the more familiar you are with the court of heaven the better shall you discharge your heavenly trust. Among all the formative influences which go to make up a man honored of God in the ministry, I know of none more mighty than his own familiarity with the mercy-seat. All that a college course can do, for a student is coarse and external compared with the spiritual and delicate refinement obtained by communion with God. While the unformed minister is revolving upon the wheel of preparation, prayer is the tool of the great potter by which he molds the vessel. All our libraries and studies are mere

---

25. Spurgeon, *Greatest Fight*, 43.

emptiness compared with our closets. We grow, we wax mighty, we prevail in private prayer.[26]

To lead others to pray, you must pray. This was Spurgeon's life practice and his encouragement to other church leaders. By praying for and praying with our members, the culture of a praying church will take shape.

Pneumatology

In the last chapter we looked at Spurgeon's statements giving his strong belief in and dependency upon the Holy Spirit and His power to do the Great Commission. Spurgeon knew the work of the Holy Spirit is what made preachers and all evangelistic endeavors effective: "Only as the Holy Ghost overshadows a man's mind can he influence other minds in a right manner."[27]

On the occasion of Spurgeon's Jubilee service celebration of his fiftieth birthday, Spurgeon gave a distinct glimpse of his and the church at Metropolitan Tabernacle's success through sharing all they attempted was done consciously on the Holy Spirit's power. At this service conducted on the Wednesday of June 18, 1884, Spurgeon's opening statements were:

> But let me say this for my speech: the blessing which I have had here, for many years, must be entirely attributed to the grace of God, and to the working of God's Holy Spirit among us. Let that stand as a matter, not only taken for granted, but as, a fact distinctly recognized among us. I hope, brethren, that none of you will say that I have kept back the glorious work of the Holy Spirit. *I have tried to remind you of it, whenever I have read a chapter, by praying that God the Holy Spirit would open that chapter to our minds. I hope I have never preached without an entire dependence on the Holy Ghost* [emphasis added].[28]

The Holy Spirit's role and activity in ministry involving a pastor's and the people's work for Christ was a conviction for Spurgeon—and was such to the people of the Metropolitan Tabernacle. It was only He, the Holy Spirit, who could keep the church in a culture of unity to affect the Great Commission. Jesus prayed in John 17:22 just before His death for the church to know unity so it could do His work, "that all of them may

---

26. Spurgeon, *Lectures*, 43.
27. Spurgeon, *Sword and Trowel* 19, 263.
28. Spurgeon, *Autobiography*, vol. 4, 243.

be one, Father, just as you are in me and I am in you. May they also be in us so that the world may believe that you have sent me." Spurgeon stated in his last address to gathered pastors, "For the keeping of our people together, and for the building of them up into a holy temple, we must look to him [the Holy Spirit]."[29] He added to this, *the Holy Ghost will not dwell where there is strife . . . I fear you cannot expect much blessing, for the Holy Dove does not dwell by troubled waters: he chooses to come where brotherly love continues.*[30]

This member of the Trinity was not simply a theological fact to Spurgeon, but a living Person with a specific divine assignment for guiding and empowering the church to fulfill her purpose. To Spurgeon and the Metropolitan Tabernacle, He was required and leaned upon for the Great Commission work of the Savior. Spurgeon's words about this are clear: "Blessed Spirit of the Lord, forgive us that we have done thee such despite, by our forgetfulness of thee, by our proud self-sufficiency, by resisting thine influences, and quenching thy fire! Henceforth work in us according to thine own excellence. Make our hearts tenderly impressible, and then turn us as wax to the seal, and stamp upon us the image of the Son of God."[31]

This was what Spurgeon taught and encouraged pastors and churches to understand and live. The book, *An All-Round Ministry*, was taken from Spurgeon's Presidential addresses at the Annual Conferences of the Pastors' College. (Spurgeon spent more time preparing these addresses than his normal practice for sermons.) In his message on "Faith" he gave this call to his hearers to appreciate and value the Holy Spirit in their ministries:

> We have an equal confidence, beloved brethren, in *the Holy Spirit*. We unfeignedly believe in His Deity and personality. We speak of His influences, because He has influences, but we do not forget that He is a Person from whom those influences stream; we believe in His offices, for He has offices, but we rejoice in the Person who fills them, and makes them effectual for our good. *Devoutly would each one of us say, "I believe in the Holy Ghost."* Yet, my brethren, do you believe in the Holy Ghost? "Yes," you say unanimously, spontaneously, and emphatically. "Yes," say I also; but be not grieved if I ask you yet again if you verily and indeed

---

29. Spurgeon, *Greatest Fight*, 52.
30. Spurgeon, *Greatest Fight*, 63.
31. Spurgeon, *Greatest Fight*, 53.

> believe in Him; for there is a believing and a believing... Have we such a reliance upon the Holy Ghost? Do we believe that, at this moment, He can clothe us with power, even as He did the apostles at Pentecost?... For this reason, I mournfully conclude that there is not, in the Church, such a belief in the Holy Ghost as there ought to be; and yet, as certainly as we hear the voice which saith, "Power belongeth unto God;" as surely as we hear the Divine voice of the Son, saying, "Ye believe in God, believe also in Me;" so truly does the third Person of the blessed Trinity claim our loving confidence, and woe be unto us if we vex Him by our unbelief! When we have a full faith in the Triune God, then shall we be "strong in the Lord, and in the power of His might [emphasis added]."[32]

Spurgeon knew the individual pastor and the individual church must be holy; they must be in a condition whereby the Holy Spirit can fill them. He knew and counted on the Holy Spirit's ability to reveal the methods and strategies making effective evangelism possible through a local church. He will lead to a farm system practice in local churches to multiply believers and more churches birthed to carry out the Great Commission. Our God promises the Holy Spirit's power and guidance if we will seek Him for this gift in our lives and ministries—Luke 11:11–13.

Churches and pastors of each generation must come to know the workings and power and Person of the Holy Spirit if they are to see a gospel life-changing farm system develop.

Processing New Members

Spurgeon believed all Christians wanted to be useful to the Lord Jesus' service: "First, then, I will take it for granted that every believer here wants to be useful. If he does not, I take leave to question whether he can be a true believer in Christ."[33] Careful church growth research has documented all healthy churches which multiply believers practice wise new member processing systems. Spurgeon and Metropolitan Tabernacle did this and he trained his Pastors' College men to do the same in their churches: "By all means let us bring true converts into the church, for it is a part of our work to teach them to observe all things whatsoever Christ has commanded them; but still, this is to be done to disciples, and not to mere professors; and if care be not used, we may do more harm than good at

---

32. Spurgeon, *All-Round Ministry*, 8–9.
33. Spurgeon, *Soul-Winner*, 277.

this point. To introduce unconverted persons to the church, is to weaken and degrade it; and therefore an apparent gain may be a real loss."[34]

Spurgeon and Metropolitan Tabernacle practiced a six-step process for receiving members into the church: (1) the prospective member met with two of the elders for initial inquiry of the person's testimony, (2) next, the associate pastor met with the person approved by the elders (early in Spurgeon's pastorate he met with people individually [he would talk with as many as forty people in four hours], but as the church grew this necessitated help from others), (3) if the associate pastor was satisfied, he nominated an elder or church member to visit nearby neighbors of the member candidate to verify their moral character and reputation, (4) if this went well, the candidate was invited to the next church meeting (held monthly) to come before the church and reply to questioning, (5) following questions by the church body, the candidate then withdrew from the meeting and the assigned neighborhood visitor gave his report, and (6) the vote of the church was then taken.[35] The Tabernacle church family found this approach never tended to keep converted ones out, but many times strengthened or corrected the belief and commitment of those joining.

It was serious work for Spurgeon and the Tabernacle church: "Alas! I fear there has been great laxity in the admission of members, and the quality of our churches has become defiled and debased by 'the mixed multitude,' among whom all manner of evil finds a congenial dwelling-place."[36] Spurgeon was interviewed by the Pall Mall Gazette (an evening newspaper in London during Spurgeon's time) and he stated the following as to how people were received into membership at the Tabernacle:

> Every member who joins my church is expected to do something for his fellow creatures. After I have had a talk with him and satisfied myself as to his sincerity, I say to him: "My good fellow, you seem to be a converted man, and I hope that you are truly a Christian; but, suppose you join the church, what are you going to do for your fellow-men? If, after you are admitted, you will do nothing for them, I cannot help it; we have made a bad bargain, that's all; but no one shall enter with my good will who does not promise beforehand to undertake, if at all possible, some useful work for the benefit of others". In many cases the

---

34. Spurgeon, *Soul-Winner*, 17.
35. Spurgeon, *Metropolitan Tabernacle*, 90; *Autobiography* vol. 4, 82.
36. Spurgeon, *All-Round*, 295.

idea never seems to have struck them that this was an essential part of Christian duty. It makes them think of what they can do and in most cases they profess their readiness to do whatever I think would be most useful.[37]

Spurgeon understood all this took time and many wanted faster actions regarding membership. But he knew it was needful and wise. He told his Pastors' College men,

> Yes, I believe Judas was a man exactly of that kind, very clever at deceiving those around him. We must mind that we do not get any of these into the church if we can anyhow keep them out. You may say to yourself, at the close of a service, "Here is a splendid haul of fish!" Wait a bit. Remember our Saviour's words, "The kingdom of heaven is like unto a net, that was cast into the sea, and gathered of every kind; which, when it was full, they drew to shore, and sat down, and gathered the good into vessels, but cast the bad away." Do not number your fishes before they are broiled; nor count your converts before you have tested and tried them. This process may make your work somewhat slow; but then, brethren, it will be sure. Do your work steadily and well, so that those who come after you may not have to say that it was far more trouble to them to clear the church of those who ought never to have been admitted than it was to you to admit them.[38]

Meetings for tea were conducted for all those coming into the church "The pastor presided and counseled them with regard to the duties and privileges of their position."[39] Spurgeon realized when people were too easily admitted as members, they just as easily lapsed into unfruitfulness. "Our members must be the most devout and the most devoted in the community . . . The holiest church will one day be the most powerful church."[40]

In addition to communicating up front the expectations of Christian service involvement through the church's ministries, new members were directed from Scripture of the value of regular participation in the Lord's Supper. The Tabernacle conducted the Lord's Supper every Sunday evening, except the second Sunday, with a major gathering of members

---

37. Hayden, *Spurgeon's Tabernacle*, 80–81.
38. Spurgeon, *Soul-Winner*, 43.
39. Cook, *Wit and Wisdom of Spurgeon*, 186.
40. Pike, *Life and Works of Spurgeon*, vol. 5, 45–46.

the first Sunday evening of each month. The second Sunday opportunity was offered after the morning worship service so those members, a good number of them, who were involved in Sunday afternoon mission work: extension Sunday Schools, open-air preaching meetings, and other forms of missions work they could participate in.[41]

A communion card was issued to every new member. The card was divided and perforated into twelve parts, one of which was to be turned in at a communion service monthly. If a member missed three months, an elder called on them and ministered to them and a formal report was submitted updating the member's spiritual condition. Open communion was practiced, but guests were counseled to join the church, or find another church to commit to, after the third such participation in communion.[42]

What Spurgeon and the Tabernacle understood and practiced has been documented by studies one hundred years after Spurgeon's ministry. Those churches which expect of their members and who have a clear process for members to follow to grow in Christ are much healthier in their overall work for Christ. Spurgeon encouraged and challenged pastors in his last conference with them to follow the practice of the German minister/missionary J. G. Oncken:

> The German churches, when our dear friend, Mr. Oncken, was alive, always carried out the rule of asking every member, "What are you going to do for Christ?" and they put the answer down in a book. The one thing that was required of every member was that he should continue doing something for the Savior. If he ceased to do anything it was a matter for church discipline, for he was an idle professor, and could not be allowed to remain in the church like a drone in a hive of working bees. He must do or go.[43]

Pastors and churches must exercise the courage to honor and follow Scripture in the way, as well the who, they bring into church membership. How members begin their journey with Christ upon entering membership into the local church will mark and define to a great degree their health and service for Christ for the duration of their membership. No sports team and no church team can ever build a solid

---

41. Spurgeon, *Autobiography*, vol. 3, 71–72.

42. Wayland, *Spurgeon*, 193; *Autobiography*, 4:72; Spurgeon, *Metropolitan Tabernacle History*, 90–91.

43. Spurgeon, *Greatest Fight*, 44.

farm system without earnest and committed members being brought on to the team rosters.

PASTORAL LEADERSHIP

Spurgeon believed the pastor was to be the leader of the church. It was his God-given responsibility and was to be understood as such. Spurgeon taught his Pastors' College minister prospects: "What am I, and what are you, that we should be lords over God's heritage? Dare any of us say . . . I am the most important person in the church? If so, the Holy Spirit is not likely to use such unsuitable instruments; but if we know our places and desire to keep them with all humility, He will help us, and the churches will flourish beneath our care."[44]

Spurgeon believed in leading with certitude and doing so with grace. He understood if a pastor becomes ensnared in his heart with the fear of man, his leadership effectiveness is nullified. When Spurgeon was called from Waterbeach to London, one of his deacons prayed that God would keep the young pastor from the *bleating of the sheep*. The meaning of this baffled Spurgeon, but later it all became clear:

> He meant to ask the Lord that I might live above the fear of man, so that, when some persons said to me, "How much we have been edified today!" I might not be puffed up; or if another said, "How dull the discourse was today!" I might not be depressed. There is no leader of the flock who will not occasionally wish to be delivered from the bleating of the sheep, for they bleat such different tunes sometimes. There is some old bellwether, perhaps, that is not bleating in the right style, and one is apt to be troubled about it; but it is a great thing to feel, "Now, I am not going to be influenced by the way these sheep bleat. I am set to lead them rather than to let them lead me, and I am going to be guided by something far more reliable than the bleating of the sheep, namely, the voice of the Great Shepherd." I soon found that the best way to be delivered from the bleating of the sheep was to seek to be filled with the spirit of the Good Shepherd.[45]

He encouraged pastors to think big by having faith in a great God. There was too much on the line to be thinking small as Spurgeon understood the call of God, the commission of Jesus, and the desperate

---

44. Spurgeon, *Lectures*, 199.
45. Spurgeon, *Autobiography*, vol. 1, 296.

need of the lost. "Go in for great things, brethren, in the name of God; risk everything on His promise, and according to your faith shall it be done unto you."[46] The risks had to be for God and based on God's calling. As Spurgeon said, "He who doubts as to whether he is sent of God, goes hesitatingly."[47]

What had mastered the Savior's heart must master His servant's heart as well. When a pastor so walks with and for God, a definite and distinct confidence is known and lived out with the people God has called him to serve and lead. Spurgeon said the right kind of pastoral leadership "demands and commands an audience" in communicating the gospel call to people to come to Christ and serve Him with their lives.[48]

But this pastoral leadership Spurgeon taught was earned leadership. The pastor must lead from a heart firmly in love with the Savior and His Great Commission instructions (these instructions again underscore the call to train people to do all Jesus' commands—the first being to totally love God with everything, and then to love all others as oneself). Such a pastor's heart would do all possible to love and help the members do the same with their lives. "The man of God, who feels the force of holy fatherhood, would do anything and everything, possible and impossible, for the sake of his spiritual children; he gladly spends and is spent for them."[49] Spurgeon gave more specific instruction of how and what such pastoral leadership must model: "If you desire to be a father in the church that you may have his special honor, you see the way to it: it comes of self-denial, patience, forbearance, love, zeal, and diligence."[50]

What Spurgeon understood with absolute clarity and Scripture guided conviction is *what the leaders model, the members do*. This axiom applies in all venues of life: sports, business, home, the church. Jesus taught and practiced this (Matt 4:19; Mark 3:14) and Paul did as well (1 Cor 11:1; Phil 4:9). Spurgeon explained it this way: "The other servants will take their cue from us . . . A minister soon gets round him people like himself: 'like priest, like people.' Oh, that we may always be alive and earnest in the service of the Lord Jesus, that our people may be alive

---

46. Spurgeon, *All-Round*, 185.
47. Spurgeon, *All-Round*, 13.
48. Spurgeon, *All-Round*, 13.
49. Spurgeon, *All-Round*, 241.
50. Spurgeon, *All-Round*, 243.

also!"⁵¹ He gave further insight on this by stating, "Many beginners take readily to an earthly model; they find it more natural to copy a godly man, whom they have seen, than to imitate the Lord Jesus, whom they have not seen."⁵²

Spurgeon believed if the pastor grows in grace and knowing Christ, his leadership effectiveness grows, and his church will grow. He knew if the pastor is growing in holiness and wisdom, this inspires members in the same direction. As this happens, the church begins to see more fruit of the Spirit being evidenced in the body. With this experience comes more lives being impacted with the gospel as the members share their lives with the lost. Churches then begin to see disciples being multiplied. Spurgeon explained this principle of growing pastors—growing churches:

> I believe that many weak ones in our churches are seriously injured, if not entirely broken down, by following the example of their ministers in matters wherein they come short of the Lord's mind. How grievous it would be if any believers were dwarfed through our conduct! May we not fear that there are some in our churches today who are not what they might have been had we properly guided them? No doubt some have been coddled into weakness, and others have been allowed to grow more in one direction than in others. *Do you say, "We cannot help this; it is no business of ours"? I tell you it is our business. Strangers may talk in a careless way, but fathers are conscious of great responsibility as to their children. If a family is not well ordered, a wise father begins to mend his own ways. If our people do wrong, we fret and blame ourselves. If we were better, our church-members would be better. It is little use to scold them; our wiser way is to humble ourselves before God, and find out the reason why our ministry does not produce better results* [emphasis added].⁵³

At the celebration of Spurgeon's fiftieth birthday, *Mr. Spurgeon's Jubilee* as it was commonly called, one of the Metropolitan Tabernacle deacons gave an interesting observation of Spurgeon's leadership of the church over the history of his pastoral tenure. After reading salutations from various groups, including the professors of the Southern Baptist Theological Seminary of Louisville, Kentucky, a deacon, B. W. Carr, shared insights explaining how Spurgeon led the church:

---

51. Spurgeon, *All-Round*, 258.
52. Spurgeon, *All-Round*, 245.
53. Spurgeon, *All-Round*, 246.

As our Minister, you are known to the utmost ends of the earth. Richly endowed by the Spirit of God with wisdom and discretion, your conduct as our Ruling Elder has silenced contention and promoted harmony. The three hundred souls you found in fellowship at New Park Street Chapel have multiplied to a fellowship of nearly six thousand in this Tabernacle. And under your watchful oversight the family group has increased without any breach of order . . .

Your natural abilities never betrayed you into indolent habits. The talents you possessed gave stimulus to your diligence. A little prosperity did not elate you, or a measure of success prompt the desire to settle down in some quiet resting place. You spread your sails to catch the breeze. The ascendancy you began to acquire over the popular mind, instead of making you vainglorious, filled you with awe, and increased the rigor of that discipline you have always exercised over yourself . . . To your unwavering faith in his guardian care we venture to attribute the coolness of your head and the courage of your heart in all the great adventures of your life . . . The retrospect of your career, to those who have followed it throughout, appears like one unbroken series of successes; but as our memory retraces the steps you have taken, we can testify to the exhaustive labors in which you have blithely engaged, the constant self-denial you have cheerfully exercised, and the restless anxieties that have kept you and your comrades incessantly calling on the name of the Lord. By such an experience you have enlarged the field of evangelical enterprise in the various institutions of the church . . . Your skillful generalship has laid ten thousand happy donors to your charities under lasting obligations to you for providing outlets for their benevolence. It has pleased the Lord to make whatever you do to prosper. You braved much calumny on the outset of your career, and you have outlived it . . . Your kindness to everybody has made everybody kind to you. You have illustrated the force and the fullness of a divine proverb which has puzzled many a philosopher: 'When a man's ways please the Lord, he maketh even his enemies to be at peace with him.'[54]

Such leadership does not come without resistance from Satan, our flesh, and others. There is a militant motif throughout Scripture describing the Christian experience. Spurgeon encouraged his Pastors' College men to not quit in the fight for souls and leading churches forward to victorious Christian service. His words to pastors were clear on this needed

---

54. Spurgeon, *Spurgeon's Jubilee*, 11–12.

leadership: "'Forward' is the watchword of our Conference, let it ring through your ranks. Onward, ye elect of God! Victory is before you; your very safety lies in that direction. To retreat is to perish."[55] Often pastors have given up because of just a few people in the church being resistant.

Spurgeon understood the value and need of holy courage and loving perseverance. It came through faith in God—and God alone. Spurgeon knew this and lived on this premise of Scripture. He said, "The man who believes in God, . . . will stay himself upon the Lord alone . . . and when he has most human helps, he sedulously endeavors still to wait only upon God. If you lean upon your helpers . . . you will realize the terrible meaning of that ancient word, 'Cursed be the man that trusteth in man, and maketh flesh his arm' [Jer 17:5]."[56] What was true for Spurgeon, as has been true for all pastors throughout history, was that confidence in God causes confident pastoral leadership. Spurgeon's words for pastors were, "Dependence upon God is the flowing fountain of success." He went on to say in this same message, "Brothers, it would be a great calamity if it could be said of any one of you, 'He had an excellent moral character, and remarkable gifts; but he did not trust God.' Faith is a chief necessary. 'Above all, taking the shield of faith,' was the apostolic injunction."[57] Our lives as pastors and church leaders will always be measured by our Savior's words: "According to your faith be it unto you." The need and opportunity of each pastor and church leader in churches is to receive and experience faith from Jesus as Spurgeon learned. This will create confidence to develop a farm system which will multiply disciples and birth more churches.

Priesthood of the Believer

Spurgeon could see no clergy versus laity dichotomy when it came to Christians serving the Lord. All were called into Christ's service of extending His Kingdom. Spurgeon looked at and treated his people as what they were called in Scripture, 'servants of Jesus Christ.' His understanding of each believer's calling, potential and responsibility to follow and obey Christ was founded in Scripture. He preached and believed in a radical conversion.

---

55. Spurgeon, *All-Round*, 32.
56. Spurgeon, *All-Round*, 19.
57. Spurgeon, *All-Round*, 183–84.

As revealed in chapter six above, Spurgeon's theology caused him to preach and cast the vision of every believer's calling to know and make Christ known. In his message "How to Win Souls for Christ" delivered to his Monday night prayer meeting body, Spurgeon challenged and called the members of the Tabernacle to be champions for Christ in His work. He instructed those in attendance,

> Our object is to turn the world upside down; or, in other words, that where sin abounded grace may much more abound. We are aiming at a miracle: it is well to settle that at the commencement. Some brethren think that they ought to lower their note to the spiritual ability of the hearer; but this is a mistake. According to these brethren, you ought not to exhort a man to repent and believe unless you believe that he can, of himself, repent and believe. My reply is a confession: I command men in the name of Jesus to repent and believe the gospel, though I know they can do nothing of the kind apart from the grace of God; for I am not sent to work according to what my private reason might suggest, but according to the orders of my Lord and Master. Ours is the miraculous method which comes of the endowment of the Spirit of God, who bids His ministers perform wonders in the name of the holy child Jesus . . . If the champion's locks be shorn, the Philistines will laugh at him; if the Lord be gone from a man, he has no power left for useful service . . . Unless your walk be close with God, unless you dwell in that clear light which surrounds the throne of God, and which is only known to those who are in fellowship with the Eternal, you will go forth from your chamber, and hasten to your work, but nothing will come of it.[58]

Spurgeon simply, but with confident expectation, imparted to his members what God through His Word had taught him through personal experience. He led his church with the understanding that God had called each member to bear fruit to Jesus. John 15:1–16 was a conviction and a theological framework by which the members of the Tabernacle were taught to believe and live. Every child of God was given this high calling. As his hero Paul had taught the Philippian church "I press toward the mark of the high calling of God in Christ Jesus . . . Those things, which you have both learned, and received, and heard, and seen in me, do" (Phil 3:14; 4:9), Spurgeon taught the same to his members.

---

58. Spurgeon, *Soul-Winner*, 164–65.

Spurgeon understood his church to be an army of believers united under Christ to serve Him and His purposes. They were united in Him and His love. That love was undiminishable and never ceasing. This was his belief in God and his belief in its effect on his members. They could expectantly go forward together under Christ to accomplish His purposes as pastor and people because of Christ's unfailing love and commitment to them. They were called of God equally and individually. Their roles and responsibilities in Christ's service were per God's appointment and gifting, but each was a contributor to the kingdom's advancement. In his message to the Metropolitan church family based upon James 5:19–20, Spurgeon gave this encouragement:

> Now, beloved, what comes out of this but these suggestions? Let us long to be used in the conversion of sinners. James does not speak concerning the Holy Ghost in this passage, nor of the Lord Jesus Christ, for he was writing to those who would not fail to remember the important truths which concern both the Spirit and the Son of God; *but yet it may be meet here to remind you that we cannot do spiritual good to our fellow-creatures apart from the Spirit of God, neither can we be blessed to them if we do not preach to them "Jesus Christ and Him crucified." God must use us; but, oh, let us long to be used, pray to be used, and pine to be used! Dear brethren and sisters, let us purge ourselves of everything that would prevent our being employed by the Lord. If there is anything we are doing, or leaving undone, any evil we are harbouring, or any grace we are neglecting, which may make us unfit to be used of God, let us pray the Lord to cleanse, and mend, and scour us, till we are vessels fit for the Master's use. Then let us be on the watch for opportunities of usefulness; let us go about the world with our ears and our eyes open, ready to avail ourselves of every occasion for doing good; let us not be content till we are useful, but make this the main design and ambition of our lives. Somehow or other, we must and will bring souls to Jesus Christ* [emphasis added]. As Rachel cried, "Give me children, or I die," so may none of you be content to be barren in the household of God. Cry and sigh until you have snatched some brand from the burning, and have brought at least one sinner to Jesus Christ, that so you also may have saved a soul from death, and covered a multitude of sins.[59]

---

59. Spurgeon, *Soul-Winner*, 312–13.

Such convictions gained from Scripture's instruction and arranging opportunities for their implementation in each local church's life, is what makes possible building a farm system.

PREPARING PREACHERS

This is the objective in the life of each local church and is simply the practical and intentional application of 2 Tim 2:2. Again, Spurgeon said, "It is no small blessing when a church can find her pastors in her own midst; the rule is to look abroad; but, perhaps, if our home gifts were more encouraged, the Holy Spirit would cause our teachers to come forth more frequently from among our own brethren."[60] The ministries of the Metropolitan Tabernacle such as the Monday evening school, the Saturday training classes, the colportage work, the Pastors' College—were all parts of the whole machinery put into place to see preachers and proclaimers of the Gospel raised up.

But the work of preparing preachers began well before the teen and young adult years of those ministered to by the Metropolitan Tabernacle. Spurgeon strongly valued and encouraged Sunday School work. He saw in this the potential for future church leaders through reaching and teaching children for Christ:

> Children need to be saved; children may be saved; children are to be saved by instrumentality . . . The conversion of a child involves the same work of divine grace, and results in the same blessed consequences as the conversion of the adult . . . To reclaim the prodigal is well, but to save him from ever being a prodigal is better. To bring back the thief and the drunkard is a praiseworthy action, but so to act that the boy shall never become a thief or a drunkard is far better; hence Sabbath-school instruction stands very high in the list of philanthropic enterprises, and Christians ought to be most earnest in it. He who converts a child from the error of his way, prevents as well as covers a multitude of sins.
>
> Moreover, this gives the Church the hope of being furnished with the best of men and women. The Church's Samuels and Solomons are made wise in their youth; David and Josiah were tender of heart when they were tender in years. Read the lives of the most eminent ministers, and you shall usually find that their Christian history began early. Though it is not

---

60. Spurgeon, *Autobiography*, vol. 1, 307.

> absolutely needful, yet it is highly propitious to the growth of a well-developed Christian character, that its foundation should be laid on the basis of youthful piety. I do not expect to see the Churches of Jesus Christ ordinarily built up by those who have through life lived in sin, but by the bringing up in their midst, in the fear and admonition of the Lord, young men and women who become pillars in the house of our God. If we want strong Christians, we must look to those who were Christians in their youth. Trees must be planted in the courts of the Lord while they are yet young if they are to live long and to flourish well.[61]

Spurgeon believed in calling out the called as he pastored the Metropolitan Tabernacle and he believed God was calling a portion of the members into vocational Christian service. In his message "Preach the Gospel," delivered August 5, 1855, he closed the message by calling out the called in his congregation. His words reflect his understanding of the priesthood of the believer and his faith in God calling out people to serve His Son's ministry vocationally as leaders in the Kingdom. In a special ceremony for the dedication of the new church building was conducted prior to the official opening of the Metropolitan Tabernacle. On August 20, 1860, before the building was completed for the church, Spurgeon shared this:

> We pledge ourselves to the Christian public that they shall be no losers by us. While this work has been going on we have done as much as any other Church for all other agencies—as much at least as it was possible for us to do. We hope to help other places, by first giving to our young men education when God has called them to the ministry, and afterwards helping them when they are settled. We wish to become a fruitful mother of children, and pray that God may make this place a center, out of which many rays of truth, and light, and glory, may be dispersed through the darkness of the land.[62]

Spurgeon believed from Scripture the local church was to make disciples and also make disciple-making leaders. It was the passion of his life to see this happen and what eventuated the Pastors' College ministries of the church. Because of the theology which gripped his mind, he was focused on calling out and preparing preachers of the gospel. L. R. Scarborough had a good grasp of what this calling out work was based upon:

---

61. Spurgeon, *Soul-Winner*, 314–16.
62. Spurgeon, *New Park Street Pulpit* vol. 6, 360.

God calls men into salvation and into special service. A divine call is a spiritual necessity to successful work in the Kingdom of Grace, either in preaching or in missions. The prophets, apostles, preachers and evangelists of the Bible were divinely called into God's service. Christ's command was "pray ye the Lord of the harvest that He may thrust forth laborers into His harvest." He must do the calling. Pastors, churches, anxious parents or loving friends must not do the calling of preachers and missionaries. Nothing can fill the place of a divine inner call. God is calling many in the churches and in our schools into the special fields of labor. *Many years of constant prayer, extended observation and inquiry convince me that in almost every church in all of our land where the fires of evangelism and mission burn, God is secretly dealing with the hearts of young men and women on this question. The writer has asked pastors and evangelists to press this matter of calling out the called in their churches and meetings and everywhere the report is that God is calling. God is doing his part. Will we do ours?*

There is a human side to a divine call. God calls and man calls out [emphasis added]. It is doubted whether there is a preacher or missionary in all the world who was not influenced by some word of some wise friend or loved one at the time of his surrender to God's will. There may be a few exceptions. These would have been in the service earlier if some wise word had been spoken to them at the proper times . . . The writer began to give special attention to this matter ten years ago. In the colleges and churches where he has been, in private and public, he has tried to call out the God-called and in these years more than 450 have publicly surrendered to do God's will to preach or do mission work. [Scarborough would eventually see 5000 respond to God's call during his 1920–25 work in the "Seventy-Five Million Campaign"].[63]

Spurgeon's assessment about the college at the Metropolitan Tabernacle made clear the aim to prepare preachers: "It appears to us that the maintenance of a truly spiritual College is probably the readiest way in which to bless the church."[64] He believed every church should have a 'strong back-bone of preaching men.' And that to have a 'college' to train her men was the most common-sense matter of business for any and every church. Because of his own experiences in the Lay Preachers'

---

63. Scarborough, *Recruits for World Conquests*, 24–25.
64. Harte, *Historical Tablets of College*, 14.

Association Spurgeon valued this training and the evangelism-preaching opportunities it afforded young men. It led him to the formal training of men who indicated desires to serve Jesus Christ. He knew by exposing them to experiences of preaching and evangelism, there would be opportunity to lead them into further preparation and service for Christ. He was confident this would help the church he pastored be a functioning and fruitful farm system for multiplying disciples and leaders for the kingdom of our God.

These seven principles from Spurgeon's and the Tabernacle's experience, grounded in the Word of God, can serve every generation of pastors and churches. They are guiding lights for each generation of Christ's servants to impact their world for Him. If we carefully seek our Lord and give ourselves to holy experimentation and obedience to Him in applying these principles, we (and those who follow us) will be much happier and fruitful workers in the Savior's harvest.

8

Confident Pastoral Leadership

WE'VE ESTABLISHED EVERY PASTOR and leader needs character, competence, and chemistry (or to say credibility, capabilities, and compassion)—the most important being character. I appreciate Rick Warren's words in *Purpose Driven Church* "Developing the character of Christ is life's most important task' . . . .'When you put knowledge of the Word, perspective, conviction, and the corresponding skills together, the resulting product is character! First you know it; then you understand it; then you believe it with your whole heart; then you do it. The result of these four is character."[1] Spurgeon helps us with proper self-awareness (how we see ourselves), social awareness (how we read our members and our harvest field), and Spirit of God awareness (how we personally relate to God—this informs and guides all our attitudes and actions towards others). This is what wisdom is and what it does for us. It results in God-inspired leadership.

The need for confident pastoral leadership generated from solid character, cannot be overemphasized in Christendom. Howard Hendricks often stated in class lectures at Dallas Seminary, the greatest need in America was competent leaders: leaders who understand and embrace integrity and can lead people to accomplish worthy goals. When I first began my seminary training journey in 1975, Dr. Frank Schmidt at Liberty University's School of Divinity posed a challenging insight in

---

1. Warren, *Purpose Driven Church*, 360, 362.

his Leadership course which startled and challenged my total theological framework. He placed before us this consideration: if two pastors equally love the Lord, His Word, and winning souls to the Savior—if one understands leadership and the other does not, the one who can lead well will take a church to one thousand while the other who doesn't understand how to lead well can only take a church to one hundred. He wasn't prizing numbers so much as effectiveness. If you carefully consider this, regardless of how much theology or evangelism knowledge and insights a pastor may have, if he does not understand effective leadership, he will not see the lives impacted by the gospel he hopes to. This is the genius of 2 Tim 2:2. We must always look to the Savior and study what He practiced and the principles He applied, particularly His investing in the Twelve and why He gave more time to Peter, James, and John.

It's intriguing to observe the parallels between good athletic coaching and good pastoring. Having a background in sports I was always intrigued with good coaches and their ability to lead teams to championships. Reading the lives of these coaches and how they handled players and led their teams has been very profitable. John Wooden's autobiography (he was voted coach of the twentieth century by ESPN magazine) *They Call Me Coach* is an excellent study in character and its influence in sports. Interviews made with Jim Craig, Mike Eruzione, and Buz Schneider of the 1980 US Olympic Hockey team gave insights on their team and the coach's influence. They discussed the confidence and character coach Herb Brooks demonstrated in leading the team through their trainings and games leading up to their unfathomed upset of Russia (Russia had won the gold for twenty-four years in the Olympics, except for 1960) for the 1980 gold medal. His confident leadership inspired and instilled confidence in the players to give their best and execute exceptionally as a team. They stated, "You are as confident as your coach is."[2] This works the same in local churches between pastors and people. Scripturally, the passages of Deut 31 and Josh 1 are classic studies on character and confident leadership. God calls pastors to be strong and courageous in Him for the work of His Son.

Good pastoral leadership, like good coaching, helps members of the team (the church family) to know their objective and how to work together to achieve it. This is what Spurgeon did with the Metropolitan Tabernacle. Starting with what Scripture said about each person, Spurgeon

2. Craig et al., *Miracle* ESPN Roundtable, 2004.

handled and led the people accordingly. This is the path of confident pastoral leadership. John Wooden said of coaching teams, "It is amazing how much can be accomplished if no one cares who gets the credit."[3] Wooden developed an ABCD philosophy of coaching that guided his work: (1) appreciate your players, (2) believe in them, (3) crown their every accomplishment, and (4) take responsibility to develop them. Paul Bear Bryant's, famed football coach of Alabama, philosophy in coaching was (1) if we win, *they* (the team) *did it*, (2) if we did "so-so," then *we did it*, and (3) if we lost, *I did it*. Wooden and Bryan were similar in their values. Wooden said regarding character, "Ability may get you to the top, but it takes character to keep you there."[4] The above words apply to pastors.

God wants every pastor (and member) to grow in the grace and wisdom of Christ. If we grow, our people grow. As pastors and people grow, their ministries grow as more and more lives are impacted by Christ's love and message. The pastor inevitably plays a pivotal role in leading a church's health and growth to affect a farm system which multiplies disciples and ultimately more churches from their church. Spurgeon was referred to as the *governor* by the leaders of the Metropolitan Tabernacle. It was not due to dictatorial practices but earned through respect gained by how he loved and led his people. The characteristics of his life and the wisdom in leadership he demonstrated can serve any pastor and church leader in growing as an effective and confident leader.

There are four life perspectives we want and need to keep developing to effectively lead a local church to accomplish the Lord Jesus' Great Commandment and Great Commission and carry out 2 Tim 2:2. Perspective comes out of our beliefs and determines what one sees and expects in life. Pastors and church leaders have great responsibilities and opportunities for influencing their members for Christ. The following four areas are pivotal in the pursuit of the Savior's life and call: (1) how a pastor sees God, (2) how a pastor sees himself, (3) how a pastor sees his church, and (4) how a pastor sees his community and world. By growing in all four areas, a pastor can lead a church to be faithful and fruitful in Christ's kingdom expansion. These life perspectives, as observed in Scripture and through what Spurgeon demonstrated, can be wisely developed through grace and can make a pastor confident in leading a church to realize a farm system which multiplies disciples and more churches.

3. Wooden, *They Call Me Coach*, 104.
4. Wooden, *They Call Me Coach*, 152.

Before looking at the first perspective (character and how it is developed and its role in confident leading as a pastor), we consider the question are leaders born this way from birth or are they developed? Life circumstances always factor into what a person becomes. These can take on many faces of what would be considered unfortunate and fortunate. What has been proven is that God's grace can invade any kind of life circumstance and forge persons of leadership from them. This is why God guides us into unique roles; He tells us different gifts are expressed in different ways for Christ's kingdom work (1 Cor 12:4–6). He knows what He is doing and has a unique race lane (Heb 12:2) for each of His servants to run in to accomplish His glory and others' good in helping them come to know His Son.

Leadership is something which can be learned by any person willing to apply him or herself. Jesus calls us to follow Him, and this inherently means learning to be a leader due to this intimate connection with the greatest leader of all history. A well-documented life principle is people do what people see. A person following Christ will grow to understand how to work with, lead, and influence people. I had to settle this in my own heart many years ago as a young ministerial student. After reading many publications from the American Management Association and authors like Robert Greenleaf (who influenced MIT's Sloan School of Management and the Harvard Business School) and Bennis and Nanus (leadership researchers at University of Southern California) and combining this with reading church leaders' lives and numerous journal and periodical studies—but most importantly Scripture, it revealed effective leadership can be learned. It's not a gift given by one's birth; it is an acquired characteristic and ability. Every pastor and church leader learn this through following Christ and studied attendance to, and application of, Scripture precepts and principles. The better we see Christ, the better we see how leadership is to be done. This is aided through carefully observing wise leadership in others. Spurgeon can give much help with this.

CHARACTER: HOW A PASTOR SEES GOD

Jesus had/has the perfect balance of grace and truth. If we are to be leaders in His church, we need to develop an intimate relationship with Jesus Christ. It is His church and our leading in His work is about winning and developing people to be like Him—so as His leaders we must seek to know Him better. Beyond developing intimacy with Jesus, studying the lives of others who have loved Him dearly and have followed Him solidly can bring help and encouragement. Spurgeon can be a historical mentor and friend who helps pastors be more effective and confident in their responsibilities to God and His people. His life passion was to know Christ as noted from his secret diary and from his applied theology. How he saw God offers a great example to pastors—and all church leaders.

Spurgeon knew the work of a pastor was to represent Christ and lead others to know and represent Christ—so they could lead others to know and serve Him. This high calling was only possible as Christ leads and works through His undershepherds. Spurgeon explained, "*Men infer the Master from the servant; . . . You cannot dissociate . . . the Lord from His representative . . . this is no small matter. It will need the Lord Himself to be both our wisdom and our strength, or we shall surely fail* [emphasis mine]."[5] Spurgeon understood having Christ preeminent in life required humility and being a servant: "He is highest who makes himself lowest; he is greatest who makes himself less than the least."[6] Spurgeon genuinely wanted to learn what his mentor Paul the Apostle embraced: "Here is a trustworthy saying that deserves full acceptance: Christ Jesus came into the world to save sinners—of whom I am the worst" (1 Tim 1:15). This conviction directly impacts the pastor's leading a church and how he serves the members as Spurgeon explained,

> Ministers are for churches, and not churches for ministers. In our work among the churches, we must not dare to view them as estates to be farmed for our own profit, or gardens to be trimmed to our own taste . . . *A pastor's work is an anxious one. All sorts of difficulties occur with our fellow-servants; and, alas! unwise stewards make a great many more than there need be by expecting perfection in others, although they do not possess it themselves* [emphasis added]. Our fellow-servants are, after all, wisely selected; for He who put them into His household knew what He was doing; at any rate, they are *His* choice, and not ours. It is not our place to find fault with our Lord's own election.[7]

Humility was fueled by the Savior's love in Spurgeon's life. He knew and lived well on the principle of John 10: *you must love them before you can lead them.* Spurgeon taught other pastors "I have no power but that

---

5. Spurgeon, *All-Round*, 267–69.
6. Spurgeon, *All-Round*, 255.
7. Spurgeon, *All-Round*, 256–57.

which gentleness and love have brought me . . . Self-display is death to power."[8] Again, his life instruction to his Pastors' College men was, "*the less you think of yourself, the more will people think of you; and the more you think of yourself, the less will people think of you* [emphasis mine]."[9]

Spurgeon knew this in his life because he saw God loom large in all areas of his life as a great and gracious Heavenly Father. This attitude learned from Christ made him, as it makes all pastors and all Christians, want to see people grow in Christ and sinners experience such a great salvation. It gave him influence with and effective leadership of his people.

Spurgeon daily understood God's love for him, and he lived in the certitude of its reality. It informed and defined how he treated others. Spurgeon's encouragement to pastors was "You must have a real desire for the good of the people if you are to have much influence over them. Why, even dogs and cats love the people who love them, and human beings are much the same as these dumb animals . . . Do you not notice that men succeed in the ministry, and win souls for Christ, just in proportion as they are men with large hearts?"[10] He further explained and challenged, "When a man has a large, loving heart, men go to him as ships to a haven, and feel at peace when they have anchored under the lee of his friendship. Such a man is hearty in private as well as in public; . . . No pride and selfishness chill you when you approach him; he has his doors all open to receive you, and you are at home with him at once. Such men I would persuade you to be, every one of you."[11] Spurgeon observed that love of children and cheerfulness were the ingredients which made for effective leadership and soul winning abilities; they were a good estimate of character.[12]

All these grace blessings which shape our character into Christ's character come from God. Spurgeon embraced with absolute clarity God must become at home in our hearts and minds; this occurs when we have genuinely committed our lives solely for His kingdom service as Jesus taught us to pray in the Lord's Prayer. "When you are fullest of the fruits of the Spirit bow lowest before the throne, and serve the Lord with fear. 'The Lord our God is a jealous God.' Remember that God has come unto us, not to exalt

---

8. Spurgeon, *All-Round*, 277, 332.
9. Spurgeon, *Soul-Winner*, 80.
10. Spurgeon, *Soul-Winner*, 77–78.
11. Spurgeon, *Lectures*, 169.
12. Spurgeon, *Lectures*, 169–70.

us, but to exalt *himself*, and we must see to it that his glory is the one sole object of all that we do. '*He* must increase, and I must *decrease*.'"¹³

All character comes from knowing God's holiness. Spurgeon held this with conviction and consistently communicated this life principle to his people and especially to his pastor students. His example and instruction were to do as Peter commanded in 2 Pet 3:18, "Grow [i.e. grow and keep on growing] in the grace and knowledge of our Lord Jesus Christ." In his *Lectures to My Students* Spurgeon said,

> We need to know ourselves. The preacher should be great in the science of the heart, the philosophy of inward experience. There are two schools of experience, and neither is content to learn from the other; let us be content, however, to learn from both . . . Know where Adam left you; know where the Spirit of God has placed you. Do not know either of these so exclusively as to forget the other . . . So let us for ever [sic] abide under the sweet influence of Jesus' love. Dwell in God, brethren; do not occasionally visit him, but abide in him . . . Brethren, as the outcome of this, if we are to be strong men, we must be conformed to our Lord. Oh, to be like him! Blessed be that cross on which we shall suffer, if we suffer for being made like unto the Lord Jesus. If we obtain conformity to Christ, we shall have a wondrous unction upon our ministry, and without that, what is a ministry worth?
>
> In a word, we must labor for holiness of character. What is holiness? Is it not wholeness of character? A balanced condition in which there is neither lack nor redundance? It is not morality: that is a cold lifeless statue; holiness is life. You must have holiness; and, dear brethren, if you should fail in mental qualifications (as I hope you will not), and if you should have a slender measure of the oratorical faculty (as I trust you will not), yet, depend upon it, a holy life is, in itself, a wonderful power, and will make up for many deficiencies; it is, in fact, the best sermon the best man can deliver.¹⁴

This personal growth in the pastor brings growth to the members. Growing pastors means growing people. Growing people means growing churches. Spurgeon's conviction was fixed, "The other servants will take their cue from us. A steward, who is dull, inert, and slow, will have a slow team of servants about him, and the business of his lordship will

---

13. Spurgeon, *Lectures*, 203.
14. Spurgeon, *Lectures*, 214–16.

fare badly."[15] Spurgeon drives this home more clearly stating, "A minister soon gets round him people like himself: 'like priest, like people.' Oh, that we may always be alive and earnest in the service of the Lord Jesus, that our people may be alive also! I have read of a Puritan divine, that he was so full of life that his people said he lived like one who fed on live things. Oh, for a life sustained by living bread!"[16]

Such character formation in Christ naturally leads to wanting to see those without His grace be told of, and won to, His redeeming love and power to transform. Spurgeon's passion was his Savior's: "My earnest desire is that all of us may really be—SOUL-WINNERS."[17] Spurgeon participated in evangelism through open air preaching, personal work while riding to and from his meetings, and especially labored this carefully in his pulpit ministries. He was wise to not be locked into any one method for leading his church to reach people for Christ. He taught the same to pastors: "In order to secure this end of gathering around you a band of Christians who will themselves be soul-winners, I should recommend you *not to go to work according to any set rule,* for what would be right at one time might not be wise at another, and that which would be best for one place would not be so good elsewhere."[18] He once commented on methods being used in America (referring to camp meetings) and how thousands were being reached with the gospel. He reflected how it might be done in England and finished by saying: "Not only must *something* be done to evangelize the millions, but *everything* must be done, and perhaps amid variety of effort the best thing would be discovered. 'If by any means I may save some' must be our motto, and this must urge us onward to go forth into the highways and hedges and compel them to come in. Brethren, I speak as unto wise men, consider what I say."[19]

LEADERSHIP: HOW A PASTOR SEES HIMSELF

As seen in this entire story of Spurgeon's life and ministry, Christ was his everything. He sought to honor and obey and know better and better His Master with his life. The attitudes and actions of the Savior were

15. Spurgeon, *All-Round*, 258.
16. Spurgeon, *All-Round*, 258.
17. Spurgeon, *All-Round*, 236.
18. Spurgeon, *Soul Winner*, 128–29.
19. Spurgeon, *Lectures*, 253.

Spurgeon's desire. He, like his hero Paul expressed in Phil 3:8–14, desired to know Christ and make Him known. The passions and aims of Christ informed and guided the leadership practices of Spurgeon.

The Lord Jesus was always in control of situations and people throughout His ministry. He controlled without people feeling it, although it made a huge difference in what was done and experienced. Even in the Garden of Gethsemane when the soldiers and officials from the chief priests and Pharisees came to arrest Him, His person and demeanor caused the soldiers to fall backward in fear. The Bible says Jesus will come back like He left (Acts 1:11). He is coming back to this world on a great white horse to conquer (Rev 19:11–18); He left taking with Him captives and dividing spoils from His victory at Calvary (Eph 4:8).

The only way for our Savior to win was through the grave, i.e., the Cross. It is what He taught as the only way for His followers to win: "take up your cross daily and follow Me" (Luke 14:27). His plan was and is for total and exclusive commitment to Him and His command in our lives. Jesus calls people to follow Him and die to self—lose life for His purposes to find and fulfill the life purpose God has for each. So, Spurgeon, like again his hero Paul, was held by the Cross of Christ. His message "The Three Crosses" from Gal 6:14 gives much insight to his beliefs and understanding of the Cross.

Jesus does call us to our own grave experiences with Him through the Cross, and through this grace experience He does call us to win in life. In the messages to the seven churches in Rev 2–3, it is clear Jesus calls His followers to overcome. Spurgeon knew the conviction of Paul "I can do all things [including how to lead a church to fulfill the Great Commission] through Christ who strengthens me" (Phil 4:13). The instructions and call of the Savior is for His church to move forward, "and the gates of hell shall not prevail against it" (Matt 16:18). This leadership of the Lord and Savior influenced and shaped the leadership Spurgeon practiced and he believed it was what each pastor should practice.

Spurgeon understood the right kind of pastoral leadership as a pastor came by knowing Christ's leadership over his own life. This is what allows a pastor to see himself as Christ sees him; it colors how the pastor will look at himself, his work, his people, his calling in the Great Commission's execution. This kind of leadership means doing the work of the Lord Jesus as a team—pastor and people respecting each other and one another's gifts, worth, and callings. Clearly this is Scripture: God calls His children to serve as a team of believers together as the Savior prayed for us to do just before His going to the Garden of Gethsemane in John 17—that we would be a team like He and the Father and the Holy Spirit are. This understanding of ourselves and others in the body of Christ enables confident pastoral leadership. Spurgeon stated,

> For my part I should loathe to be the pastor of a people who have nothing to say, or who, if they do say anything, might as well be quiet, for the pastor is Lord Paramount, and they are mere laymen and nobodies. I would sooner be the leader of six free men, whose enthusiastic love is my only power over them, than play the dictator to a score of enslaved nations. What position is nobler than that of a spiritual father who claims no authority and yet is universally esteemed, whose word is given only as tender advice, but is allowed to operate with the force of law? Consulting the wishes of others he finds that they first desire to know what he would recommend, and deferring always to the desires of others, he finds that they are glad to defer to him. Lovingly firm and graciously gentle, he is the chief of all because he is the servant of all.[20]

Genuine looking unto Jesus as Scripture directs in Heb 12:1–2 causes the pastor to look at himself as in a race. The passions and pursuits of Jesus become more and more his passions and pursuits. This has a direct impact on his leadership of those God has tasked him to serve and lead. The pastor and people mold together as an army for Christ. This was a prominent feature in the life and work of Spurgeon and the Metropolitan Tabernacle. An example is seen in one of Spurgeon's letters to a Sunday School class,

> Begin by doubling your own numbers, which I believe could be done if you laid it to heart, and resolved each one to introduce, at the least, one newcomer. Make each meeting full of life, power, prayer, love, and zeal . . . Push into the unconquered regions. There ought to be more work done close at home around the Tabernacle. The time for outdoor services will soon be upon us; see what you can do beyond what is yet done. Sunday-schools in many places are pining for want of teachers, and Ragged-schools still more so. Where there is a gap, fill it.[21]

Confident leadership is never cocky, and it is what those serving in the organization desire. They want to be a part of a winning team as Jim

---

20. Spurgeon, *Lectures*, 198.
21. Spurgeon, *Autobiography*, vol. 3, 120.

Collins so ably documented in the outstanding work, *Good to Great*. People understand this requires confidence in those who lead them. It features the consistent practice of respect being exercised in both directions: the leader to people and the people to the leader—motivated by leaders who understand this practice starts with them. This kind of leadership generates united, concerted action. The best companies, the best teams, the best churches practice this. Collins noted great companies were distinct in how people described them: "we were struck by the continual use of words like disciplined, rigorous, dogged, determined, diligent, precise, fastidious, systematic, methodical, workmanlike, demanding, consistent, focused, accountable, and responsible."[22] John Wooden used the adjectives *disciplined, determined, dedicated* to describe the play of his teams at UCLA. His words about leadership and people (in his case players) creating great teams are instructive: "It is not necessary for everyone to particularly like each other to play well together, but they must respect each other and subordinate selfishness to the welfare of the team... Poise and confidence will come from condition, skill, and team spirit."[23] This is what Jesus instructed in His final prayer for the church. Four times He asks the Father to make us one because our fulfilling His Great Commission hinges on our knowing His power and presence which creates teamship (unity) like He and the Father and the Holy Spirit practice. We cannot do His work without practicing His spirit and standards between us as pastor and people. A pastor who knows God and His love intimately sees himself forgiven, graced and called, and so behaves himself toward those he works with. He understands and appreciates the call of God in Micah 6:8: to love mercy, do justly, and walk humbly with God.

The manner in which Spurgeon viewed himself through the eyes of His Lord created the culture of teamship at the Metropolitan Tabernacle. It was especially noted in the leadership of the church—proving the principle of what the members see in the leaders, the members practice themselves. The following gives a glimpse of church life among the leaders at the Tabernacle and how and why Spurgeon was called 'governor' by the elders:

> All my church-officers are in a very real sense my brethren in Christ. In talking to or about one another, we have no stately modes of address. I am called "the Governor," I suppose,

---

22. Collins, *Good to Great*, 127.
23. Wooden, *They Call Me Coach*, 90.

because I do not attempt to govern; and the deacons are known among us as "Brother William," "Uncle Tom," "Dear Old Joe, "Prince Charlie," "Son of Ali," and so on . . . On going into the Tabernacle, one day, I gave directions about some minor alterations that I wished to have made, not knowing at the time that I was canceling the orders given by the deacon who had the main care of the building resting upon him. When he arrived, in the evening, he saw what had been done, and at once asked who had interfered with his instructions. The reply was, "the Governor, sir." The spirit of unquestioning loyalty at once asserted itself over any temporary annoyance he may have felt, and he said, "Quite right; there must be only one captain in a ship;" and, for a long while, that saying became one of our most familiar watchwords. I have often been amazed, at the devotion of our brethren; I have told them, many a time, that, if they would follow a broomstick as they have followed me, the work must succeed. To which Mr. William Olney, as the spokesman for the rest, has answered, "Yes, dear Pastor; but it is because we have such absolute confidence in your leadership that we are ready to follow you anywhere. You have never misled us yet, and we do not believe you ever will do so."[24]

The Metropolitan Tabernacle had both deacons and elders. Spurgeon believed from his study of Scripture both officers were needed in the church. Shortly after coming to New Park Street in 1854, he began to teach from the Scriptures of the two offices in the church. He didn't rush the change on the church as the office of elders was not launched until 1859. Spurgeon said, "I did not force the question upon them I only showed them that it was Scriptural, and then of course they wanted to carry it into effect."[25]

The way Spurgeon viewed himself colored how he viewed these men and their work. The fraternity of dedication, discipline, accountability, and respect was very apparent in the work and attitudes of these leaders at the Tabernacle. Spurgeon shared,

> I have always made it a rule to consult the existing officers of the church before recommending the election of new deacons or elders, and I have also been on the lookout for those who have proved their fitness for office by the work they have accomplished in their private capacity . . .

---

24. Spurgeon, *Autobiography*, vol. 3, 20–21.
25. Spurgeon, *Autobiography*, vol. 3, 22.

> My elders have been a great blessing to me; they are invaluable in looking after the spiritual interests of the church. The deacons have charge of the finance; but if the elders meet with cases of poverty needing relief, we tell them to give some small sum, and then bring the case before the deacons. I was once the unseen witness of a little incident that greatly pleased me. I heard one of our elders say to a deacon, "I gave old Mrs. So-and-so ten shillings the other night." "That was very generous on your part," said the deacon. "Oh, but!" exclaimed the elder, "I want the money from the deacons." So the deacon asked, "What office do you hold, brother? Oh!" he replied, "I see; I have gone beyond my duty as an elder, so I'll pay the ten shillings myself; I should not like 'the Governor' to hear that I had overstepped the mark." "No, no, my brother," said the deacon; "I'll give you the money, but don't make such a mistake another time."[26]

Spurgeon explained how the elders of the Tabernacle were active in the spiritual concerns of the membership and the deacons saw to the fiscal policies and needs of the church. The elders were models of soul-winning and disciple-making. They were instrumental in leading people to Christ following the close of the worship services. Their involvement and leadership in establishing mission posts in other parts of South London and beyond led to many of these efforts becoming autonomous churches. They emulated the zeal of their pastor for Christ and souls. The deacons maintained comparable values and practices. Spurgeon's conviction and confidence from Scripture on leadership was this: "In some way or other, the Lord will make a holy life to be an influential life. It is not possible that a life which can be described as a following of Christ should be an unsuccessful one in the sight of the Most High. 'Follow Me,' and there is an 'I will' such as God can never draw back from: 'Follow Me, and I will make you fishers of men.'"[27]

Spurgeon was resolute in a pastor's responsibility to be zealous in the Lord's work. He knew its benefit as recorded about Baruch in Neh 3:20. Spurgeon understood it was necessary to inspire others in the Lord's harvest calling; he knew without it pastors would not motivate others for the Savior's work. He said, "It is an unhappy thing that there should be men calling themselves ministers of Christ to whom it never seems to occur that they are bound to display the utmost industry and zeal. They

---

26. Spurgeon, *Autobiography*, vol. 3, 23.
27. Spurgeon, *Soul-Winner*, 287.

seem to forget that they are dealing with souls that may be lost for ever [sic] or saved for ever, souls that cost the Saviour's heart's blood. They do not appear to have understood the nature of their calling, or to have grasped the Scriptural idea of an ambassador for Christ."[28]

This zeal was not anything short of the Spirit of God. It was not something worked up in the strength of the flesh. Spurgeon said, "Zeal,—what is it? How shall I describe it? Possess it, and you will know what it is. Be consumed with love for Christ, and let the flame burn continuously; not flaming up at public meetings, and dying out in the routine work of every day."[29] He asserted zeal and earnestness and heart were from Christ and by faith in Him: "Serve God with all your might while the candle is burning, and then when it goes out for a season, you will have the less to regret. Be content to be nothing, for that is what you are. When your own emptiness is painfully forced upon your consciousness, chide yourself that you ever dreamed of being full, except in the Lord."[30]

As Paul told Timothy, so Spurgeon told and taught pastors; you must stir up the gifts placed in you by God. They are there but a pastor must cooperate with God for them to mature and become usable. Earnestness, enthusiasm, zeal are all gifts from God and only from God. Spurgeon taught his Pastors' College men: "Remembering then, dear brethren, that we must be in earnest, and that we cannot counterfeit earnestness, or find a substitute for it, and that it is very easy for us to lose it, let us consider for a while the ways and means for retaining all our fervor and gaining more . . . and I know of but one—the flame of the love of Christ."[31] How can this be experienced and possessed in a the pastor's life? Spurgeon's counsel was, "*Feed the flame, my brother, feed it frequently;* feed it with holy thought and contemplation, especially with thought about your work, . . . the helps that are waiting for you, and the grand results of it if the Lord be with you. Dwell much upon the love of God to sinners, and the death of Christ on their behalf, and the work of the Spirit upon men's hearts."[32] The work of ministry is never to be attempted with half-heartedness. The command of our Savior is to love God with all our hearts. Spurgeon encouraged, "Brethren, we must wait upon God continually.

---

28. Spurgeon, *All-Round Ministry*, 163.
29. Spurgeon, *All-Round Ministry*, 49.
30. Spurgeon, *Lectures*, 164.
31. Spurgeon, *Lectures*, 313.
32. Spurgeon, *Lectures*, 314.

The habit of going to Him for our orders must be cultivated . . . We must be serious as death in this solemn work."[33]

Such zeal and earnestness and enthusiasm if truly of God will be considerate, honest, and forthright in communicating truth, not just in the pulpit, but perhaps even more importantly, in personal communications. Spurgeon's encouragement and challenge to pastors was, "May you also possess *the grand moral characteristic of courage!* By this, I do not mean impertinence, impudence, or self-conceit; but real courage to do and say calmly the right thing, . . . I am astonished at the number of' Christians who are afraid to speak the truth to their brethren."[34] No leader, especially the pastor, will have the respect of people if they cannot speak honestly, face-to-face when it's needed. John Maxwell conducted Leadership conferences for pastors across America in the 1980's and 1990's. He discovered in working with hundreds of pastors that 95% of these leaders would not caringly confront someone in the church membership or church leadership team when needed.[35]

A key means Satan uses to kill holy confidence in pastors is getting them to compare themselves with themselves. At the close of our Savior's time on earth, He had to counsel his disciples not to compare themselves with one another. His departing words to Peter were to keep his eyes on Him. He helped Peter by teaching him it was not *his love* that would see him through, but *the object of his love*. He could not have this focus while comparing himself with others. Many pastors fall short because they compare themselves too often and too much with another pastor on the Master's team. Spurgeon always believed in being himself, and he encouraged the same to pastors:

> When each of us was made, the mould was broken;—a very satisfactory circumstance in the case of some men, and I greatly question whether it is not an advantage, in the case of us all. If we are, however, vessels for the Master's use, we ought to have no choice about what vessel we may be. There was a cup which stood upon the communion table when our Lord ate that passover which He had so desired to eat with His disciples before He suffered; and, assuredly, that cup was honored when it was put to His lips, and then passed to the apostles. Who would not be like that cup? But there was a basin also which the Master took,

---

33. Spurgeon, *All-Round*, 260, 272.
34. Spurgeon, *All-Round*, 48.
35. Maxwell, "Confrontation in Pastoral Leadership", 1991.

into which He poured water, and washed the disciples' feet. I protest that I have no choice whether to be the chalice or the basin. Fain would I be whichever the Lord wills so long as He will but use me. But this is plain,—the cup would have made a very insufficient basin, and the basin would have been a very improper cup for the communion feast. So you, my brother, may be the cup, and I will be the basin; but let the cup be a cup, and the basin a basin, and each one of us just what he is fitted to be. Be yourself, dear brother, for, if you are not yourself, you cannot be anybody else; and so, you see, you must be nobody.[36]

Spurgeon's perspective on himself grew directly out of what he saw His Savior seeing in Him. This grew in him an opinion and perspective of his fellow man, especially his own church members. This guided his vision and gave him the faith to believe God for the humanly impossible because he did not see things through a human perspective only. He was, through grace and the Scripture's lenses, able to look at God and his world and his church and see a harvest of souls reachable because Christ had purchased and prepared them for His call to redemption and relationship with Himself. This drove Spurgeon and became his life purpose, passion, and power; it made (and makes) him a helpful servant of Christ to learn from.

By studying and learning from what God taught Spurgeon, the pastor and the church leader can be inspired, guided, and encouraged. We each will be able to see more clearly and understand more confidently what must be done and how the work should be carried out. Our churches will be strengthened and be made more fruitful in our Savior's work and honor. This is help that each pastor, church leader, and church can be eternally grateful for and gladdened over.

HOW A PASTOR SEES HIS CHURCH (HIS ECCLESIOLOGY)

The challenge of leading a church family to follow the Savior and grow by means of conversions and disciple-making is a challenging assignment. It is desired by pastors and members, but not easily achieved. The work takes time as Spurgeon counseled his Pastors' College men. The church in Jerusalem as studied in Acts grew seemingly overnight, but Jesus and others had painstakingly laid the groundwork for three years.

36. Spurgeon, *All-Round*, 73.

It is important to observe the presence of persecution in this phenomenal growth; persecution has been normative throughout church history when churches have grown and spread rapidly.

A key reason why churches do not grow is that the nature of the church and its individual members has been misunderstood as noted in the prior chapter under "Priesthood of the Believer." It is a widely established principle in any kind of leadership work that what a leader sees in others, i.e., how associates are viewed, largely determines the kind and amount of work produced. There are leadership and coaching skills involved with this, but the perception of the people's potential on the part of the leader always impacts what happens. A pastor or church leader with real faith in God will communicate a real hope to the members for their potential. The maxim is true: a Godly leader, like his Savior, sees people for what they can become, not just for what they are.

A prime reason for churches being plateaued is because pastors do the work of the ministry and missions alone without engaging the members into the work alongside them. Because the pastor does much of the work of the church himself, he defaults to a maintenance ministry instead of a missional equipping work. Some of this has been affected by theological training in schools which has stressed maintaining doctrine without balancing training in missions and leadership. Donald McGavran shared,

> During my lifetime I have served as a faculty member in nine theological seminaries. I have lectured in many more and met many fellow theological professors in several continents. Though I have never done a careful research on the subject, I believe that I am correct when I state that most theological training schools do not count evangelism or church growth an essential part of their curricula. In a few schools a two- or four-hour course on evangelism is an elective. In many, however, no course on effective evangelism [and the leadership skills for it to be carried out] is offered.[37]

McGavran went on to explain this had largely come about through following a Reformation response of evangelical theological training which was strongly biased toward defending the faith. They did not want to see doctrines compromised and redemption relegated to a works salvation practice. But the focus was not balanced with courses for the advancement of the kingdom of Christ through Great Commission leadership training.

---

37. McGavran, *Effective Evangelism*, 1.

Jesus modeled what needs to be the perception of the pastor towards his members. He staked His entire kingdom on guys who blew their tempers, spoke without thinking, and some were so shy they were never recorded to have said anything in the Gospels. Jesus saw what could be done in lives through the impact of grace afforded through the Cross. He knew the human heart longed to be connected with God and would grow and change to become more capable of bearing His fruit with time and encouragement.

This same perspective marked Spurgeon in how he viewed his own church and what he could see in them for kingdom expansion. In his final message delivered to the annual College Conference, later published as *The Greatest Fight in the World*, Spurgeon told the gathered pastors there were three key matters: "(1) *our armory*, the Word of God; (2) *our army*, the Church of God; and (3) *our strength*, the Holy Spirit."[38] He viewed and prayed and worked to see his church be an active army winning spiritual victories in Christ's name for Christ's cause. He saw their potential if wisely loved, encouraged, equipped, and engaged for Christ's service.

Such thinking and life perspective was generated from the gospel Spurgeon believed in. At the end of his life, Spurgeon stated to the pastors gathered to hear him one last time, "The very root of holiness lies in the gospel of our Lord Jesus Christ; and if this be removed with a view to more fruitfulness, the most astounding folly will have been committed. We have seen a fine morality, a stern integrity, a delicate purity, and, what is more, a devout holiness, produced by the doctrines of grace."[39] This kind of confidence he instilled into and taught his people so they could grow and invest the Word in others: "It was neither human reasoning, nor the force of eloquence, nor the power of moral suasion, but the omnipotence of the Spirit, applying the Word itself, that gave you rest and peace and joy through believing. We are ourselves trophies of the power of the sword of the Spirit; he leads us in triumph in every place, the willing captives of his grace."[40]

There is no clearer presentation and explaining of Spurgeon's life perspective of the local church than what he preached in a sermon delivered to his Metropolitan Tabernacle church family in 1869. Carefully read the following taking into view the scope of what has been shared

---

38. Spurgeon, *Autobiography*, vol. 4, 314
39. Spurgeon, *Greatest Fight*, 16.
40. Spurgeon, *Greatest Fight*, 18.

of Spurgeon's upbringing, conversion, early experiences and what he invested into the Pastors' College men as to their mission, values, and vision. What Spurgeon gives here defines the attitude a pastor needs to have toward his members to see them used of God to fulfill their life mission assigned by Jesus. This offers the core of Spurgeon's beliefs for accomplishing the Great Commission; it is his defining what 2 Tim 2:2 should look like in and through the local church:

> We ought to regard the Christian Church, not as a luxurious hostelry where Christian gentlemen may each one dwell at his ease in his own inn, but *as a barracks in which soldiers are gathered together to be drilled and trained for war. We should regard the Christian Church, not as an association for mutual admiration and comfort, but as an army with banners, marching to the fray, to achieve victories for Christ, to storm the strongholds of the foe, and to add province after province to the Redeemer's kingdom. We may view converted persons gathered into church-membership as so much wheat in the granary. God be thanked that it is there, and that so far the harvest has rewarded the sower; but far more soul-inspiring is the view when we regard those believers as each one likely to be made a living center for the extension of the kingdom of Jesus, for then we see them sowing the fertile valleys of our land, and promising ere long to bring forth some thirty, some forty, some fifty, and some a hundredfold. The capacities of life are enormous* [emphasis added]), one becomes a thousand in a marvelously brief space. Within a short time, a few grains of wheat would suffice to seed the whole world, and a few true saints might suffice for the conversion of all nations. Only take that which comes of one ear, store it well, sow it all, again store it next year, and then sow it all again, and the multiplication almost exceeds the power of computation. Oh, that every Christian were thus year by year the Lord's seed corn! If all the wheat in the world had perished except a single grain, it would not take many years to replenish all the earth, and sow her fields and plains; but in a far shorter time, in the power of the Holy Spirit, one Paul or one Peter would have evangelized all lands. View yourselves as grains of wheat predestinated to seed the world. That man lives grandly who is as earnest as if the very existence of Christianity depended upon himself, and is determined that to all men within his reach shall be made known the unsearchable riches of Christ[41]

---

41. Spurgeon, *Soul-Winner*, 204–5

Notice Spurgeon states how a pastor should view his church. It is to be seen as an army, marching forward into Christ's harvest and gaining victories, i.e., taking souls out of Satan's club and placing them into the company of the committed to Christ. Spurgeon places before us the reality of the capabilities of the members to multiply disciples as they are led by pastors to make disciple-making disciples per the Great Commission. He gives the call to Christians to see themselves predestined by God to Christianize their communities through spreading the gospel; this requires their pastors to see them as such.

Spurgeon was so deeply impacted by the gospel personally he looked at other Christians as having the same opportunities of grace and calling from the Lord Jesus. He stated, "We claim no priesthood over and above that which belongs to every child of God."[42] He viewed himself as a priest of the Lord knowing he had a calling to fulfill, and he took the same view toward his members because he understood from Scripture, they were priests of Jesus Christ just as well. So, he led them as such.

Spurgeon seeing the church body as servants of Jesus Christ and calling them an "army" came directly from Scripture. Paul writes describing the Christian's attitude and daily discipline being that of a soldier in Eph 6:10–20. He writes this encouragement to Timothy, his younger associate, instructing him to develop pastor leaders through the Ephesus church ministry as soldiers leading soldiers (2 Tim 2:1–7). A true spiritual battle was taking place. This thinking of pastoring guided Spurgeon throughout his leadership of the Metropolitan Tabernacle. In 1860, as they anticipated moving into the new building, he wrote to his church family this pastoral letter:

> Comrades in battle, we are also co-heirs of victory. May the Lord, whom I serve in the gospel of His Son, abundantly bless you, and return into your bosoms a thousand-fold those acts of love, and those words of affection, by which you so perpetually prove your earnest attachment to me! Never had pastor a better flock; never did a minister more sincerely long for the good of his people. And now, brethren, suffer the word of exhortation which I address to you: . . . [then he wrote regarding the elders and the church members] Rally round the officers of our little army, and submit yourselves to their guidance and counsel. Let every member know the elder who presides over his district; and should that brother fail to visit him, let the member visit the

---

42. Spurgeon, *Lectures*, 186–87.

elder, and remind him that he has overlooked one of the sheep of his flock. *Endeavor to maintain meetings for prayer in each district of this great city; and if there be a door for other agencies, use them to the utmost of your ability. Each district, with its elder should be a regiment with its officer; and then all the different bands, when called to united action, would be ready to achieve an easy victory* [emphasis added].[43]

Interestingly the last sentence above reveals there was a ministry strategy like what Paul Cho and Ceaser Costellanos utilized nearly a century later in their respective cell group vision strategies. This quote from Spurgeon reveals the fraternity, the accountability, the excitement and enthusiasm of being in service together under Christ as a church. It presents encouragement as to why the local church can and should be viewed as an army for Christ by pastors. What we read in the book of Acts, throughout church history (such as Moravians and the Methodist movement under Wesley and Asbury), and in our current generation (such testimonies Ying Kai and Steve Smith reporting in their 2011 book *T4T: A Discipleship ReRevolution*—the report of God saving one million and seven hundred thousand souls and planting over one hundred and fifty thousand churches from 2001–11 in southeast Asia) where Great Commission movements have occurred through everyday Christians being seen by their leaders, and seeing themselves, as called ambassadors for Christ. God taught Spurgeon this attitude about himself and his people—to be soldiers of the Cross: "We labor to hold forth the cross of Christ with a bold hand among the sons of men, because that cross holds us fast by its attractive power. Our desire is, that every man may hold the truth, and be held by it; especially the truth of Christ crucified."[44]

VISION: HOW A PASTOR SEES HIS WORLD (THE HARVEST)

It was a special privilege God allowed me to study at Liberty University and Liberty School of Divinity from 1973–80. Attending chapels at school and church services at Thomas Road Baptist Church gave repeated opportunities to hear Dr. Jerry Falwell Sr. He constantly held before us the understanding "The difference between mediocrity and greatness

---

43. Spurgeon, *Autobiography*, vol. 2, 306–7.
44. Spurgeon, *Autobiography*, vol. 2, 150.

is vision." One other axiom constantly affirmed to all students was "You do not determine a person's greatness by what they know or what they possess, but what it takes to discourage them"; this referred directly to the prior perspective considered. Eleven years after finishing work at Liberty and completing work at Southwestern Seminary and a dissertation on Spurgeon, it struck me how many parallels were apparent in the ministries of Charles Haddon Spurgeon and Jerry Falwell: passion for Christ and souls, impact beyond their local Jerusalem, and training institutions producing leaders for Christ's cause around the world. They both were familiar with the Savior.

When a pastor's heart and eyes are guided by Scripture and shaped by the Holy Spirit to see God properly, it causes him to see his harvest field with eyes of faith. By looking to Jesus, a pastor takes on the burden of Jesus for the lost. How much we see and know God in our hearts will be revealed in our passion for the lost. This drives a pastor to have vision—and is accompanied by a believing faith it can be done. This is our Jesus: "I have come to seek and to save that which is lost." Isa 6:1–8 presents this truth.

The pastor who knows God also knows man. It is often in life, and Christ's work is no exception, that a vision movement will need to be started by a single person—in this case, the pastor. He must believe God and the vision He has put in his heart when others do not. Other believers will question its validity, but a pastor must be confident in God's ability to bring about the vision through faithful obedience. Spurgeon's counsel is this:

> Very likely you will have almost everything to do in connection with the work; at all events, expect that it may be so, and then you will not be disappointed if it so turns out. It may be otherwise; but you will be wise if you go into the ministry expecting not to find any very great assistance from the people in the work of soul-winning. Anticipate that you will have to do it yourself and to do it alone; and begin doing it alone, sow the seed, tramp up and down the field, always looking to the Lord of the harvest to bless your labour, and also looking forward to the time when through your efforts, under the divine blessing, instead of a plot of land that is apparently covered with nettles, or full of stones, or weeds, or thorns, or partly trodden down, you shall have a well-tilled farm in which you may sow the seed to the best advantage, and on which you shall have a little army of fellow-labourers to aid you in the service. Yet all that is the work of time.[45]

---

45. Spurgeon, *Soul-Winner*, 127–28.

A great Christ-honoring dream and enthusiasm birthed from God will draw others to join in its execution. Spurgeon did not agree with small thinking on the part of pastors in relation to the Great Commission call of our Savior. He stated,

> It is essential that we should exhibit faith in the form of *confidence in God* . . . Go in for great things, brethren, in the Name of God; risk everything on His promise, and according to your faith shall it be done unto you.
>
> The common policy of our churches is that of great prudence. We do not, as a rule, attempt anything beyond our strength. We measure means, and calculate possibilities with economical accuracy; then we strike off a large discount for contingencies, and a still larger percentage as provision for our ease, and *so we accomplish little because we have no idea of doing much* [emphasis added].[46]

The attitude he encouraged pastors to live in toward the Great Commission call of the Savior was "Brethren, be filled with a great ambition; not for yourselves, but for your Lord. Elevate your ideal! Have no more firing at the bush. You may, in this case, shoot at the sun himself; for you will be sure to shoot higher, if you do so, than if some grovelling object were your aim. Believe for great things of a great God."[47] This requires courage and confidence which only comes for knowing God properly as we've discussed, but the possibilities for Christ's work are beyond what we can think or imagine: "Who knows but what thou art come to the kingdom for such a time as this? If thou hast grit in thee, quit thyself like a man. If thou hast God in thee, then thou mayest yet do marvels."[48]

In Spurgeon's message on Matt 9:36–38 reveals how he gave confidence and conviction to his people to go with their Savior into His harvest fields:

> He said to his disciples, "Lift up now your eyes, behold the fields are white already to the harvest." Now, when people are ready to hear the word, then it is that the fields are ripe; and our Lord meant that as the wheat ears do not oppose the sickle, but stand there, and a man has but to enter into the field, and use the sickle, and the result will surely follow, so there are times when nothing is wanted but to preach the gospel, and the souls which

---

46. Spurgeon, *All-Round*, 184–85.
47. Spurgeon, *All-Round*, 360.
48. Spurgeon, *All-Round*, 361.

otherwise would perish, will surely be ingathered. *I do not believe, my brethren, that at any time the world has had a dull ear to the gospel . . . He bids us know that though God could reap his harvest without men, he will not do it.* Could he not bring forth a spiritual reaping machine? Modern invention has done this for the farmer, and the same idea could be carried out in spiritual things, and so thousands would be converted in an hour without human agency. *But the Lord asks for no such inventions, he does not direct us to ask for spiritual reaping machines, but to pray the Master to send laborers into the harvest.* [It is to be life-on-life; this is God's way to fulfill the Great Commission through Great Commandment living: lives changed by grace influencing lives by that same grace] . . . *"Pray ye," that is the stress of the whole text—"Pray ye therefore the Lord of the harvest, that He would thrust forth laborers into his harvest," that these fields may not rot before our eyes. Will ye pray it, my brethren? This text is laid on my heart; it lies more on my heart than any other in the Bible; it is one that haunts me perpetually, and has done* [so] *for many years* [emphasis added].[49]

God calls pastors to lead His people to do the works of Christ. The pastor must have vision to cast vision. What he sees and what he models will become the people's vision and work. Prov 29:18 is true, "Without a vision, the people perish"—*inside the church and outside*. A pastor should look at his community as his and his membership's responsibility to reach for Christ. Could not he and his army of believers aim to see 10 percent of their harvest field brought to Christ through their direct efforts? As Spurgeon said, aiming higher we cannot be discouraged more by the results than from aiming lower. Such vision thinking and faith would involve starting other churches as leaders are raised and called out. Spurgeon shared his own vision for South London where the Metropolitan Tabernacle was located:

> God sparing my life, if I have my people at my back, I will not rest until the dark county of Surrey is covered with places of worship. I look on this Tabernacle as only the beginning; within the last six months, we have started two churches,—one in Wandsworth and the other in Greenwich, and the Lord has prospered them, the pool of baptism has often been stirred with converts. And what we have done in two places, I am about to do in a third, and we will do it, not for the third or the fourth,

---

49. Spurgeon, *Treasury of the Bible*, vol. 5, 156–59.

but for the hundredth time, God being our Helper. I am sure I may make my strongest appeal to my brethren, because we do not mean to build this Tabernacle as our nest, and then to be idle. We must go from strength to strength, and be a missionary church, and never rest until, not only this neighborhood, but our country, of which it is said that some parts are as dark as India, shall have been enlightened with the gospel.[50]

As revealed in this book, Spurgeon loved Calvin and claimed himself a Calvinistic Baptist. But he always learned a hot heart and passionate mind from Christ which steeled the eyes of his soul to the Great Commission. He, as his Savior, was riveted to this work. His passion was as the Savior's: "As the Father has sent me, so send I you" (John 20:21).

Vison, faith, a growing church, and dreaming are all challenging when churches are flat-lined. Non-growth is the experience of most churches. How do we face the challenge of wanting growth when the reality is—it's not happening? This book was written in part to answer this question. The encouragement, faith, and confidence Spurgeon learned from Jesus Christ is also ours. It will be learned the same way Spurgeon did—by seeking God with all our hearts and studying all we can to know Scripture and wisdom to apply it faithfully and wisely. We will need to fellowship with Godly leaders and workers passionate for Christ and His work. What God has taught others, He can teach us. He also uses those He has taught His Scriptures in seeing lives changed and churches added to and multiplied to teach us how to see the same.

There will always be tension between faith and works, between sovereignty and human responsibility—because we are in the mix. But we have so great a Coach to play under on this heaven-sent team. Scripture teaches we are colaborers with Christ and we team up with Him in this divine calling and work called the Great Commission—always recognizing secretly and publicly without Him we can do nothing. But we live in the constant assurance He is always at work and His love towards us and those around us never diminishes nor loses its potency. Spurgeon told his Pastors' College men, "Cling to the two great collateral truths of Divine Sovereignty and Human Responsibility. Live near to God, and love the souls of men."[51]

---

50. Spurgeon, *Autobiography*, vol. 2, 329.
51. Spurgeon, *Autobiography*, vol. 3, 155.

Conclusion

ALL OF US NEED a template, an example to follow to get it right in whatever endeavor we undertake. Research institutions and the field of psychology have documented the influence and impact upon us by those we associate with; it is a definite warning and encouragement emphasized in Proverbs. In life and in ministry we need wise and proven patterns to learn from and be helped by. Charles Spurgeon was not perfect, but his life and ministry work afford us a biblically dedicated and fruitful example of the Savior's calling to help us better follow, honor, and serve our Wonderful Counselor and Mighty God in the particular roles and responsibilities He has called each of us to fulfill.

It was repeated many times over my academic and ministry pilgrimage by different leaders, "You are a product of the people you meet and the books you read." These are pivotal influences upon our lives and perspectives, and factor significantly into the efforts we put forth in Christ's work. In all my classes I constantly kept in mind who was teaching the subject being studied. I wanted to understand and discern the professor's ministry experience and the character and integrity he brought to the course discipline. Studying Spurgeon and the church families he served can give us understanding and wisdom in our Lord's ways and work to know how to be effective representations of Him and disciple makers for Him which can set in motion the multiplying principles of 2 Tim 2:2 in our lives and ministries.

The life of being a Christ-follower, especially a leader in the Christian ministry, is challenging. There is the discouragement of our own flesh, external distractions of the world around us, and the persistent deception work of Satan to keep us spiritual dwarfs and spiritually impotent for our Savior's work. What is so great about our salvation is that we carry out our Christian experience under the greatest Coach who has ever lived! There are very few instances in sports history where a coach was found to be able to always win at any school he or she coached at. Our Savior is always able to coach us to victory in every setting, situation, and circumstance. He knows exactly where and how we can best serve Him and others, and will guide us for this. He wants to make each of His servants effective and productive in His harvest fields (John 15:16); our great Savior doesn't want any of His followers (players) sitting on the sidelines.

Spurgeon's words "If He had not chosen me, I would have never chosen Him" come right out of John 15:16: "you did not choose me, but I chose you and appointed you so that you might go and bear fruit—fruit that will last—and so that whatever you ask in my name the Father will give you." The verses which precede verse sixteen make clear we can only bear fruit as we stay close to the Savior with our lives. In John 14–17, Jesus made definite the condition of our being fruitful was our having a love affair with Him. Spurgeon gives us a faithful template to understand how this takes place in our lives. His life and ministry explain and encourages a sure and simple love relationship with Jesus as the foundation for experiencing fruitfulness for Jesus. Jesus made this principle clear in Mark 3:14: He appoints us first to be with Him before we can be effective for Him. Spurgeon's example and work gives a clear path to knowing how to accomplish the Savior's work with fellow believers to multiply disciples and more leaders for the Savior's service. Our Savior is always about others; He never wants a ministry to be dependent or focused on just a single individual—He is always about developing others and increasing His kingdom through more leaders being raised up.

Like our Savior and also like Spurgeon, we must see the potential in those we serve in His church. In order for pastors and churches to see the fruit of multiplying disciples and kingdom leaders, and to see more churches started, there must be the continuing belief that Christ is calling and wants to use His people (those sitting in our pews) to do this! In coaching, this is referred to as positive self-talk. "It has been said that the most intimate and influential messages come from what we say to ourselves. Because this is so and because performance is initiated by self-talk it becomes very apparent that controlling self-talk is essential to a positive performance. It is also apparent that if our self-talk is negative [or in error] our performance will suffer."[1] Jesus said we make all mistakes in Christianity from not correctly knowing Scripture and from not knowing God's power, i.e., the Holy Spirit's filling us—which comes from rightly applying Scripture to our lives (Matt 22:29). Spurgeon can be an assistant coach to the Savior in helping pastors and church leaders to get it right on both, i.e., knowing the Savior and knowing His Word effectively applied to our lives and to the lives of those we serve. If we are following Him and His instructions, the work we participate in will always be about others in a holy, life-giving way.

We all need the benefit of steady, sure, and proven coaching/mentoring in following and serving our Savior. Spurgeon can be a trusted friend for this help. The Spurgeonic principles are applicable for today. His understanding of needful practices to develop leaders for Christ's work through a farm system are effective and proven. They need to be practiced more in Christendom. They are unthought of, at least to the degree Spurgeon embraced them, by many (maybe correctly said "most") Christian leaders and churches. They enable focused attention and commitment to Scripture's directives. As we apply them to our ministries and develop them more through God's grace and leading, pastors and churches will see more men and women, boys and girls brought to Christ and developed into leaders for His kingdom.

Spurgeon helps us understand how to carry out the calling and business of our Lord and Savior. He provides a rich resource for churches to draw assistance from and be encouraged by to see Christ's purposes carried out: "Then Jesus came to them and said, 'All authority in heaven and on earth has been given to me. Therefore, go and make disciples of all nations, baptizing them in the name of the Father and of the Son and of the Holy Spirit, and teaching them to obey everything I have commanded you. And surely, I am with you always, to the very end of the age.'" (Matt 28:18–20)

---

1. Vernacchia et al., *Coaching Mental Excellence*, 75.

Bibliography

Bacon, Earnest W. *Spurgeon: Heir of Puritans*. London: Allen & Unwin, 1967.
Bailey, Ivar. "The Challenge of Change; A Study of Relevance Versus Authority in the Victorian Pulpit." *Expository Times* 86 (1974): 18–22.
Carlisle, J[ohn] C. *Charles H. Spurgeon*. London: The Religious Tract Society & Kingsgate, 1933.
Collins, Jim. *Good to Great*. New York: HarperCollins, 2001.
Conwell, Russell H[erman]. *Life of Charles H. Spurgeon*. Boston: Hastings, 1892.
Cook, Richard Briscoe. *The Wit and Wisdom of Charles H. Spurgeon*. Baltimore: R. H. Woodword & Co., 1892.
Craig, Jim, et al. *Miracle* ESPN Roundtable with Linda Cohn, 2004.
Dallimore, Arnold. *C. H. Spurgeon*. Chicago: Moody, 1984.
Day, Richard Ellsworth. *Shadow of Broad Brim*. Philadelphia: Judson, 1934.
Douglas, James. *Prince of Preachers*. London: Morgan & Scott, n.d.
Engel, James F. and Norton, H. Wilbert. *What's Gone Wrong with Harvest? A Communication Strategy for the Church and World Evangelism*. Grand Rapids: Zondervan, 1975.
Fant, Clyde E., Jr., and Pinson, William J. *20 Centuries of Great Preaching*. 13 vols. Waco: Word, 1971.
Fisher, George Park. *History of Christian Church*. New York: Charles Scribner's and Sons, 1897.
Fullerton, Y. C. *C. H. Spurgeon*. London: Williams & Norgate, 1920.
Glover, Willis B. *Evangelical Nonconformists and Higher Criticism in the 19th Century*. London: Independent, 1954.
Harte, G. W. *Historical Tablets of the College Founded by Charles Haddon Spurgeon*. Southport, Eng: Thomas Seddon, 1951.
Hayden, Eric W. *A Centennial History of Spurgeon's Tabernacle*. Pasadena, TX.: Pilgrim Publications, 1971.

Hendricks, Howard and Hendricks, William. *Iron Sharpens Iron*. Chicago: Moody, 1995.

Hope, Eva. *Spurgeon: The People's Preacher*. London: Walter Scott, n.d.

Johnson, W. Charles. *Encounter in London: The Story of the London B. Association, 1865–1965*. London: Carey Kingsport, 1965.

Lewis, Peter. *The Genius of Puritanism*. Haywards Heath, Sussex: Carey, 1975.

Livingston, James C. *Modern Christian Thought: From the Enlightenment to Vatican II*. New York: Macmillan, 1971.

Lorimer, George C. *C. H. Spurgeon*. Boston: James H. Earle, 1892.

Maxwell, John. "Confrontation in Pastoral Leadership." Keynote address, Bootcamp Pastors' Conference, Euless, TX, May 13–15, 1991.

McBeth, H. Leon, *The Baptist Heritage*. Nashville: Broadman, 1987.

McCarty, Doran. "The Serving Example of Jesus." Devotional presentation, annual meeting of the Association of Ministry Guidance Professionals, San Antonio, TX, July 27–29, 2011.

McGavran, Donald Anderson. *Effective Evangelism: A Theological Mandate*. Phillipsburg, New Jersey: Presbyterian and Reformed, 1988.

———. *Understanding Church Growth*. Grand Rapids: Eerdmans, 1980.

Needham, George Carter. *The Life and Labors of Charles H. Spurgeon*. Boston: D. L. Guernsey, 1882.

Nicoll, Wm. Robertson. *Princes of the Church*. London: Hodder & Stoughton, 1921.

Nicholls, Michael. "Charles Haddon Spurgeon Educationalist; Part 1: General Education Concerns." *Baptist Quarterly* 31 (1986): 384–401.

———. "Charles Haddon Spurgeon Educationalist; Part 2: The Principle and Practices of the Pastors' College." *Baptist Quarterly* 32 (1987): 73–94.

Northrop, Henry Davenport. *Life and Works of Charles Haddon Spurgeon*. Chicago: Monarch, 1890.

Payne, Ernest A. *The Baptist Union–A Short History*. London: Carey Kingsgate, 1959.

———. *The Free Church Tradition in the Life of England*. 3rd ed., rev. London: S.C.M., 1951.

Pike, G. Holden. *Life and Works of Charles H. Spurgeon*. 6 vols. London: Cassell, n.d.

Poole-Conner, Rev. E. J. *Evangelicalism in England*. New Rev. ed., with a foreword by D. Martyn Lloyd-Jones. Worthing, Sussex: Walter, 1966.

Ray, Charles. *Life of Charles Haddon Spurgeon*. Introduction by Thomas Spurgeon. London: Passmore & Alabaster, 1903.

Robinson, Darrell W. *Total Church Life*. Revised and expanded edition, with a foreword by Billy Graham. Nashville: Broadman, 1993.

Ryken, Leland. *Worldly Saints: The Puritans as They Really Were*. Grand Rapids: Zondervan, 1986.

Scarborough, Lee Rutland. *Recruits for World Conquests*. Fort Worth, Tx: Southwestern Baptist Theological Seminary, 1914.

Shindler, R. *From the Usher's Desk to the Tabernacle Pulpit; The Life and Labors of Charles Haddon Spurgeon*. New York: A. C. Armstrong and Son, 1892.

Skinner, Craig. *Lamplighter and Son*. Nashville: Broadman, 1984.

Spurgeon, Charles Haddon. *An All-Round Ministry*. Pasadena, TX: Pilgrim, 1973.

———. *The Autobiography of Charles Haddon Spurgeon*. Compiled and edited by Susannah Spurgeon and J. W. Harrald. 4 vols. Philadelphia: American Baptist Society, n.d.

———. *The Early Years 1834–1859*. Revised Ed. of Autobiography compiled and edited by Susannah and J. W. Harrald. London: Banner of Truth, 1962.

———. *Full Harvest 1860–892*. Revised Ed. of Autobiography compiled and edited by Susannah and J. W. Harrald. Edinburgh: Banner of Truth, 1973.

———. *Greatest Fight in the World: Conferences Addresses*. Toronto: Gospel Witness, n.d.

———. *John Ploughman's Pictures: or, More Plain Talk for Plain People*. Pasadena, TX: Pilgrim, 1974.

———. *Lectures to My Students*. New ed. London: Marshall, Morgan, and Scott, 1954.

———. *Memories of Stambourne*. New York: American Tract Society, 1891; Chicago: University of Chicago, Joseph Regenstein Library Department of Photoduplication, 1972.

———. *The Metropolitan Tabernacle: It's History and Work*. London: Passmore & Alabaster, 1876.

———. *Metropolitan Tabernacle Pulpit*. 63 vols. London: Passmore & Alabaster, 1861–1917.

———. *New Park Street Pulpit*. 6 vols. London: Passmore & Alabaster, 1856–1861. Reprint, Grand Rapids: Baker, 1990.

———. *The Saint and His Saviour: The Progress of the Soul in the Knowledge of Jesus*. London: Hodder & Stoughton, 1892.

———. *Soul Winner: How to Lead Sinners to the Savior*. Grand Rapids: Eerdmans, 1963.

———. *The Spurgeon Jubilee Album*. London: Passmore & Alabaster, n.d.

———. *Spurgeon's Sermons*, 10 vols. New York: Robert Carter & Brothers, 1883 as *Sermons of C. H. Spurgeon of London*. Reprint, Grand Rapids: Baker, 1984.

———. *The Sword and Trowel*. 27 vols. London: Passmore & Alabaster., 1865–1891.

———. *The Treasury of the Bible*. Grand Rapids: Baker, 1988.

Stroope, Michael W. "Eschatological Mission: Its Reality and Possibility in the Theology of Karl Barth and Its Influence on Modern Mission Theology." PhD diss. Southwestern Baptist Theological Seminary, 1985.

Thielicke, Helmet. *Encounter with Spurgeon*. Cambridge, England: James Clarke, 1964.

Torbet, Robert G. *A History of Baptists*. Rev. ed., with a foreword by Kenneth Scott Latorette. Valley Forge, PA: Judson, 1950.

Underwood, A. C. *History of English Baptists*. London: Kingsgate, 1947.

Vernacchia, Ralph A, et al. *Coaching Mental Excellence*. Portola Valley, CA: 1996.

Warren, Rick. *Purpose Driven Church*. Grand Rapids: Zondervan, 1995.

Wayland, H[eman] L[incoln]. *Charles H. Spurgeon, His Faith and Works*. Philadelphia: American Baptist Society, 1892.

Whitley, W. T. *The Baptists of London*. London: Kingsgate, 1955.

———. *A History of British Baptists*. London: Charles Griffith, 1923.

Williams, W[illiam]. *Personal Reminiscences of Charles Haddon Spurgeon*. London: Religious Tract Society, 1895.

———. *Charles Haddon Spurgeon*. Rev. and ed. by his daughter. n.p.; n.d.

Wooden, John. *They Call Me Coach*. Rev.ed., with foreword by Denny Crum. Chicago: Contemporary, 1989.

Wuest, Kenneth S. *Wuest's Word Studies*. 3 vols. Grand Rapids: Eerdmans, 1973.

Subject Index

Abingdon Association 6
American Christianity xviii, 1
Anabaptists 3
Ananias xviii
Angus, Joseph 20
Army 155, 171, 185, 193–97, 199
Atmosphere 3, 10, 41, 96, 107–8, 119–21, 153
Aunt Ann 26, 30, 33

Balanced 42, 128, 182, 192
Baptist Mission Society 2
Baptist Union 2, 8–9, 12, 108, 206
Bartlett, Lavinia Strickland 120–21
Baxter, Richard 40–42, 45
Bedford jail 25
Bi-vocational 34, 90
Booth, Abraham 7
Bristol College 18, 108
Browne, Robert 4
Bunyan, John 15, 25, 41
Burr's Hotel 79

Calling 89–91, 97–98, 119, 124, 126, 128, 144, 147–48, 153, 166, 168–69, 170, 173–74, 180, 184, 188–89, 195, 200

Calvin, John 4, 41, 125
Calvinism 7–8, 53, 73, 94
Calvinistic Baptists 200
Cambridge (town) 4, 45, 62–64, 66–68, 70–71, 76, 83, 106, 207
Cambridge University 45, 64
Campbell, John 106
Carey, William 2
Carr, B. W. 167
Character xvi, 4, 15, 21, 25, 29, 30, 34, 41, 46, 49, 59, 61, 89, 100, 108, 115, 120–21, 124, 126, 132, 141, 148–49, 162, 169, 173, 176–83, 190, 201
Chemistry 102, 126, 196
Church of England 3, 4–5, 14, 39, 45–46
Church plants (planting) ix, xi, 70, 95, 102
Clifford, John 11–12
Coach (Coaching) 147–48, 177, 186, 192, 200, 202–3
Colchester 26, 33–34, 37, 45–46, 57, 59, 63
Communion 5, 8, 32, 64, 158, 164, 190–91
Competence 126, 176

Subject Index

Confidence xix, 10–12, 30, 50–51, 58–59, 71, 74, 84, 89, 92, 132–33, 135, 148, 152, 160–61, 166, 169, 177, 186–88, 190–91, 198, 200
Confident leadership 177, 185
Courage 71–71, 140, 143, 150, 164, 168–69, 177, 190, 198
Crisp, Tobias 7
Cross 55, 57, 60, 68, 78, 96, 116, 119, 133, 137, 150, 155, 184, 193, 196
Culture xv, 15, 33, 50, 108, 120, 148, 153, 158–59

Darwin, Charles 11
Davies, G. H. 108
Deacon Coe 74
Devotions (devotional) 36, 63, 108
Difficulties 72, 103, 113, 118, 139, 180
Doctrine of the Fall 9
Doddridge, (Philip) 72, 93
Downgrade Controversy 72, 111

Earnestness 29, 31, 34, 45, 49, 51, 56, 61, 66, 71, 73–74, 85, 89, 95, 100, 113, 121, 131, 136–37, 156, 165–66, 172, 180, 183, 189–90, 194–95
Edinburgh University 20
Elder 26–27, 29, 32, 37, 153, 162, 164, 168, 180, 186–88, 195–96
Election 8, 50, 53, 116, 131–33, 142
Encouragement xvii, xviii, xix, 5–6, 16, 21, 27, 30–31, 66, 68, 69, 75, 78, 88, 94, 98–99, 101–5, 108–10, 120–21, 127, 130, 144, 147–48, 151, 154, 156, 159–60, 164–65, 168, 171–72, 180–81, 189–91, 193, 195–203
Essex 24–26, 29, 36, 58, 180
Everett, J. D. 49
Example xii, xvi, 9, 26–27, 29–30, 33–34, 40, 49, 78, 88, 120–22, 125, 167, 180, 182, 185, 201–2

Faith xii, xviii, 1, 9–10, 14, 17, 28–29, 34–35, 40, 43, 46–47, 56, 59, 61, 72, 87, 90, 93, 101, 112, 116, 128, 130, 132–33, 135–36, 138, 141, 143–46, 151, 154, 156, 160–61, 166, 168–69, 173, 189, 191–92, 197–98, 200, 202
Farm system xii, xix, 8, 13, 50, 60, 68, 115–18, 121, 123, 125, 145, 147–49, 151, 153–59, 161, 163, 165, 167, 171–73, 175, 178, 203
Fawcett, John 7
Fishers (of men) 65, 107, 124, 152, 188
Friday Lectures 143
Fuller, Andrew 2
Fundamentals 9

General Baptists 4, 6, 8
German rationalism 111
Gill, John 7, 16
Gospel x–xi, xvii, 2, 7, 8–10, 13–14, 18, 29–30, 36, 50, 54, 56–60, 64, 66, 71–74, 76–78, 80, 85–85, 88–93, 96–97, 99, 103–4, 109, 116–20, 126–28, 130–38, 140, 145, 148, 151–54, 156, 161, 166–67. 170. 172–73, 177, 183, 193, 195, 198–200
Gout 40, 46, 105
Grace 4, 7–8, 17, 28, 30, 35, 39, 45, 50–51, 53–58, 61, 68, 76, 89, 93, 98–99, 102, 109, 111, 113, 115–16, 118, 125, 127–33, 135, 137, 141, 143, 148–49, 151–53, 155, 159, 165, 167, 170–72, 174, 178–79, 181–84, 186, 191, 193, 195, 199, 203
Great Commandment xii, xvii, xviii, 122, 147, 178, 199
Great Commission xii, xiii, xvii–xviii, 12, 21, 39, 43, 56, 72, 75, 77, 89, 92, 95–97, 117–18, 121–25, 137, 145, 147–48, 155, 157, 159–61, 166, 178, 184, 186, 192, 194–96, 198–200

Hall, Robert 8, 64
Harvard University 45
Harvest xix, 45, 73, 76, 78, 92, 95, 111, 115, 119, 122–25, 127, 142, 144–45, 147, 174–76, 188, 191, 194–99, 202
Helwys, Thomas 4
Hendricks, Howard 22, 38, 59, 176

Subject Index

Hermeneutics 12
Holiness 42, 52–53, 56, 131, 134, 141, 151, 167, 182, 193
Holy Spirit 1, 10, 16–17, 40, 59, 65, 98, 110, 114–16, 124, 129, 130, 133, 135, 138–40, 155, 159–61, 165, 172, 185–86, 193–94, 197, 203
Humility 34, 61, 165, 180
Humor xi, 29, 34, 108

Internships 147

Jerry Falwell xvi, 145, 196
Juvenile Magazine 35

Keach, Benjamin 7, 14, 16
Kimball, Edward xviii
Kindness 133, 168
Knill, Richard 36, 78
Knowledge 7, 12, 17, 38, 45, 49, 51, 53–54, 74, 89, 91, 95, 103, 106, 133, 142, 144, 153, 176–77, 182
Knowles, James Sheridan 108

Laity v, 22, 49–50, 118–19, 169
Lay Preachers' Association 64, 66, 68–70, 72
Leadership xii–xiii, xix, 5–6, 8–9, 16, 18–20, 22, 31, 33, 64, 77, 80, 107, 117, 121–22, 141–42, 147, 157, 165–69, 176–79, 181, 183–93, 197, 199
Leeding 45, 63–64, 72
London Baptists 9
London Baptist Confession 3
London Bridge 19
Lorimer, George C. 106
Love ix–xi, xiii, xvi, xviii, 1, 2, 4, 12, 17, 25, 27–29, 33, 35, 37–39, 43–44, 53–55, 57, 59–62, 66–67, 71–72, 75–77, 85, 87–89, 93, 95–96, 107–8, 112–13, 115–16, 118–19, 122, 124–26, 128–31, 133, 137, 141–43, 151–52, 154, 160, 166, 171, 177–78, 180–83, 185–86, 189–90, 193, 200, 202
Luther, (Martin) 3, 28, 36, 48, 83, 94, 125

Manton, Thomas 40, 155
Mary King 49, 50
McBeth, Leon 4
McGavran, Donald 1, 97, 156, 192
Medhurst, Thomas 122
Mentone 40, 62, 104
Mentor (mentoring) ix, 33, 39, 147, 180, 203
Model xii, xv–xvi, 33, 74, 98, 108, 116, 121, 139, 143, 148, 154, 156–57, 166–67
Moody, D L xviii

New Park Baptist x, xviii, 2, 7, 14, 16, 18, 20–22, 27, 68, 73, 78–83, 85–89, 94, 109, 112, 118, 120, 122, 142, 168, 187
Newmarket School 49, 59, 65
Nicoll, William Robertson 13
Nonconformists 3, 15, 24, 39, 92, 106

Owen, John 40, 42
Oxford University 39, 45, 106

Particular Baptists 5, 7–8
Pastors' College Conference 110–11, 138, 157
Pike, G. Holden 27
Popery Unmasked 47
Priesthood of Believer 22, 97, 149, 169, 173, 192, 195
Pulpit 7, 10, 15, 17, 30, 32, 43, 53, 57, 62, 77, 79, 97–98, 154–57, 183, 190
Puritans 4–5, 29, 39–42, 45, 105, 129

Richardson, Will 28
Rider, William 14
Rippon, John 18
Roads, Thomas 31
Rogers, George 95, 143

Saint Andrews Baptist 8, 153
Saint Augustine College 46, 62
Scarborough, L. R. 89. 173–74
Scholars 10, 12, 39, 99
Scholarship 70, 80, 97–98, 106
Schleiermacher, Friedrich 10
Second Timothy 2:2 xix, 64

Self-confidence 89
Send (sending) 60, 64–65, 68, 70, 73,
    77, 84, 93, 96, 100, 111, 117,
    119, 122–23, 134, 140, 147–48,
    199, 200
Separatists 5, 6
Septuagint 72, 76
Siberia 78
Sin 7, 21, 28, 31, 35, 46, 51–53, 55–56,
    72–73, 86, 90, 118, 121, 128–30,
    132–36, 151–52, 170–73
Smith, James 20
Soul winning 53, 117, 150, 188, 197
Spurgeon, James & Sarah 26
Spurgeon, Job 25
Spurgeon, John & Eliza 25, 33, 36
Spurgeon, Susannah 36, 39, 60–61, 80
Stambourne 26–28, 30–32, 35–36, 44
Stepney College 20, 75, 108
Stinton, Benjamin 16
Southern Baptist Theological Seminary
    167
Stockwell School 45–46
Suffolk 2, 27, 49
Swindell 49, 60
Sword and Trowel 27, 94–96, 100, 102,
    110, 114–15, 148

Teversham 67, 70
Timothy (Timothies) 117, 122, 189, 195

Tracts 59, 65–66, 76, 88, 122
Training systems 84
Trinity 17, 160–61
Taylor, Dan 7–8
Taylor, Hudson 111
Thielicke, Helmet 13, 55

Vinter, James 66–67
Vision xi, xix, 68, 70, 82, 84, 88–89,
    91–92, 97, 102, 104, 110, 112,
    117, 120, 145, 156, 170, 191,
    194, 196–97

Walters, William 21
Waterbeach 70, 73–77, 79, 81, 84–85,
    94, 165
Watts, Isaac 30
Wesley, John 14, 196
Williams, William 29
Wisdom xvi-xviii, 1, 3, 68, 75, 111, 115,
    117, 126, 141, 153, 158, 163,
    167–68, 176, 178, 180, 200–201
Worship 4–5, 14–15, 20–21, 28, 30, 37,
    39, 41, 57, 64, 71, 79–81, 144,
    153, 164, 188, 199

Yorkshire Association 9

Zwingli, Ulrich 4